hell's
cartographers

hell's cartographers

Some Personal Histories of
Science Fiction Writers

with contributions by

Alfred Bester
Damon Knight
Frederik Pohl
Robert Silverberg
Harry Harrison
Brian W. Aldiss

Edited by

Brian W. Aldiss
Harry Harrison

HARPER & ROW, PUBLISHERS
New York, Hagerstown, San Francisco, London

Note:
The editors wish to state that the individual
contributors to this volume are responsible
only for their own opinions and statements.

Library of Congress Cataloging in Publication Data
Main entry under title:

Hell's cartographers.
    Bibliography: p.
    1. Authors, American—Biography. 2. Aldiss, Brian Wilson, 1925–
    —Biography. 3. Science fiction, American—History and criticism—
Addresses, essays, lectures. 4. Science fiction—Authorship. I. Aldiss,
Brian Wilson, 1925–   II. Harrison, Harry.
PS129.H4 1975   813'.0876 [B]   75-25074
ISBN 0-06-010052-4

76 77 78 79 10 9 8 7 6 5 4 3 2 1

Contents

A section of illustrations follows page 122

Introduction

A few years ago, there was a man living down in Galveston or one of those ports on the Gulf of Mexico who helped make history. He did not enjoy that honour – a feeling shared by many who find themselves in that position.

His name was Claude Eatherly, and at one time he was something of a legend. For all I know, he still lives down in Galveston, for all I know he still feels himself to be one of the scapegoats of history. For Major Claude Eatherly, back in 1945, piloted the weather plane which flew over Hiroshima and reported that cloud conditions were suitable for the dropping of the first A-bomb.

The responsibility for the deaths which followed rode hard on Eatherly's shoulders, although nobody until then had mistaken him for a thinking man. He liked drink, gambling, women, and horseplay, and read nothing more profound than comic books. Then he got mixed up with lethal technology.

After the war, Eatherly became a misfit and eventually a jailbird, before being turned into a myth-figure by some of the dark father-figures of our time – politicians, psychiatrists, philosophers, preachers, and publicists. Even Bertrand Russell weighed in.

1

It was not the importance of Eatherly's life as such. The extraordinary crucifying incident in which he was involved was what gave him significance.

This volume contains brief autobiographies by six eminent science fiction writers. With only one exception, we are all within a few years of the same age. We were all old enough to appreciate the spectacle of the mushroom clouds rising over Hiroshima and Nagasaki. There are few things more vexing than modesty exercised upon someone else's behalf, so I trust my contributors will forgive me if I say that some of our interest is, like Eatherly's, extrinsic.

For the atomic bomb meant something particular to science fiction writers and readers. Despite our differences, we held at least two items of faith unshakably. One of them was – and it is curious to look back to the forties and see how absolutely bizarre, lunatic even, was this faith then – that space travel waited just round the corner (well, so it did, and we were right, although on many of the details we were instructively wrong).

The other item of faith concerned science fiction itself, by which was meant at that time magazine science fiction, disreputable stuff which has only recently been graced by such sociologists' terms as Alternative Literature. We believed that sf was of genuine merit. More, we saw those merits as being unique.

Whatever else the A-bomb meant to Eatherly and all the rest of mankind, to a small handful of us it meant vindication. We who had been regarded as mad were proved dangerously sane. The Future had happened, and blown the lid off the Old Order.

From then on, we wrote sf with greater confidence, treated it more seriously, and were ourselves treated by our critics with slightly less scorn and by our readers with positive veneration. Never have critics and readers in any field been more divided than they are over sf.

Science fiction, to my mind, is not a matter of prediction, and never has been, although prediction is one of the ingredients which makes it fun. Rather, it mirrors the present in such a way as to dispense with inessentials and dramatize new trends. In my own fiction, each decade would typically present some central image which differed from the one before: in the forties and early fifties, a bleak landscape cleared of people by some almost-forgotten catastrophe; in the fifties, men imprisoned in huge spaceships and technologies; in the sixties, men's minds altered by drugs or engines; and now – well, maybe a great windjammer, fully automated and computerized, bearing the goods that formerly went by air, its complex rig of sails operated without the need of human crew. . . . There's always a new scenario round the corner.

My thought was to invite the men who have been most successful in inventing such fictional scenarios to write a brief memoir of themselves. They were asked to be as frank as possible about their lives and to discuss their involvement in the world of science fiction.

The result is a book of unique significance. We have been the weather men flying above alien cities, and we have not delivered our reports before. When we began to write, it seemed as if we were doomed by our beliefs to work in obscurity. Yet it turned out that there was something prodromic in our approach to life; what we had to say proved to be on a subject with which millions of people of our generation were concerned; and, as a result, our books have been reprinted and translated all round the world (not least in Eatherly's old target, Japan, one of sf's global capitals). We are an entirely new sort of popular writer, the poor man's highbrows.

We wrote against the grain and were accepted against it. We wrote for kicks and ha'pence. There is a certain emphasis on finance in our memoirs, and with reason; for the smaller the payment, the larger it looms. We had faith in what we were doing; individualists though we were, it transpired that the faith virtually created a movement. A lot of people needed to re-dream our nightmares.

What we see today is the too-easy acceptance of sf. The sharp idiom we created has blurred to become one of the bland flavourings of mass media; the unembarrassed muse we espoused is one of the jades of television. And the younger writers now writing have an entirely different approach to their art. They have found how easy it is to rely on formula, or how simply success can come through self-advertisement.

For us it was different.

Well, that's a good motto for this volume. Where I think the difference showed in our work was that, for all our sleight-of-hand with the wonders of space-and-time, our fiction gained its power by having as unspoken topic one of the great issues of the day: the sense that the individual's role in society is eroded as society itself becomes wealthier and more powerful. This is certainly so with novels as unalike as Pohl and Kornbluth's *The Space Merchants*, Silverberg's *The Time Hoppers*, and Knight's *A for Anything*. Harrison and Bester, in their most characteristic fiction, allow the individual much more latitude; their heroes can save worlds or defeat the solar system; but nobody who ever meets them is likely to forget the oppressions of the decadent society in *Tiger! Tiger!* or of the hunger-line crowds of *Make Room! Make Room!*

I chose the men I did because they were friends of mine, though not always particularly close friends, since the Atlantic separates us much of the time; although it is true to say that I have danced the samba with Damon Knight's wife, Kate Wilhelm – and (darn it) Damon at the same time, because it was one of those mad nights in Rio de Janeiro; while I have been reasonably stoned with Fred Pohl and his wife Carol in the Tokyo hotel room of our Russian pal Julius Kagarlitski; and so on.

They were also chosen because I admired their innovations in sf. Knight published *In Search of Wonder,* the first book of critical reviews of sf, and it would be hard to overestimate the influence of his cool appraisals in a field over-fond of puffery. Bester was quite simply the popular writer who showed greatest verve and swagger in short stories and novels; although he does not realize it, he is something of a cult figure in England. One man in his time plays many parts; Pohl has played all the parts in the sf world, fan, editor, writer, adviser, ambassador. Among his other lesser virtues, he was the first guy in the States to buy one of my stories. Silverberg made a great deal of money from sf; in his exemplary piece, he relates how sf made him a millionaire – and it is a story which gives me a great deal of pleasure. He provides a deep insight into what it means to be a popular writer.

Harrison had to be in here, simply because we co-edit books. We co-edit books because we work well together and get pleasure from so doing. I cannot recall all the odd places in which Harrison and I have found ourselves together. My life would be poorer in many ways without his friendship.

The sixth writer is me because I could not bear to be left out. I originally approached seven writers. The seventh was Michael Moorcock. Because there has always been a bond between Moorcock and me; because I am one of the handful of people who know just how much lifeblood Moorcock gave to his sf magazine. Moorcock was the only guy who said he could not talk about himself. True modesty.

The rest of us, happily, have no such qualms. I hope at a future date to produce a second – who knows, even a third and fourth – volume of Hell's Cartographers, since I am convinced that this is the way in which I can most easily earn posterity's gratitude. And the book, in a sense, follows naturally after my history of science fiction.

The overall interest in this volume resides, I think, in the fact that vital parameters of our six lives lie between the Bomb and the Apollo. These two events mark out our sceptical approach to life from both those writers of a generation before us and those of a later generation. We have all been keeping the reading public reading for two or more decades; this is how and why we did it.

My particular thanks go to Miss Nancy Neiman of Weidenfeld & Nicolson for all her understanding and assistance.

Heath House   Brian W. Aldiss
Southmoor
February 1974

Robert Silverberg:

sounding brass, tinkling cymbal

'... *and even Silverberg, who sometimes, with all his skill and knowledge and sophistication, does tend to the androidal....*'
John Clute in New Worlds 5

Though I speak with the tongues of men and of angels, and have not charity, I am become as sounding brass, or a tinkling cymbal.

And though I have the gift of prophecy, and understand all mysteries, and all knowledge; and though I have all faith, so that I could remove mountains, and have not charity, I am nothing.
I Corinthians, 13

At last to speak of one's self. An odd temptation, which mostly I have resisted, in the past, maintaining that I'm not yet ready to undertake a summing up, or that I'm in the midst of some intricate new transition still not fully understood, or that I'm bored with myself and talking about myself. Yet I have granted all sorts of interviews, and spoken quite explicitly, all the while protesting my love of privacy; the one thing I've never attempted is explicit written autobiography. I manage to hold all poses at once, modest and exhibitionistic, esthete and man of commerce, puritan and libertine: probably the truth is that I have no consistent positions at all. We'll see.

Autobiography. Apparently one should not name the names of those one has been to bed with, or give explicit figures on the amount of money one has earned, those being the two data most eagerly sought by readers; all the rest is legitimate to reveal. Very well. The essential starting point, for me, is the confession (and boast) that I am a man who is living his own adolescent fantasies. When I was sixteen or so I yearned to win fame as a writer of science fiction, to become wealthy enough to indulge in whatever amusements I chose, to know the love of fair women, to travel widely, to live free from the pressures and perils of ordinary life. All these things have come to me, and more; I have fewer complaints to make about the hand destiny has dealt me than anyone I know. Here at what I assume is my midpoint I feel a certain inner security, a self-satisfaction, which I suppose borders occasionally on smugness. (But not on complacency. The past is unchangeable and the present delightful, yet the future still must be regarded warily. I live in California, a land where the earth might literally open beneath my feet this afternoon; and I've already once had, in my pre-California incarnation, the experience of awakening before dawn to find my world in flames.)

Because my life has been so generally satisfactory, and because I'm a literary enough man to know the dangers of *hubris*, I sometimes affect a kind of self-deprecatory shyness, a who-*me*? kind of attitude, whenever I am singled out for special attention. This pose gets more and more difficult to maintain as the years go on and the accomplishments and money and awards pile up; by now certain objective measures of achievement exist, for me, and there's an element of hypocrisy in trying to deny them purely for the sake of trying to avoid the fate that chops down the boastful.

Sounding Brass, Tinkling Cymbal

Ten years ago, or even five, I probably would have refused the opportunity to contribute to this book, claiming that I was unworthy (and privately fearing that others would say so if I did not). To hell with that now.

I am the youngest of the six contributors here: the youngest by nearly a decade, I suspect, since as I write this I'm still more than a year short of my fortieth birthday, and my companions, I know, all cluster around the half-century mark. A familiar feeling, that one. I was always the youngest in any group, owlishly precocious, a nastily bright little boy who was reading at three, writing little stories at six, spouting learned stuff about European dynasties and the sexual habits of plants at seven or eight, publishing illegible magazines at thirteen, and selling novels at eighteen. I was too unruly and too clever to remain in the same class at school with my contemporaries, so I grew up two years younger than all my friends, thinking of myself as small and weak and incomplete. Eventually, by surviving, I caught up with everyone. I am the oldest in my immediate circle of friends, with a beard alas now tinged with grey, and I am as tall as most and taller than many, and within the tiny world of science fiction I have become something of an elder statesman, and the wounds I received by being fourteen years old in a universe of sixteen-year-olds are so well sheathed in scar-tissue now that I might as well consider them healed. And yet it still is strange to be included as an equal in this particular group of writers, since three of them – Alfred Bester, Damon Knight, Frederik Pohl – were among my own literary idols when I was indulging in those adolescent fantasies of a writer's career twenty-odd years ago. A fourth, Harry Harrison, had not yet begun writing seriously then himself, but he was the editor who first paid me for writing anything, in 1953; and only Brian Aldiss, the originator of this project, played no part in shaping me in my teens, for I had never heard his name until I myself was an established writer. Yet I make no apologies for being here among my elders. Here we all are: professional writers, diligent craftsmen, successful creators – artists, if you will. And good friends as well.

9

I am an only child, born halfway through the Great Depression. (There would have been a sibling, I think, when I was about seven, but it miscarried; I often wonder what pattern my life would have taken had I not grown up alone, pampered, self-indulgent.) My ancestors were Jews from Eastern Europe, and my grandparents, three of whom survived well into my adulthood, were reared in Poland or Russia in villages beyond my easy comprehension. My father was born in London in the first year of this century, and came to the United States a few years thereafter. My mother was born in Brooklyn, New York, and so was I.

I have no very fond recollections of my childhood. I was puny, sickly, plagued with allergies and freckles, and (I thought) quite ugly. I was too clever by at least half, which made for troubles with my playmates. My parents were remote figures; my father was a certified public accountant, spending his days and many of his evenings adding up endless columns of red figures on long yellow sheets, and my mother taught school, so that I was raised mainly by Lottie, our mulatto housekeeper, and by my loving and amiable maternal grandmother. It was a painful time, lonely and embittering; I did make friends but, growing up in isolation and learning none of the social graces, I usually managed to alienate them quickly, striking at them with my sharp tongue if not my feeble fists. On the other hand, there were compensations: intelligence is prized in Jewish households, and my parents saw to it that mine was permitted to develop freely. I was taken to museums, given all the books I wanted, and allowed money for my hobbies. I took refuge from loneliness in these things; I collected stamps and coins, harpooned hapless butterflies and grasshoppers, raided the neighbours' gardens for specimens of leaves and flowers, stayed up late secretly reading, hammered out crude stories on an ancient typewriter, all with my father's strong encouragement and frequent enthusiastic participation, and it mattered less and less that I was a troubled misfit in the classroom if I could come home to my large private room in the afternoon and, quickly zipping through the too-easy homework, get down to the serious business of the current obsessional hobby.

10

Children who find the world about them distasteful turn readily to the distant and the alien. The lure of the exotic seized me early. These were the years of World War II and real travel was impossible, but in 1943 a friend of my father's gave me a subscription to the *National Geographic Magazine,* and I was off to Zanzibar and Surinam and Jamaica in my imagination decades before I ever reached those places in actuality. (Typically, I began buying old *National Geographics* with lunatic persistence, and didn't rest until I had them all, from the 1880's on. I still have them.) Then, an hour's journey from home on the subway, there was the American Museum of Natural History, with its mummies and arrowheads, its mastodons and glyptodons, above all its brontosaurs and tyrannosaurs; Sunday after Sunday my father and I made the pilgrimage, and I revelled in the wonders of prehistory, soberly lecturing him on the relative chronological positions of Neanderthal and Peking and Piltdown Man. (Yes, Piltdown, this was 1944, remember.) From dinosaurs and other such fantastic fossils to science fiction was but a short journey: the romantic, exotic distant past is closely tied to the romantic, exotic distant future in my imagination.

So there was Jules Verne when I was nine – I must have taken that voyage with Captain Nemo a hundred times – and H. G. Wells when I was ten, most notably *The Time Machine* (which promised to show me all the incredible eons I would never live to know) but also *The Island of Dr Moreau* and *War of the Worlds,* the myriad short stories, and even an obscure satire called *Mr Blettsworthy on Rampole Island,* to which I often returned because Mr Blettsworthy encountered living ground-sloths. There was Twain's *Connecticut Yankee in King Arthur's Court,* which also I read repeatedly. (How early my fascination with time travel emerged!) I dabbled in comic books, too, and I have gaudy memories of Buck Rogers and *Planet Comics.* But somehow I missed Edgar Rice Burroughs altogether; and it was not until early 1948, when I was already a veteran of scores of hardbound science fiction books, that I even knew such things as science fiction magazines existed.

The magazines mostly repelled me by their covers and

their titles. I did buy *Weird Tales* – my first one had an Edmond Hamilton novelette about the Norse gods, which delighted me since I had gone through whole libraries of Norse mythology in early boyhood. I bought *Amazing Stories*, then the sleaziest representative of the genre, because it happened to publish an uncharacteristically respectable-looking issue about then. I bought John Campbell's dignified little *Astounding Science Fiction*, but found the stories opaque and unrewarding to my thirteen-year-old mind. Because I was rather a snob, I would not even open magazines with names like *Thrilling Wonder Stories* and *Famous Fantastic Mysteries* and *Startling Stories*, especially since their covers were bright with paintings of hideous monsters and scantily clad damsels. (Sex was very frightening to me just then, and I had sworn never to have anything to do with women.) More than a year passed before I approached those magazines in what was by then an unquenchable thirst for science fiction, and discovered they were publishing some of the best material of the day.

Then there were the books: the wondrous Healy-McComas *Adventures in Time and Space*, the big Groff Conklin titles, Wollheim's *Pocket Book of Science Fiction*, and the other pioneering anthologies. My father was more than a little baffled by my increasing obsession with all this trash, when previously I occupied myself with decent books on botany and geology and astronomy, but he saw to it that I bought whatever I wanted. One collection in particular had enormous impact on me: Wollheim's *Portable Novels of Science*, published in 1945 and discovered by me three years later. It contained Wells' *First Men in the Moon*, which amused me; Taine's *Before the Dawn*, which fed my always passionate interest in dinosaurs; Lovecraft's *Shadow Out of Time*, which gave me that peep into unattainable futures that originally led me to science fiction; and above all Stapledon's *Odd John*, which spoke personally to me as I suppose it must to any child who is too bright for his own good. I was up almost till dawn reading that book, and those novels marked me.

I was at that time still talking of some sort of career in the sciences, perhaps in botany, perhaps in paleontology, perhaps astronomy. But some flaws in my intelligence were making themselves apparent, to me and to my teachers if not to my parents: I had a superb memory and a quick wit, but I lacked depth, originality, and consistency; my mind was like a hummingbird, darting erratically over surfaces. I wanted to encompass too much, and mastered nothing, and though I always got high marks in any subject that caught my interest, I noticed, by the time I was thirteen, that some of my classmates were better than I at grasping fundamental principles and drawing new conclusions from them. I doubt that I would have been of much value as a scientist. But already I was writing, and writing with precocious skill – for school newspapers and magazines, for my own abominably mimeographed magazine, and, without success, for professional science fiction magazines. Off went stories, double-spaced and bearing accurate word-counts (612, 1814, 2705). They were dreadful, naturally, and they came back, usually with printed rejection slips but sometimes – when the editors realized they were dealing with a bright child of thirteen or fourteen and not with a demented adult – with gentle letters suggesting ways I might improve my style or my sense of plot. And I spoke openly of a career in writing, perhaps earning my living as a journalist while writing science fiction as a sideline.

Why science fiction? Because it was science fiction that I preferred to read, though I had been through Cervantes and Shakespeare and that crowd too. And because writing science fiction allowed me to give free play to those fantasies of space and time and dinosaurs and supermen that were so gratifying to me. And because I had stumbled into the world of science fiction fandom, a world much more comfortable than the real world of bullies and athletes and sex, and I knew that my name on the contents page of *Astounding* or *Startling* would win me much prestige in fandom, prestige that I could hardly hope to gain among my classmates.

So, then, the stories went forth, awkward imitations on a miniature scale of my favourite moments out of Lovecraft or Stapledon or Taine or Wells, and the stories came back, and I read textbooks on the narrative art and learned a good deal, and began also to read the stories in the science fiction

13

magazines with a close analytical eye, measuring the ratio of dialogue to exposition, the length of paragraphs, and other technical matters that, I suppose, few fifteen-year-olds study as carefully as I did. Nothing got published, or even came close, but I was growing in skill.

I was growing in other ways, too. When I was about fourteen I went off, for the first time, to summer camp, where I lived among boys (and girls) of my own age and no longer had to contend with being the youngest and puniest in my peer-group. I had always been known as 'Robert', but at camp I was speedily dubbed 'Bob', and it seemed to me that I was taking on a new identity. *Robert* was that spindly misfit, that maladjusted, isolated little boy; *Bob* was a healthy, outgoing, normal young man. To this day I wince when some stranger presumes on my public persona and addresses me as Robert – it sends me rocketing backward in time to the horrors of being ten again. Although I sign my stories *Robert* for reasons of formality, my friends know me as *Bob*, and my parents managed the transition fairly gracefully at my request (though my father sometimes slips, a quarter of a century after the change), and when I occasionally encounter some childhood friend I let him know, rapidly, the name I prefer and the reason I prefer it.

This new Bob was able to cope. He grew to a reasonable height, halting just a bit short of six feet; he became a passable athlete; he discovered how to sustain friendships and how to manage conversations. For a few years I led a split life, introverted and lonely and secretive at home, open and lighthearted and confident during the summers; and by the time I was about seventeen, some integration of the two lives had begun. I had finished high school (where I had become editor of the high-school newspaper and was respected for my skill as a writer) and, by way of surrendering some of my precocity, had declined to go immediately into college. Instead I spent a few months reading and writing, and a few months working in a furniture warehouse on the Brooklyn waterfront, among rough, tough illiterates who found my cultivated manner a charming novelty rather than a threatening intrusion, and then I went off to the summer camp, not as a camper but as an employee. In the autumn I entered Columbia University with old slates wiped clean: I was no longer morbidly too young, I was free of the local playmates who could never forget the maladjustments of my childhood, I was able to begin in the *Bob* persona, without hauling the burden of my past problems.

I lived away from home, in a little apartment of my own. I manifested previously unknown skills for drinking and carousing. I discovered that women were not really very frightening after all. I plunged myself into new worlds of the mind: into Aquinas and Plato, into Bartok and Schoenberg, into Kafka, Joyce, Mann, Faulkner, Sartre. I continued to read science fiction, but dispassionately, with the eye of one who was soon to be a professional; I was less interested in visions of ultimate tomorrows and more in seeing how Messrs Bester, Pohl, Knight, Sheckley, Dick etc, carried off their tricks. One of my stories was published – for a fee of $5, I think – by an amateur magazine called *Different*, operated by a poetess named Lilith Lorraine. Harry Harrison asked me to do an article about fandom for a science fiction magazine he was editing, and I turned in a competent journalistic job and was paid $30. That was in September 1953. I sent a short story called 'Gorgon Planet' off to a magazine called *Nebula*, published in Scotland by Peter Hamilton, and in January 1954 he notified me that he would use it, and sent me his check for $12.60.

That same month I sold a novel to a major American publisher. The earlier sales could be brushed aside as inconsequential – two weak short stories accepted by obscure magazines, and one specimen of mere journalism – but the novel was something else. I was not yet nineteen years old, and I was a professional writer. I had crossed the threshold.

That novel! Its genesis went back almost three years. When I was editor of my high-school newspaper in 1951 a book appeared for review, a science-fiction novel for boys, published by the Thomas Y. Crowell Company, an old-line New York firm. Steeped as I was in Wells and Heinlein and Stapledon and such, I reviewed this clumsy, naive book scornfully, demolishing it so effectively that in the summer of 1953 the publishing company invited me to examine and criticize, prior to publication, the latest manuscript by that author. I read it and demolished it too, with such thoroughness that the book was never published. This time the Crowell editor asked me to the office and said, in effect, 'If you know so much about science fiction, why don't you try a novel for us yourself?' I accepted the challenge.

I had attempted a novel once before, at the age of thirteen. It began as two short stories, but I subsequently combined them, elaborated, padded most shamefully, and ended up with an inch-thick manuscript that must have been one of the least coherent hodgepodges ever committed to paper. The outline of the book I suggested to Crowell in September 1953 was better, but not much. It concerned the trip of four young space cadets to Alpha Centauri on a sort of training cruise. No plot, not much action. The cadets are chosen, leave for space, stop at Mars and Pluto, reach Alpha Centauri, become vaguely entangled in a revolution going on there, become disentangled and go home. Some novel.

Every weekend that autumn I wrote two or three chapters, working swiftly despite the pressures of college. When eight chapters were done I submitted them and received an encouraging note urging me to complete the book. It was done by mid-November: nineteen chapters, 145 pages of typescript. I sent it in, heard nothing for two months, and on a Sunday in January 1954, received a stunning telephone call from the Crowell editor: they were sending me a contract for my novel. Of course, some changes would be required before it could be published.

In March I was sent a severe four-page letter of analysis. Anticlimax after anticlimax, they said; first part of book fine, last half terrible. Though immensely discouraged, I set to work rewriting, trying to build complications and a resolution into my rudimentary story. On 5 June this revision came back to me: I had allowed my main protagonist to achieve his goal by default rather than by positive action, and the publishers wouldn't let me get away with that. I promised to spend the summer considering ways to restructure the book;

meanwhile Crowell would consult an outside reader for suggestions and evaluations.

The summer passed. I did no writing, though I began vaguely to hatch a completely new plot turning on my hero's climactic conversion to the revolutionary party. At the end of October the long-awaited reader's report on the manuscript landed in the mailbox of my campus apartment. It made the job I had done on that unpublished book the year before look like praise. What was wrong, I learned, was that I really didn't know how to write. I had no idea of characterization or plotting, my technique was faulty, virtually everything except my typing was badly done. If possible, the reader said, I should enroll in a writing course at New York University.

A year earlier, I might have been crushed; but by the autumn of 1954 I had sold a couple of competent if uninspired short stories, I had written five or six more that seemed quite publishable to me (ultimately, I sold them all), and I felt that I had a fairly firm technical grasp on the art of fiction, however faulty the execution of my novel might be at the moment. Instead of abandoning the project, I spent three hours considering what I could do to save it, and in the afternoon I telephoned my editor to tell her that I proposed a total rewrite based on the conversion-to-revolution theme. By this time she must have come to doubt her original faith in my promise and talent, but she told me to go ahead.

I knew this was my last chance. The first step was to throw out the first nine chapters, which had survived intact through all the earlier drafts. They were good, solid chapters – it was the end of the story that was weak, not the beginning – but they had little relevance to my new theme. I compressed them into two pages and got my characters off to the Alpha Centauri system as fast as I could. In six weekends of desperate work the new novel, wholly transformed, was done. And on 2 January 1955 – one year almost to the hour since I had been notified that a contract would be offered me – I received a telegram: CONGRATULATIONS ON A WONDERFUL REVISION JOB ALL SET TO GO.

Revolt on Alpha C was published in August 1955, to generally indifferent reviews. ('inept and unreal . . . a series of

17

old-hat adventures,' said the *New York Times*.) Perhaps that was too harsh a verdict: the book is short, innocent, a little foolish, but not contemptible. It remained in print, in its Crowell edition, for seventeen years, earning modest but steady royalties until the printing was exhausted. A paperback edition published in 1959 still seems to enjoy a healthy life, having been through seven or eight printings so far, and in 1972 the book was reissued on two microfiche cards as part of the Xerox Micromedia Classroom Libraries series. This strange persistence of a very young author's very unimportant first novel does not delude me into thinking I must have created a classic unrecognized in its own day, nor do I believe it has much to do with my latter-day prominence in science fiction. That *Revolt on Alpha C* remains in print after nearly twenty years is no more than an odd accident of publishing, but one that I find charming as well as profitable. My father never ceases to ask if the book still brings in royalties, and he is as wonderstruck as I that it does.

I was launched. On the strength of having sold a novel and a few short stories, I was able to get an agent, Scott Meredith, and he has represented me now for two decades. (There are writers and publishers who will tell you that drawing and quartering is too gentle a fate for him, and there are other writers who have been with him longer than I, with every intention of continuing the relationship until time's end. I think every agent evokes a similarly wide spectrum of responses.) I sent my agent all the unsold short stories in my file, and, assuming that manuscripts bearing his sponsorship would sell far more readily than ones coming in unsolicited from an unknown writer, I awaited a flow of publishers' checks. The flow was a bit sluggish, though. Two trifling stories sold to minor magazines in June 1954 and February 1955 for a total of $40.50; in May 1955 came $49.50 for a rather more elaborate piece. But several quite ambitious stories, which I thought worthy of the leading magazines of the time, failed to sell at all, from which I began to draw a sinister conclusion: that if I intended to earn a livelihood writing fiction, it would be wiser to use my rapidly developing technical skills to turn out mass-produced formularized stories at high speed, rather than to lavish passion and energy on more individual works that would be difficult to sell.

In the summer of 1955, just as that sombre insight was crystallizing in me, Randall Garrett appeared in New York and rented a room in the hotel near Columbia University where I was living. Garrett was about eight years older than I, and had had some two dozen stories published, including several in *Astounding*, the premiere magazine of the era. Alone in a strange city, down on his luck, he struck up a curious friendship with me. We were markedly different in personal habits and rhythms, in philosophy, in background; but somehow these differences were a source of vitality rather than disharmony in the collaborative partnership that swiftly evolved. We complemented one another. Garrett was an established professional writer, but his discipline had collapsed and he was writing very little; I was unknown but ambitious, and could force an entire short story out of myself at a single sitting. Garrett had had a scientific education; mine was literary. Garrett was an efficient storyteller, but his prose was mechanical; I had trouble constructing internally consistent plots, but I wrote smoothly and with some grace. Garrett's stories rarely delved into character; I was already concerned, as much as I could be at the age of twenty, with emotional and psychological depth. We began to work together.

Until then, I had submitted all my stories by mail or else through my agent. Garrett took me to editorial offices. I met John Campbell of *Astounding*, Bob Lowndes of the esteemed but impoverished *Science Fiction Stories*, Howard Browne of *Amazing*, Larry Shaw of the newly founded *Infinity*. Editors, Garrett said, bought more readily from writers they had met than from strangers who had only postal contact with them, and lo! it was so. I sold five stories in August 1955, three in September, three in October, six in November, nine in December. Many of these were collaborations with Garrett, but quite a few were stories I did on my own, capitalizing on contacts I had made with his help. Suddenly I was something more than a beginner, here in my final year of college: I was actually earning a living, and quite a good living, by writing. I think the partnership with Garrett accelerated the progress of my career by several years.

Unfortunately there were negative aspects. Once I had assumed, naively, that if I merely wrote the best stories that were in me, editors would recognize their merits and seek my work. Now I was coming to see that there was a quicker road to success – to live in New York, to visit editors regularly, learn of their issue-by-issue needs and manufacture fiction to fit them. I developed a deadly facility; if an editor needed a 7500-word story of alien conquest in three days to balance an issue about to go to press, he need only phone me and I would produce it. Occasionally I took my time and tried to write the sort of science fiction I respected as a reader, but usually I had trouble selling such stories to the better markets, which reinforced my growing cynicism. By the summer of 1956 – by which time I had graduated from college and had married – I was the complete writing machine, turning out stories in all lengths at whatever quality the editor desired, from slam-bang adventure to cerebral pseudo-philosophy. No longer willing to agonize over the gulf between my literary ambitions and my actual productions, I wrote with astonishing swiftness, selling fifteen stories in June of 1956, twenty the following month, fourteen (including a three-part serial, done with Garrett, for *Astounding*) the month after that.

This hectic productivity was crowned at the World Science Fiction Convention in September 1956, when I was voted a special Hugo as the most promising new writer of the year. The basis for the award could only have been my ubiquity, since most of what I had published was carefully-carpentered but mediocre, and much was wholly opportunistic trash. It is interesting to note that the writers I defeated for the trophy were Harlan Ellison, who at the time had had only one or two dismal stories published, and Frank Herbert, whose impressive *Under Pressure* had appeared in *Astounding* the year before. A week after the convention I went with my bride, Barbara, to the first Milford Science Fiction Writers' Workshop, an awesome assembly of titans – Theodore Sturgeon, Fritz Leiber, Cyril Kornbluth, Lester del Rey, Damon Knight, Frederik Pohl, James Blish, William Tenn, and a dozen more of equal stature. Ellison and I were the only neophytes present. Harlan had not yet begun to show a shadow of his future abilities, and he made an easy whipping-boy for the patriarchs, but I was a different matter: self-contained, confident, quite sure of what I was doing and why.

Del Rey and a few others tried to shake my cynicism and persuade me to aim higher than sure-thing potboilers, but it was clear that potboilers were what I wanted to write, and no one could argue with my success at hammering out penny-a-word dreadfuls. I was only a boy, yet already my annual income was beyond that of anyone in the field except Asimov, Heinlein, Clarke, and Bradbury, those long-enshrined demigods. What I dared not say was that I had opted to write mechanical junk because I had no faith, any longer, in my ability to write anything better. It had been my experience that whenever I assayed the kind of fiction that Sturgeon or Leiber or Kornbluth wrote, I had trouble getting it published. My craftsmanship was improving steadily, in the narrow sense of craft as knowing how to construct a story and make it move; possibly some fatal defect of the soul, some missing quality, marred my serious work, so that it was idle of me, I thought, to try to compete with the Sturgeons and Leibers. I will leave art to the artists, I said quietly, and earn a decent living doing what I do best.

By the end of 1956 I had more than a million published words behind me. I lived in a large, handsome apartment in what was then a desirable neighbourhood on Manhattan's Upper West Side. I was learning about fine wines and exotic foods and planning a trip to Europe. The collaboration with Garrett had long since ended, but the impetus he had given me was sufficient and reliable. (A few, notably Horace Gold of *Galaxy*, swore at me for ruining a potentially important talent, but Horace bought my artfully aimed *Galaxy*-type potboilers all the same.) My fellow writers viewed me with alarm, seeing me as some sort of berserk robot that would fill every page of every magazine with its output; they deplored my utter lack of literary ambition, yet accepted me as one of their number, and I formed strong friendships within the close-knit science fiction fraternity. And I wrote, and I sold, and I prospered, and with rare exceptions abandoned any pretence at literary achievement. I wanted to win economic security – to get enough money into the bank so that I would be insulated against the financial storms that had buffeted most of the writers I knew, some of the greatest in the field among them. Lester del Rey pointed out to me that simply on the money-making level I was going about things the wrong way. The stuff I was writing earned me a cent or two a word and then dropped into oblivion, while stories written with more care, with greater intensity of purpose, were reprinted again and again, earning their authors fees far beyond the original sale. I knew that this was so, but I preferred to take the immediate dollar rather than the hypothetical future anthology glory.

So it went through 1957 and 1958. I grew a beard and acquired other, less superficial, stigmata of sophistication. I journeyed to London and Paris, to Arizona and California, treating myself at last to the travels I had not had in boyhood. I learned the lore of the investment world and made some cautious and quite successful forays into the stock market, seeking always the financial independence that I believed would free me from the karmic wheel of high-volume hackmanship.

Not everything I wrote was touched by corruption. I still loved science fiction for its soaring visionary expansiveness, for its mind-liberating power, and however dollar-oriented I became I still yearned to make some valuable contribution to the field, and felt guilty that the stuff I was churning out was the sort of thing I had openly scorned in my fan-magazine critical essays seven or eight years before. I recall in particular a Sunday afternoon party at Harlan Ellison's Manhattan apartment in 1957 where I talked shop with Cyril Kornbluth, Algis Budrys, James Blish, and one or two other sf writers of their level, and went home in an abyss of self-contempt because these men, my friends, were trying always to publish only their best while I was content to do my worst. Whenever I felt the sting, I put aside hackwork and tried to write honest fiction.

Scattered through my vast output of the late 1950's, then,

are a good many quite respectable stories, not masterpieces – I was still very young, and much more callow than most people suspected – but decently done jobs. Occasionally even now they find their way into anthologies. They were my comfort in those guilt-ridden days, those stories and the novels. In longer lengths I was not so commercially-minded, and I genuinely hoped to achieve in books what was beyond me in the magazines. There were few publishers of science fiction novels then, however: the market consisted, essentially, of three houses, Doubleday, Ballantine, and Ace. With the leading writers of the day keeping the first two well supplied with books, I found no niche for myself, and turned of necessity to Donald Wollheim's Ace Books. This small company published scores of novels a year in a rather squalid format, and was constantly searching for new writers to meet its hunger for copy. The shrewd and experienced Wollheim worked miracles on a tiny budget and produced an extraordinarily broad list, ranging from juvenile action stories to superb novels by Philip K. Dick, A. E. van Vogt, Clifford D. Simak, Isaac Asimov, and other luminaries. Wollheim saw potential in me, perhaps as a mass-producer of action fiction and perhaps as something more than that, and encouraged me to offer him novels. He purchased the first, *The Thirteenth Immortal*, late in 1956, and I wrote nine more for him, I think, in the next seven years.

My Ace novels would be fruitful material for somebody's thesis. The first was melodramatic, overblown, a little absurd, yet sincerely conceived; its faults are those of its author's youth, not his cynical approach toward his trade. The second, *Master of Life and Death* (1957), was something of a *tour de force*, a maze of plot and sub-plot handled, I think, with some dexterity. *Invaders from Earth* (1958), the third, attempts a sophisticated depiction of psychological and political realities. I liked those two well enough to allow them to be reprinted a decade later. *Stepsons of Terra* (1958) was an intricate time-paradox novel with a certain van Vogtian intensity. On the evidence of these four books alone I would seem an earnest and ambitious young writer striving constantly to improve. But the rest of the novels I wrote for Wollheim were slapdash adventure stories, aiming no higher than the least of his line; I had learned there was little money and less prestige in doing books for Ace, and without those rewards I was content to do the minimum acceptable job. (A few of my later Ace books were better than that, but they were aimed at better markets and went to Wollheim only after others had rejected them.) I know that Wollheim was disappointed in the trend my work for him had taken, but I was too far gone in materialism to care.

During the high-volume years I wrote a good deal that was not science fiction – crime stories, a few westerns, profiles of movie stars, and other odds and ends. Some of this work came to me on assignment from my agent, and some I sought because my rate of productivity was now so high that the science fiction field could not absorb all the wordage I was capable of turning out. I had the conviction, though – shared by a surprisingly large number of science fiction writers – that to write sf was the One True Task, and any other kind of writing was mere hack-work done to pay the bills. This was a legitimate enough attitude when held by people like James Blish or William Tenn, who in their early days were forced to write sports fiction and other trivia because the sf market was so tiny; but it was a bit odd for me to feel that way when virtually everything I wrote, sf or not, was pounded out in the same cold-blooded high-velocity manner. Still, I did feel that way, and whatever my private feelings about the quality of most of my science fiction at that time, I still saw it as a higher endeavour than my westerns and crime stories.

Then, late in 1958, the science fiction world collapsed. Most of the magazines for which I was writing regularly went out of business as a result of upheavals in distribution patterns, and those that survived became far more discriminating about what they would publish. My kind of mass production became obsolete. To sustain what had become a comfortable standard of living I found it necessary to leave the cozy, incestuous science fiction family and look for work in the general New York publishing scene.

The transition was quick and relatively painless. I was facile, I was confident, and my friends had friends. I hired out to any editor who would undertake to pay on time; and, though I continued to write some science fiction in 1959 and 1960, my records for those years show all sorts of strange pseudo-nymous stories and articles: 'Cures for Sleepless Nights', 'Horror Rides the Freeway', 'I Was a Tangier Smuggler', 'Hot Rod Challenge', 'Buried Billions Lie in Wait', and so many others that it strains my own credulity. I recall writing one whole piece before lunch and one after lunch, day in, day out; my annual output climbed well above a million words in 1959 and went even higher in 1960 and 1961.

These were years of wandering in the wilderness. I was earning more money than I had in science fiction, and I had no problems of guilt, for in pouring out this grotesque miscellany I did not need to flagellate myself with the knowledge that I was traducing a literature I loved. On the other hand, I had no particular identity as a writer. In the past, when people asked me what I did, I had answered that I wrote science fiction; now, working anonymously in twenty different sub-literate markets, I had no ready reply, so I went on saying I was a science fiction writer. In truth I did have the occasional story in *Galaxy* or *Astounding*, and an Ace book now and then, to make the claim legitimate. I was mainly a manufacturer of utilitarian prose, though, churned out by the yard. It was stupefyingly boring, and, as the money piled up, I invested it shrewdly and talked of retiring by the time I was thirty, living on my dividend income, and spending my days travelling, reading, and studying. Already I was doing a good bit of that. In the winters my wife and I fell into the habit of going to the West Indies, where we became skin-divers and explored coral reefs. In the summers we made other journeys – Canada in 1959, Italy in 1960, the American Northwest in 1961. I was working only four or five hours a day, five days a week, when at home, which left me ample leisure for my private interests – contemporary litera-ture and music, art, ancient history. There was an almost total split between my conscienceless commercialized working-hours self and the civilized and fastidious man who replaced him in early afternoon. I was still only about twenty-five years old.

Unexpectedly the seeds of a new writing career began to sprout. One of my few science fiction pieces of 1959 was a little novel for children, *Lost Race of Mars*, published by the notable house of Holt, Rinehart and Winston. (My earlier connection with Crowell had fallen apart in 1956, after their rejection of my proposed successor to *Revolt on Alpha C*, and this was my first contact with a major publishing house since then.) *Lost Race of Mars* was short and simple, but it was an appealing book; the *New York Times* chose it as one of the hundred best children's books of the year, and the publisher expressed eagerness to do more of my work. (*Lost Race* is still in print and selling well, both in hardcover and a paperback edition.) I had visited Pompeii while in Italy in 1960, and now I saw a way of capitalizing on my interest, strong since childhood, in antiquity and its remains: I suggested a book for young readers on the excavation of Pompeii.

The people at Holt, Rinehart and Winston considered the idea for quite a while but ultimately declined it. Henry Morrison, who then was handling my affairs at the Scott Meredith agency and who since has become an important agent in his own right, told me he thought the project would fare better if I wrote not about one ancient site but several – say, Chichén Itzá and Angkor and Babylon as well as Pompeii – and he even offered me a title for the expanded book, *Lost Cities and Vanished Civilizations*. When I agreed he sold the book, on the basis of a brief outline, to a Philadelphia house of which I knew nothing, Chilton Books.

With my agent's help I began to emerge from that wilderness of anonymous potboilerie. I began to work in book-length non-fiction, and displayed gifts for quick, comprehensive research and orderly uncluttered exposition. For a minor paperback company called Monarch, now defunct, I did books on the American space program, the Rockefeller family, and the life of Sir Winston Churchill; and for Chilton, in the summer of 1961, I wrote my lost-cities book.

None of this was art, but it was far from despicable work. I used secondary sources and wrote with journalistic speed, but what I produced was clear, generally accurate, an honest kind of popularized history. Chilton liked *Lost Cities* and hastened to accept my next proposal, for a book on underwater archaeology. Early in 1962 a suggestion for a young readers' book on great battles found favour at the old-line house of G. P. Putnam's Sons. In April of that year *Lost Cities and Vanished Civilizations* was published and – to my amazement, for I thought of it as no more than a competent rehash of other writers' books – was chosen as one of the year's five best books for young people by an annual awards committee in the field of juvenile publishing, and was selected by the Junior Literary Guild, an important book club. Once again I found myself launched.

Many of New York's leading hardcover publishing houses were willing, on the strength of the success of *Lost Cities,* to give me contracts for non-fiction juvenile books on whatever subject happened to interest me. As rapidly as I dared I severed my connections with my sleazy magazine outlets and ascended into this new, astoundingly respectable and rewarding career. Chilton took another general archaeology book, *Empires in the Dust.* Holt, Rinehart and Winston accepted a biography of the great Assyriologist, Austen Henry Layard. The New York Graphic Society commissioned a book on American Indians, and Putnam one on the history of medicine.

The rhythm of my life changed dramatically. I still wrote in the mornings and early afternoons – wrote at almost the same incredible velocity as when I had been doing tales of Tangier smugglers – but now I spent the after-hours time taking notes in libraries and museums, and I began to assemble a vast private reference library at home. Although my early non-fiction books had been hasty compilations out of other popularizations, I swiftly became more conscientious, as though to live up to the high opinion others had formed of those early books; I went to primary sources whenever possible, I visited actual sites, I did intensive research in many ways. The results were visible. Within a year or two I was considered one of the most skilled popularizers of the sciences in the United States, with publishers eagerly standing in line as my changing interests took me from books on Antarctica and ancient Egypt to investigations of scientific hoaxes and living fossils. For the first time since I had become a professional writer, nearly a decade earlier, I won my own respect.

I maintained a tenuous link with science fiction, largely social, since then as now my closest friends were science fiction writers. I attended parties and conventions, and kept up with what was being published. But of actual science fiction writing I was doing very little. There seemed no commercial reason to get back into sf, even though it had recovered considerably from its 1958 swoon; I had more work than I could handle in the lucrative juvenile non-fiction hardcover field. Only the old shame remained to tweak me: I had served science fiction badly in my 1955–8 days, and I wanted to atone. When Frederik Pohl became editor of *Galaxy* he suggested that I do short stories for him and offered me absolute creative freedom: I could write what I pleased and, within reason, he undertook to buy it. In such an arrangement I could blame neither editorial shortsightedness nor constricting editorial policies for the quality of what I wrote: I was my own master. In the summer of 1962 I offered Pohl a short story, 'To See The Invisible Man', inspired by Borges, which was out of an entirely different artistic universe from anything I had written in my first go-round in science fiction – a mature, complex story. He published it and, over the next couple of years, half a dozen more of similar ambitious nature, and, bit by bit, I found myself drawn back into science fiction, this time not as a producer of commodities but as a serious, dedicated artist who turned away from more profitable work to indulge in sf out of love.

During those years – 1962 to 1965 – when I dabbled in science fiction for sheer diversion only, science fiction was undergoing radical changes. The old pulp-magazine rigidities were dissolving. New writers were everywhere: Brian Aldiss, J. G. Ballard, Roger Zelazny, Samuel R. Delany, R. A. Lafferty, Michael Moorcock, and a dozen more. In the bad old days one had to be an established writer of mighty stature, a Bester or a Blish or a Sturgeon, to 'get away' with any sort of literary adventurousness; most editors rightly thought that their readers were hostile to unusual modes of narrative, and nearly everyone wrote in an interchangeable manner, unquestioningly adopting universal conventions of style and construction. Suddenly the *way* of telling stories was released from convention. The familiar old robots and starships were being put through strange and fascinating new paces. Pulp-magazine requirements for neat plots and 'upbeat' positive resolutions were abandoned. I had been only too willing, in 1957 and thereabouts, to conform to the prevailing modes, for it seemed quixotic to try to do otherwise. Now an army of younger, or at any rate newer, writers had boldly overthrown the traditional rules, and, a trifle belatedly, I joined the revolution.

Even after I returned to science fiction, the non-fiction books remained my chief preoccupation. For one thing, to go back to the mass production of sf would be to defeat the purpose of returning; for another, I was so overwhelmed with non-fiction contracts stretching two and three years into the future, that there was no question of a full-time resumption of sf. The non-fiction was becoming ever more ambitious and the books took longer; in the summer of 1965 I spent months working on one title alone, which I had never done before. (It was a book on the Great Wall of China – no mere cut-and-paste job, but an elaborate and unique synthesis of all available knowledge about the Wall.) Then, too, science fiction had become more permissive but there was still not much money to be had in writing it, and I was continuing to pursue my goal of economic independence, which mandated my centering my career in other fields.

One gigantic item of overhead had entered my life. Early in 1962 I had purchased an imposing house – a mansion, in fact – in a lovely, almost rural enclave near the northwest corner of New York City. I had always lived in apartments; now I joined the landed classes, and had my own lawn and garden, my own giant oak trees, my own wild raccoons wandering about at night (in New York!). There was room for all my books and all I was likely to acquire for many years to come. The third floor of the house, a separate four-room suite, became my working area, and we filled the rest of the place with books and paintings and *objets d'art*. It was a magnificent house, beautiful and stately, and not at all costly in terms of my income at the time. What *was* costly was the upkeep, taxes and cleaning and heat and all, running to many thousands of dollars a year; though I still intended to retire from full-time high-volume writing as soon as possible, I recognized that by buying the house I had postponed that retirement by at least five years.

The non-fiction books grew ever more demanding as – driven by vanity, I suppose, or by intellectual pride, or merely by the feeling that it was time for my reach to begin exceeding my grasp – I tackled bigger and bigger projects. Though I still was doing books for readers in their teens, a biography of Kublai Khan and one of Socrates, a book on bridges and one on coral reefs, I was aiming primarily for older readers in much of what I did, and endeavouring now to deal with subjects that had had no serious examinations in recent times. The Great Wall book was the first of these; and early in 1966 I embarked on a far more arduous task, a book called *The Golden Dream*, a study of the obsessive quest for the mythical land of El Dorado. Working an impossible, brutal schedule, pouring out thousands of words a week, I knew more than a little about the psychology of obsession, and the book, 120,000 words long, was surely the finest thing I had ever done. It was published in an appropriately handsome edition by the Bobbs-Merrill Company, was treated with respect by reviewers, and, I grieve to report, dropped into oblivion as fast as any of my hackwork. The book earned me no income beyond the small initial advance in the United States, was never published at all in Great Britain, and achieved only one translation, in France. I was disappointed but not discouraged; it would have been agreeable to grow rich on the book, but this was secondary to the joy and challenge of having written it. I was learning to love my work for its own sake, regardless of its fate in the marketplace. Growing up, that is.

About the time of *The Golden Dream* I inaugurated still another aspect of my career by asking the publisher of some of my non-fiction juveniles to let me edit a science fiction anthology. Here at last I could put to some practical use all those years of collecting and reading sf; I had built a superb science fiction library, with literally every magazine ever published and most of the books. The anthology, *Earthmen and Strangers*, was released in the autumn of 1966. I found editing so much to my taste that I sought other anthology contracts and ultimately was devoting as much time to editing as to my own writing.

In that same period – 1965–6 – I built close associations with the two major science fiction houses of the era, Ballantine and Doubleday. When I first became a professional writer these houses were the exclusive preserves of the Clarkes and Heinleins and Sturgeons and Asimovs and Bradburys, and seemed unattainable to the likes of me; now, still having not much of a reputation in science fiction but solidly established outside the field and confident of my skills, I found no difficulty convincing Betty Ballantine of Ballantine and Larry Ashmead of Doubleday to publish my sf. (Even though I considered myself a very part-time science fiction writer in those days, I was still prolific enough to require two regular publishers.) To Ballantine I gave *To Open the Sky*, a pseudo-novel constructed from five novelettes I had written for Fred Pohl's *Galaxy*. To Doubleday I offered *The Time Hoppers*, an expansion of one of those ambitious short stories of my youth that I had had so much trouble placing in 1954. They were both good, middle-of-the-road science fiction, not exactly of Hugo quality but several notches above anything I had published in the field before.

Ballantine also agreed to do a collection of my short stories; and, in January 1966, I proposed a new novel, a book called *Thorns*, telling Mrs Ballantine, 'Much of the texture of the story will rely on background details that can't be sketched in advance. I hope you can gather enough of my intentions from the outline to go ahead with it. What I have in mind is a psychological sf novel, somewhat adventurous in style and approach and characterization, and I think I can bring it off. It's worth trying, at any rate.' She agreed to the gamble.

I spent the next few months writing the El Dorado book, and in June I fell into a mysterious illness. All energy went from me and I lost close to twenty pounds – though I was slender to begin with – in a few weeks. I had not been ill since finishing with the standard childhood maladies, indeed was not even prone to minor upsets, and this was a startling event to me. The symptoms answered well to leukemia and other dire things, but turned out to be only a metabolic change, a sudden hyperactivity of the thyroid gland. Such thyroid outbreaks, I learned, are often caused by the stress of prolonged overwork, and I think the forced marches of El Dorado had much to do with this one. I took it as a warning: I was past thirty and it was time to think realistically about slowing down. Though I had enough book contracts to keep me busy for two or three years, I resolved to reduce my output and gradually to make drastic reductions in the time I devoted to work.

Though greatly weakened, I wrote steadily – but at a slower pace – through the infernally hot summer of 1966, while at the same time planning *Thorns* and doing preliminary research for another major non-fiction work, a study of the prehistoric Mound Builder cultures of the central United States. I was still gaunt and haggard when I attended the annual science fiction convention in Cleveland at the beginning of September, but the drug therapy for my thyroid condition was beginning to take hold, and immediately after the convention I felt strong enough to begin *Thorns*. The title describes the book: prickly, rough in texture, a sharp book. I worked quickly, often managing twenty pages or more a day, yet making no concessions to the conventions of standard science fiction. The prose was often oblique and elliptical (and sometimes shamefully opaque in a way I'd love to fix retroactively); the action was fragmented in the telling; the characters were angular, troubled souls. Midway in the job I journeyed out to Pennsylvania to attend a party at Damon Knight's Milford Workshop. I knew nearly all the writers there, and they knew me. They all knew how prosperous I was, and some were aware that I had achieved worthwhile things with my non-fiction, but they couldn't have had much respect for me as a writer of science fiction. They might admire my professionalism, my productivity, my craftsmanship – but to them I was still that fellow who had written all that zap-zap space-opera in the 1950's. Their gentle and not-so-gentle comments hardly troubled me, though, for I knew I was no longer that mass-producer of garbage, and sooner or later they would all know it too. While at Milford I glanced at an Italian science fiction magazine and found a harsh review of one of my early Ace novels, recently published in Italy. Badly done and wordy, the critic said – *malcondotto e prolisse.* Perhaps it was. The next day, when I went home to finish *Thorns,* Malcondotto and Prolisse joined the cast of characters.

I regained my health by the end of the year and eventually made a full and permanent recovery. I withdrew, bit by bit, from my lunatic work schedule: having written better than a million and a half words for publication in 1965, I barely exceeded a million in 1966, and have never been anywhere near that insane level of productivity since. Though I still wrote daily except when travelling, I worked less feverishly, content to quit early if I had had a good morning at the typewriter, and I began alternating science fiction and non-fiction books to provide myself with periodic changes of rhythm. I looked forward to 1967 with some eagerness – and with much curiosity, too, for that was the year in which my first really major science fiction, *Thorns* and *The Time Hoppers* and a novella called 'Hawksbill Station', would finally be published. Would they be taken as signs of reform and atonement for past literary sins, or would they be ignored as the work of a writer who by his own admission had never been much worth reading?

I began the year by writing a short story, 'Passengers', for Damon Knight's new *Orbit* anthology series. He asked for revisions, minor but crucial, five times, and though I grumbled I saw the wisdom of his complaints and did the rewriting. I wrote a novel for Doubleday, *To Live Again,* which surpassed anything I had done in complexity of plot and development of social situation. I expanded 'Hawksbill Station' into a novel. I did my vast Mound Builder book, bigger even than El Dorado, a book that was as much a study of the myth-making process as it was an exploration of American Indian culture. (When it appeared in 1968, as *Mound Builders of Ancient America: The Archaeology of a Myth,* many reviewers, even those in the archaeological journals, assumed I was myself an archaeologist, and I received flattering if embarrassing invitations to lecture, to teach, and to write reviews. The book was greeted enthusiastically by professional archaeologists and has become a standard reference item, to be found in most libraries. Having said so many uncomplimentary things about my own writing in these pages, I think I've earned the right to be a bit boastful about this one.) There were three other big projects in this year of supposedly reduced output: the novels *The Masks of Time* and *The Man in the Maze* and another Goliath of a non-fiction work, *The Longest Voyage,* an account of the first six circumnavigations of the world.

I was, in truth, riding an incredible wave of creative energy. Perhaps it was an overcompensation for my period of fatigue and illness in 1966, perhaps just the sense of liberation and excitement that came from knowing I was at last writing only what I wanted to write, as well as I could do it. In any event I look back in wonder and awe at a year that produced *To Live Again, Masks of Time, Man in the Maze,* two 150,000-word works of history, several short stories, and – I have as much trouble believing this as you – no less than seven non-fiction books for young readers, each in the 60,000-word range. No wonder my peers regarded me as some sort of robot: I have no idea myself how I managed it all, working five hours a day five days a week, with time off for holidays in Israel and the West Indies and a week at Montreal's Expo 67.

Thorns was published in August of 1967. All of Ballantine's science fiction titles were then automatically being distributed free to the members of the two-year-old Science Fiction Writers of America, and so all my colleagues had copies in hand at the time of that year's sf convention. Many of them had read it, and – as I hoped – it shook their image of my work. At least a dozen of my friends told me, with the frankness of true friendship, that the book had amazed them: not that they thought me incapable of writing it, but rather that I would be willing to take the trouble. It seemed such a radical break from my formularized science fiction of the 1950's that they thought of it as the work of some entirely new Robert Silverberg. I was pleased, of course, but also a little pained at these open admissions that I had been judged all these years by the basest of what I had written between 1955 and 1958. *Thorns* was not all that much of a breakthrough for me; it represented only a plausible outgrowth of what I had begun to attempt in 1962's short story, 'To See the Invisible Man', and in the work that followed it over a period of four years.

Even before the publication of *Thorns* I found my position in the American science fiction world undergoing transformations. In the summer of 1967 I had become President of the Science Fiction Writers of America, succeeding Damon Knight, founder of the organization. The job was not an award for literary merit but rather a tribute to the experience I had had in building a career and dealing with publishers. Certainly I was well qualified for the job, and I felt no hesitation about accepting it, especially since the organization would have collapsed if I had declined – no one else was willing to take it on. Doubtless if I had run against some writer whose work was more highly regarded than mine, James Blish or Poul Anderson or Philip José Farmer, I would have been defeated; but willy-nilly I ran unopposed, gladly letting myself in for a year of drudgery on behalf of my fellow writers. At least *Thorns* soon showed the rank-and-file of the membership that their new President would not disgrace the organization.

Thorns did not universally give delight. Those who found pleasure in my old straightforward action stories were appalled by this dark, disturbing book. One of my dearest friends, an old-line writer conservative in his tastes, explicitly accused me of a calculated sellout to the 'new wave' of science fiction – of writing a deliberately harsh and freaky book to curry favour with the influential leaders of the revolution within science fiction. That charge was particularly painful to me. Having blithely sold out so many times as a young man to any editor with the right price in his hand, I was hurt to find myself blamed for selling out again, this time to the opposite camp, when I finally wrote something that grew from my own creative needs instead of the market's demands. Such criticisms were rare, though. *Thorns* was nominated both for the Hugo and for the Science Fiction Writers' Nebula trophy – the first time anything of mine reached the final ballot in either contest.

They won no awards, nor did 'Hawksbill Station', which was also up for a Nebula; but the critics were re-evaluating my place in science fiction, invariably invoking my seamy early work before getting around to saying how much better a writer I was nowadays. 1968 promised to be a rewarding year. It was less than six weeks old, though, when I awakened at half past three one frigid winter morning to the glare of an unaccustomed light in the house. Burglars have broken in, I thought, groping toward wakefulness – but no, there were no burglars. The glare I saw was fire.

So out into the miserable night we went and watched the house burn. Papers stored in the attic, I think, had ignited. My wife and I carried our four cats and a flock of kittens to the dubious safety of the basement, and I seized the manuscript of my current book and a few ancient artifacts and cached them in the garage; then the firemen refused to let us return to the building, and we took refuge in the house across the way. By dawn it was over. The roof was gone; the attic had been gutted; my third-floor office was a wreck; and the lower floors of the house, though unburned, were awash in water rapidly turning to ice. A priest from a nearby Catholic college appeared and, unbidden, took several Volkswagen-loads of our houseplants to safety in his cabin, lest they freeze in the unprotected house. Then he returned and offered consolation, for I was in a bad way. No Catholic I, but I had felt the hand of some supernatural being pressing against me that night, punishing me for real and imagined sins, levelling me for overweening pride as though I had tried to be Agamemnon.

Friends rallied round. Barbara performed prodigies, arranging to have our belongings taken to storage (surprisingly, most of our books and virtually all the works of art had survived, though the structure itself was a ruin) and negotiating with contractors. I was not much good for anything for days – stupefied, God-haunted, broken. We moved to a small, inadequate rented house about a mile away as the immense job of reconstruction began. I bought a new typewriter, reassembled some reference books, and, after a few dreadful weeks, began once more to work in strange surroundings.

In nine months the house was ready to be occupied again, and by the spring of 1969 the last of the rebuilding was done and the place was more beautiful than ever – an exact replica of its former self, except where we had decided on improvements. But I was never the same again. Until the night of the fire I had never, except perhaps at the onset of my illness in 1966, been touched by the real anguish of life. I had not known divorce or the death of loved ones or poverty or unemployment, I had never experienced the challenges and terrors of parenthood, had never been mugged or assaulted or molested, had not been in military service (let alone actual warfare), had never been seriously ill. The only emotional scars I bore were those of a moderately unhappy childhood, hardly an unusual experience. But now I had literally passed through the flames. The fire and certain more personal upheavals some months earlier had marked an end to my apparent immunity to life's pain, and drained from me, evidently forever, much of the bizarre energy that had allowed me to write a dozen or more books of high quality in a single year. Until 1967, I had cockily written everything in one draft, rolling white paper into the machine and typing merrily away, turning out twenty or thirty pages of final copy every day and making only minor corrections by hand afterwards. When I resumed work after the fire I tried to go on that way, but I found the going slow, found myself fumbling for words and losing the thread of narrative, found it necessary in mid-page to halt and start over, pausing often to regain my strength. It has been slower and slower ever since, and I have only rarely, and not for a long time now, felt that dynamic sense of clear vision that enabled me to write even the most taxing of my books in wild joyous spurts. I wasted thousands of sheets of paper over the next three years before I came to see, at last, that I had become as other mortals and would have to do two or three or even ten drafts of every page before I could hope to type final copy.

I hated the place where we settled after the fire – it was cramped, dirty, confused, ugly – but the rebuilding job called for thousands of dollars beyond the insurance settlement, and I had to go on writing regardless of externals. With most of my reference library intact but in storage for the duration, I was forced back into virtual fulltime science fiction, the non-fiction temporarily impossible for me. One of the first things I wrote, in the early days of the aftermath, was a curiously lyrical novella, 'Nightwings', to which I added a pair of sequels some months later to constitute a novel. Later in the year came a novel for young readers, *Across a Billion Years*, almost unknown among my recent works – a rich, unusual book that never found an audience. There was a short story, 'Sundance', a display of technical virtuosity, my favourite among all my myriad shorter pieces. And, in my despair and fatigue, I managed somehow to write a bawdy comic novel of time travel, *Up the Line*. The fire had shattered me emotionally and for a time physically, but it had pushed me, I realized, into a deeper, more profound expression of feelings. It had been a monstrous tempering of my artistic skills.

In September of 1968 I went to California for the science fiction convention – my third visit to that state, and I was struck once again by its beauty and strangeness. I was toastmaster at the convention's awards banquet, a last-minute replacement for the late Anthony Boucher, and for five hours toiled to keep a vast and restless audience amused – a fascinating, almost psychedelic experience. November saw me back in my restored house, working on the biggest of all my non-fiction books, an immense exploration of the Zionist movement in the United States. The publishers invested a huge sum of money in it, and planned to promote it to best-seller status, but, as usual, nothing came of it but good reviews: I was destined never to win wide attention for my long non-fiction works.

My science fiction, though, was gathering acclaim. *Masks of Time* failed by only a few votes to win a Nebula, as did the novella 'Nightwings'. But 'Nightwings' did take a Hugo at the St Louis convention in 1969. In the spring of that year I wrote a novel, *Downward to the Earth*, which was in part inspired by a journey to Africa (and in which were embedded certain homages to Joseph Conrad) and in part by my own growing sense of cosmic consciousness: I had never been a religious man, had never belonged to any organized church, but something had been set ticking in me by the fire, a sense of connections and compensating forces, and *Downward to the Earth* reflected it. *Galaxy* purchased it for serialization and New American Library for book publication. In the autumn – slowly, with much difficulty – I wrote *Tower of Glass,* for Charles Scribner's Sons, the publishers of Hemingway and Wolfe and Fitzgerald, now experimenting with science fiction. *Galaxy* bought that one too. And at the end of the year I wrote my strangest, most individual book, *Son of Man,* a dream-fantasy of the far future, with overtones of Stapledon and Lindsay's *Voyage of Arcturus* and a dollop of psychedelia that was altogether my own contribution. It was becoming extremely hard for me to get words on paper, despite this long list of 1969's accomplishments, and, with the expenses of the fire behind me, I was again talking of retirement. Not total retirement – writing was a struggle, but *having written* was a delight – but at least a sabbatical of some months, once I had dealt with the contractual obligations I had taken on for the sake of rebuilding my home.

The paradox of this stage of my career manifested itself ever more forcefully in 1970: I felt continual growth of my art, my power, my vision, and simultaneously it became constantly more difficult to work. I tired more easily, I let myself be distracted by trifles, and when I did write I was over-finicky, polishing and polishing so that on a good day I was lucky to get nine or ten pages written. Still an immense output, but not what I had grown accustomed to pulling from myself in the vanished days of indefatigable productivity. Nevertheless it was an active year. I did *The World*

Inside, a novel composed of loosely related short stories set within a single great residential tower; I think it and *Tower of Glass* (another story of a giant erection!) are closer to pure science fiction, the exhaustive investigation of an extrapolative idea, than anything else I have written. I did *A Time of Changes,* more emotional than most of my work and heavily pro-psychedelic. I did *The Second Trip,* a rough and brutal novel of double identity, and I wrote the last of my major non-fiction books, *The Realm of Prester John,* which I regard as a genuine contribution to scholarship. (Doubleday published it and no one bought it.)

By now it was clear that the science fiction world had forgiven me for the literary sins of my youth. My short story 'Passengers' won a Nebula early in 1970. *Up the Line* and one of the 'Nightwings' series were on the ballot also, though they failed to win. In the summer I was American Guest of Honour at the World Science Fiction Convention in Heidelberg, a little to my surprise, for though I was beginning to think I would someday be chosen for this greatest of honours in science fiction, I had assumed it was at least ten years in the future. I was a triple Hugo nominee that year too, but came away, alas, with a bunch of second and third-place finishes. Another quite improbable boyhood fantasy was eerily fulfilled for me in 1970. When I was about sixteen and *Galaxy* was the newest and most controversial of science-fiction magazines, I diverted myself one day with an amiable daydream in which I was the author of three consecutive serials in that magazine – an awesome trick, since the authors of *Galaxy's* first five novels were Simak, Asimov, Kornbluth and Merril, Heinlein, and Bester. But there I was in 1970 with *Downward to the Earth, Tower of Glass,* and most of *The World Inside* running back-to-back, and *Time of Changes* following them in 1971. I remembered my old daydream and felt a little disbelieving shiver.

My new working habits were entrenching themselves: revise, revise, revise. Projects that might have taken me two weeks in 1965 took three months in 1970. I refused to sign new contracts, knowing that I no longer had much control over the length of time it took me to finish anything, and I could not therefore guarantee to meet delivery dates. Non-

fiction in particular I was phasing out; I had had a good run
in that career for a decade, but the burden of research now
was more than I cared to carry, and the failure of my big
books to have much commercial success had eventually had
a depressing effect. Now that I was in my full stride in
science fiction, working at the top of my form and enjoying
public favour, I wanted to devote as much of my dwindling
literary energies to that field as I could.

Strangely, it was becoming impossible for me to take the
stuff of science fiction seriously any more – all those starships
and androids and galactic empires. I had come to believe
that the chances that mankind would reach and colonize the
planets of other stars were very slight indeed, and the stories
set on such worlds now seemed idle fantasy to me, not
serious projection. So too with many of the other great
themes of science fiction: one by one they became unreal,
though they continued to have powerful metaphorical and
symbolic value for me. I discovered that much of what I was
writing in 1971 was either barely sf at all (*The Book of
Skulls*) or was a kind of parody of science fiction ('Good News
from the Vatican', 'Caliban', and other short stories) or
borrowed a genuine science fiction theme for use in an otherwise 'straight' mainstream novel (*Dying Inside*). This realiza-
tion inspired flickers of new guilt in me. I no longer had to
apologize, certainly not, for shortcomings of literary quality;
but was this new Silverberg really serving the needs of the
hard-core science fiction audience? Was he providing the kind
of sincerely felt fiction about the future that the readers still
seemed to prefer, or was he doing fancy dancing for his own
amusement and that of a jaded elite?

The pattern of awards in the field reinforced these doubts.
I was getting nominated by twos and threes every year now
for the Hugo and the Nebula; indeed, I have by now
amassed more final-ballot nominations than any other writer.
In 1972 the Science Fiction Writers of America favoured me
with two Nebulas, an unusual event, for my novel *A Time of
Changes* and my short story 'Good News from the Vatican' –
but the writers have relatively sophisticated tastes, and I
have fared far less well with the Hugos, awarded by a
broader cross-section of the sf readership. Though nomi-

nated every year, my books and stories have finished well behind more conservative, 'safer' works. This causes me no serious anguish or resentment, for I have hardly been neglected in the passing around of honours in the sf world, but it does lead me to brood a bit in idle hours. Not that it affects what I write: I am bound on my own course and will stay to it. I wish only that I could be my own man and still give pleasure to the mass of science fiction readers.

In 1971 I at last achieved the partial retirement of which I had been dreaming for so many years. The press of contracts abated, and in late spring I simply stopped writing, not to resume until autumn. I had never, not since early college days, gone more than four weeks away from my typewriter; now I was away from it five whole months, and felt no withdrawal symptoms at all. I read, swam, loafed; now and then I would work on anthology editing for an hour or so in the morning, for such editing was becoming increasingly important to me, but essentially I was idle all summer. A more complete break with the old Silverberg could not have been imagined. To underscore the transformation I had spent some weeks just before the holiday revising an early novel of mine, *Recalled to Life*, for a new edition. When I wrote it, in 1957, I had exaggeratedly high regard for it, seeing it as a possible Hugo nominee and hoping it would gain me a place with Ballantine or Doubleday or some other major publishing house. Looking at this masterpiece of my youth fourteen years later, I was appalled at its crudity, and repaired it as best I could before letting it be reissued. That experience gave me a good yardstick to measure my own growth.

Further transformations of my life, unexpected ones, lay in wait for me. My wife and I were native New Yorkers, and, however extensively we travelled, we always returned to New York, the home base, after a few weeks. We loved the city's vitality, its complexity, the variety of experience it offered, and we had money enough to insulate ourselves from its inconveniences and perils. Our rebuilt house was more than a dwelling to us, it was a system of life, an exoskeleton, and we assumed we would live in it the rest of our lives. But

New York's deterioration and decline was driving away our friends. Two by two they trooped away, some to distant suburbs, many to California; and by the autumn of 1971 we found ourselves isolated and lonely in a city of eight million. New York now was dangerous, dirty, ever more expensive; taxes were rising alarmingly and the amenities we prized, the restaurants and galleries and theatres, were beginning to go out of business. We were held fast by pride and pleasure in our house – but did we want to find ourselves marooned in our magnificent fortress while everything dissolved about us? Timidly we began talking about joining the exodus. It still seemed unthinkable; we toyed with the notion of moving to California the way loyal Catholics might toy with the idea of conversion to Buddhism, enjoying the novelty and daring of such an outlandish idea, but never taking it seriously. In October, 1971 we flew to San Francisco for a reunion with many of our transplanted Eastern friends; we said we were considering moving, and they urged us to come. It was impossible to give up our house, we said. We went back to California in November, though, still hesitating but now willing to look, however tentatively, at areas where we might find a comparable place to live. And just after the turn of the year we discovered ourselves, to our amazement, boarding a plane for a sudden weekend trip west to see a house that a friend had located for us.

That house turned out not to work – it was too big even for us, and too decayed – but before the weekend was over we had found another, strange and beautiful, an architectural landmark in a park-like setting, and we placed a bid on it and after some haggling the bid was accepted, and, as if in a dream, we put our cherished New York place up for sale and made arrangements to move West. It all happened so swiftly, in retrospect – less than six months from the moment the temptation first struck to the day we arrived, with tons of books and furniture, in golden California, in the new El Dorado.

California, then. A new life at the midpoint. For reasons of climate, my 1971 scheme of working autumn and winter and

43

taking a holiday in spring and summer did not seem desirable, though I still wanted to work only half the time. I hit on a plan of working mornings, normally a cloudy time of day here, and giving myself the afternoons free, with frequent total interruptions of work for short holidays away from home. This has worked well for me. My output continues to decline: 1971 saw me write about a quarter of a million words, 1972 only some 115,000, or about what I would have done in an average month a decade earlier. Since *Dying Inside* in 1971 I have written no novels, though doubtless that datum will be obsolete before this essay is published: my major work in California has been a novella, 'Born With the Dead', but a novel soon will be upon me, I think. Mainly I have written short stories, ostensibly science fiction, though the definition has required some stretching; they are strange and playful pieces, qualities evident in the titles of the two story collections I have made of them: *Unfamiliar Territory* and *Capricorn Games*.

Though one good quiver of the San Andreas Fault could destroy all I have built in a moment, I am at present in a comfortable situation, invulnerable to the demands of the marketplace, able to write what I choose and have it published by people I respect. The work comes slowly, partly because I revise so much, partly because the temptations of lovely California are forever calling me from my desk, partly because the old pressures – to prove myself artistically, to make myself secure financially – no longer operate on me. I keep close to nature, regularly visiting the mountains and deserts nearby and, when at home, labouring in my well-stocked and ever-expanding garden; I read a good deal, I edit anthologies of original material that bring me into contact with younger writers, I maintain many friendships both within and outside the science fiction cosmos, and, as the mood takes me, I pursue such old interests – music, archaeology, the cinema, whatever – as still attract me. Though I may eventually write more non-fiction, if only for the sake of learning more about the natural environment here by studying it systematically in preparation for a book, I expect that such writing as I do henceforth will be almost exclusively science fiction, or what passes for science fiction in my consciousness these days. I still respond to it as I did as a child for its capacity to open the gates of the universe, to show me the roots of time. I have little admiration for most of the science fiction I read today, and even less for the bulk of what I wrote myself before 1965, but I do go on reading it however short it falls of my ideal vision of it, and I do go on writing it in my fashion, pursuing an ideal vision there too and always falling short, but coming closer, coming closer now and then, close enough to lead me to continue.

Alfred Bester:

my affair
with science
fiction

I'm told that some science fiction readers complain that
nothing is known about my private life. It's not that I have
anything to conceal; it's simply the result of the fact that I'm
reluctant to talk about myself because I prefer to listen to
others talk about themselves. I'm genuinely interested, and
also there's always the chance of picking up something
useful. The professional writer is a professional magpie.

Very briefly: I was born on Manhattan Island 18
December 1913, of a middle-class, hard-working family. I
was born a Jew but the family had a *laisser faire* attitude
toward religion and let me pick my own faith for myself. I
picked Natural Law. My father was raised in Chicago,
always a raunchy town with no time for the God bit. Neither
had he. My mother is a quiet Christian Scientist. When I do
something that pleases her she nods and says, 'Yes, of course.
You were born in Science'. I used to make fun of her belief as
a kid and we had some delightful arguments. We still do,
while my father sits and smiles benignly. So my homelife was
completely liberal and iconoclastic.

I went to the last Little Red Schoolhouse in Manhattan
(now preserved as a landmark) and to a beautiful new high

school on the very peak of Washington Heights (now the scene of cruel racial conflicts). I went to the University of Pennsylvania in Philadelphia where I made a fool of myself trying to become a Renaissance man. I refused to specialize and knocked myself out studying the humanities and the scientific disciplines. I was a maladroit on the crew and football squads, but I was the most successful member of the fencing team.

I'd been fascinated by science fiction ever since Hugo Gernsback's magazines first appeared on the stands. I suffered through the dismal years of space opera when science fiction was written by the hacks of pulp Westerns who merely translated the Lazy X ranch into the Planet X and then wrote the same formula stories, using space pirates instead of cattle rustlers. I welcomed the glorious epiphany of John Campbell whose *Astounding* brought about the Golden Age of science fiction.

Ah! Science fiction, science fiction! I've loved it since its birth. I've read it all my life, off and on, with excitement, with joy, sometimes with sorrow. Here's a twelve-year-old kid, hungry for ideas and imagination, borrowing fairy tale collections from the library – *The Blue Fairy Book, The Red Fairy Book, The Paisley Fairy Book* – and smuggling them home under his jacket because he was ashamed to be reading fairy tales at his age. And then came Hugo Gernsback.

I read science fiction piecemeal in those days. I didn't have much allowance so I couldn't afford to buy the magazines. I would loaf at the newsstand outside the stationery store as though contemplating which magazine to buy. I would leaf through a science fiction magazine, reading rapidly, until the proprietor came out and chased me. A few hours later I'd return and continue where I'd been forced to leave off. There was one hateful kid in summer camp who used to receive the *Amazing Quarterly* in July. I was next in line and he was hateful because he was a slow reader.

It's curious that I remember very few of the stories. The H. G. Wells reprints, to be sure, and the very first book I ever bought was the collection of Wells' science fiction short stories. I remember 'The Captured Cross Section' which flabbergasted me with its arresting concept. I think I first read

'Flatland by A. Square' as an *Amazing* reprint. I remember a cover for a novel titled, I think, *The Second Deluge*. It showed the survivors of the deluge in a sort of second ark gazing in awe at the peak of Mt Everest now bared naked by the rains. The peak was a glitter of precious gems. I interviewed Sir Edmund Hillary in New Zealand a few years ago and he never said anything about diamonds and emeralds. That gives one furiously to think.

Through high school and college I continued to read science fiction but, as I said, with increasing frustration. The pulp era had set in and most of the stories were about heroes with names like 'Brick Malloy' who were inspired to combat space pirates, invaders from other worlds, giant insects and all the rest of the trash still being produced by Hollywood today. I remember a perfectly appalling novel about a Negro conspiracy to take over the world. These niggers, you see, had invented a serum which turned them white, so they could pass, and they were boring from within. Brick Malloy took care of those black bastards. We've come a long way, haven't we?

There were a few bright moments. Who can forget the impact of Weinbaum's 'A Martian Odyssey'? That unique story inspired an entire vogue for quaint alien creatures in science fiction. 'A Martian Odyssey' was one reason why I submitted my first story to Standard Magazines; they had published Weinbaum's classic. Alas, Weinbaum fell apart and degenerated into a second-rate fantasy writer, and died too young to fulfill his original promise.

And then came Campbell who rescued, elevated, gave meaning and importance to science fiction. It became a vehicle for ideas, daring, audacity. Why, in God's name, didn't he come first? Even today science fiction is still struggling to shake off its pulp reputation, deserved in the past but certainly not now. It reminds me of the exploded telegony theory; that once a thoroughbred mare has borne a colt by a non-thoroughbred sire she can never bear another thoroughbred again. Science fiction is still suffering from telegony.

Those happy golden days! I used to go to secondhand magazine stores and buy back copies of *Astounding*. I remember a hot July weekend when my wife was away working in a summer stock company and I spent two days thrilling to 'Slan' And Heinlein's 'Universe'! What a concept, and so splendidly worked out with imagination and remorseless logic! Do you remember 'The Destroyer'? Do you remember Lewis Padgett's 'Mimsy Were The Borogroves'? That was originality carried to the fifth power. Do you remember ... But it's no use. I could go on and on. The *Blue*, the *Red* and the *Paisley Fairy Books* were gone forever.

After I graduated from the university I really didn't know what I wanted to do with myself. In retrospect I realize that what I needed was a *Wanderjahr*, but such a thing was unheard of in the States at that time. I went to law school for a couple of years, just stalling, and to my surprise received a concentrated education which far surpassed that of my undergraduate years. After thrashing and loafing, to the intense pain of my parents who would have liked to see me settled in a career, I finally took a crack at writing a science fiction story which I submitted to Standard Magazines. The story had the ridiculous title of 'Diaz-X'.

Two editors on the staff, Mort Weisinger and Jack Schiff, took an interest in me, I suspect mostly because I'd just finished reading and annotating Joyce's *Ulysses* and would preach it enthusiastically without provocation, to their great amusement. They told me what they had in mind. *Thrilling Wonder* was conducting a prize contest for the best story written by an amateur, and so far none of the submissions was worth considering. They thought 'Diaz-X' might fill the bill if it was whipped into shape. They taught me how to revise the story into acceptable form and gave it the prize, $50. It was printed with the title, 'The Broken Axiom'. They continued their professional guidance and I've never stopped being grateful to them.

I think I wrote perhaps a dozen acceptable science fiction stories in the next two years, all of them rotten, but I was without craft and experience and had to learn by trial and error. I've never been one to save things, I don't even save my mss, but I did hold on to the first four magazine covers on which my name appeared. *Thrilling Wonder Stories* (15¢). On the lower left hand corner is printed 'Slaves of the Life

Ray, a startling novelet by Alfred Bester'. The feature story
was 'Trouble on Titan, A Gerry Carlyle Novel by Arthur K.
Barnes'. Another issue had me down in the same bullpen,
'The Voyage to Nowhere by Alfred Bester'. The most
delightful item is my first cover story in *Astonishing Stories*
(10¢). 'The Pet Nebula by Alfred Bester'. The cover shows an
astonished young scientist in his laboratory being confronted
by a sort of gigantic, radioactive seahorse. Damned if I can
remember what the story was about.

Some other authors on the covers were: Neil R. Jones, J.
Harvey Haggard, Ray Cummings (I remember that name),
Harry Bates (his too), Kelvin Kent (sounds like a house name
to me), E. E. Smith, Ph.D. (but of course), and Henry Kuttner
with better billing than mine. He was in the lefthand *upper*
corner.

Mort Weisinger introduced me to the informal luncheon
gatherings of the working science fiction authors of the late
thirties. I met Henry Kuttner (who later became Lewis
Padgett), Ed Hamilton, and Otto Binder, the writing half of
Eando Binder. Eando was a sort of acronym of the brothers
Earl and Otto Binder. E. and O. Earl died but Otto continued
to use the well-known *nom de plume*. Malcolm Jameson,
author of navy-orientated space stories, was there, tall,
gaunt, prematurely grey, speaking in slow, heavy tones. Now
and then he brought along his pretty daughter who turned
everybody's head.

The vivacious compère of those luncheons was Manley
Wade Wellman, a professional Southerner full of regional
anecdotes. It's my recollection that one of his hands was
slightly shrivelled, which may have been why he came on so
strong for the Confederate cause. We were all very patient
with that; after all, our side won the war. Wellman was quite
the man-of-the-world for the innocent thirties; he always
ordered wine with his lunch.

Henry Kuttner and Otto Binder were medium sized young
men, very quiet and courteous, and entirely without out-
standing features. Once I broke Kuttner up quite un-
intentionally. I said to Weisinger, 'I've just finished a wild
story that takes place in a spaceless, timeless locale where

there's no objective reality. It's awfully long, 20,000 words, but I can cut the first 5,000.' Kuttner burst out laughing. I do too when I think of the dumb kid I was. Once I said most earnestly to Jameson, 'I've discovered a remarkable thing. If you combine two story-lines into one the result can be tremendously exciting.' He stared at me with incredulity. 'Haven't you ever heard of plot and counterplot?' he growled. I hadn't. I discovered it all by myself.

Being brash and the worst kind of intellectual snob, I said privately to Weisinger that I wasn't much impressed by these writers who were supplying most of the science fiction for the magazines, and asked him why they received so many assignments. He explained, 'They may never write a great story but they never write a bad one. We know we can depend on them.' Having recently served my time as a magazine editor I now understand exactly what he meant.

When the comic book explosion burst, my two magi were lured away from Standard Magazines by the Superman Group. There was a desperate need for writers to provide scenarios (Wellman nicknamed them 'squinkas') for the artists, so Weisinger and Schiff drafted me as one of their writers. I hadn't the faintest idea of how to write a comic book script, but one rainy Saturday afternoon Bill Finger, the star comics writer of the time, took me in hand and gave me, a potential rival, an incisive, illuminating lecture on the craft. I still regard that as a high point in the generosity of one colleague to another.

I wrote comics for three or four years with increasing expertise and success. Those were wonderful days for a novice. Squinkas were expanding, there was a constant demand for stories, you could write three and four a week and experiment while learning your craft. The scripts were usually an odd combination of science fiction and 'Gangbusters'. To give you some idea of what they were like, here's a typical script conference with an editor I'll call Chuck Migg, dealing with a feature I'll call 'Captain Hero'. Naturally, both are fictitious. The dialogue isn't.

'Now listen,' Migg says, 'I called you down because we got to do something about Captain Hero.'

'What's your problem?'

'The book is closing next week and we're thirteen pages short. That's a whole lead story. We got to work one out now.'

'Any particular slant?'

'Nothing special, except maybe two things. We got to be original and we got to be realistic. No more fantasy.'

'Right.'

'So give.'

'Wait a minute, for Christ's sake. Who d'you think I am, Saroyan?'

Two minutes of intense concentration, then Migg says, 'How about this? A mad scientist invents a machine for making people go fast. So crooks steal it and hop themselves up. Get it? They move so fast they can rob a bank in a split second.'

'No.'

'We open a splash panel showing money and jewellery disappearing with wiggly lines and – Why no?'

'It's a steal from H. G. Wells.'

'But it's still original.'

'Anyway, it's too fantastic. I thought you said we were going to be realistic.'

'Sure I said realistic but that don't mean we can't be imaginative. What we have to – '

'Wait a minute. Hold the phone.'

'Got a flash?'

'Maybe. Suppose we begin with a guy making some kind of experiment. He's a scientist but not mad. This is a straight, sincere guy.'

'Gotcha. He's making an experiment for the good of humanity. Different narrative hook.'

'We'll have to use some kind of rare earth metal; cerium, maybe, or – '

'No, let's go back to radium. We ain't used it in the last three issues.'

'All right, radium. The experiment is a success. He brings a dead dog back to life with his radium serum.'

'I'm waiting for the twist.'

'The serum gets into his blood. From a lovable scientist he turns into a fiend.'

At this point Migg takes fire. 'I got it! I got it! We'll make like King Midas. This doc is a sweet guy. He's just finished an experiment that's gonna bring eternal life to mankind. So he takes a walk in his garden and smells a rose. Blooie! The rose dies. He feeds the birds. Wham! The birds plotz. So how does Captain Hero come in?'

'Well, maybe we can make it Jekyll and Hyde here. The doctor doesn't want to be a walking killer. He knows there's a rare medicine that'll neutralize the radium in him. He has to steal it from hospitals and that brings Captain Hero around to investigate.'

'Nice human interest.'

'But here's the next twist. The doctor takes a shot of the medicine and thinks he's safe. Then his daughter walks into the lab and when he kisses her she dies. The medicine won't cure him any more.'

By now Migg is in orbit. 'I got it! I got it! First we run a caption: IN THE LONELY LABORATORY A DREADFUL CHANGE TORTURES DR – whatever his name is – HE IS NOW DR RADIUM!!! Nice name, huh?'

'Okay.'

'Then we run a few panels showing him turning green and smashing stuff and he screams: THE MEDICINE CAN NO LONGER SAVE ME! THE RADIUM IS EATING INTO MY BRAIN!! I'M GOING MAD, HA-HA-HA!!! How's that for real drama?'

'Great.'

'Okay. That takes care of the first three pages. What happens with Dr Radium in the next ten?'

'Straight action finish. Captain Hero tracks him down. He traps Captain Hero in something lethal. Captain Hero escapes and traps Dr Radium and knocks him off a cliff or something.'

'No. Knock him into a volcano.'

'Why?'

'So we can bring Dr Radium back for a sequel. He really packs a wallop. We could have him walking through walls and stuff on account of the radium in him.'

'Sure.'

'This is gonna be a great character, so don't rush the writing. Can you start today? Good. I'll send a messenger up for it tomorrow.'

The great George Burns, bemoaning the death of vaudeville, once said 'there just ain't no place for kids to be lousy any more'. The comics gave me an ample opportunity to get a lot of lousy writing out of my system.

The line '... knocks him off a cliff or something' has particular significance. We had very strict self-imposed rules about death and violence. The Good Guys never deliberately killed. They fought, but only with their fists. Only villains used deadly weapons. We could show death coming – a character falling off the top of a high building *Aiggghhh!* – and we could show the result of death – a body, but always face down. We could never show the' moment of death; never a wound, never a rictus, no blood, at the most a knife protruding from the back. I remember the shock that ran through the *Superman* office when Chet Gould drew a bullet piercing the forehead of a villain in a *Dick Tracy*.

We had other strict rules. No cop could be crooked. They could be dumb but they had to be honest. We disapproved of Raymond Chandler's corrupt police. No mechanical or scientific device could be used unless it had a firm foundation in fact. We used to laugh at the outlandish gadgets Bob Kane invented (he wrote his own squinkas as a rule) for *Batman and Robin* which, among ourselves, we called Batman and Rabinowitz. Sadism was absolutely taboo; no torture scenes, no pain scenes. And, of course, sex was completely out.

Holiday tells a great story about George Horace Lorrimer, the awesome editor-in-chief of the *Saturday Evening Post*, our sister magazine. He did a very daring thing for his time. He ran a novel in two parts and the first installment ended with the girl bringing the boy back to her apartment at midnight for coffee and eggs. The second installment opened with them having breakfast together in her apartment the following morning. Thousands of indignant letters came in and Lorrimer had a form reply printed 'the *Saturday Even-*

ing Post is not responsible for the behaviour of its characters between installments.' Presumably our comic book heroes lived normal lives between issues; Batman getting bombed and chasing ladies into bed, Rabinowitz burning down his school library in protest against something.

I was married by then and my wife was an actress. One day she told me that the radio show, *Nick Carter*, was looking for scripts. I took one of my best comic book stories, translated it into a radio script and it was accepted. Then my wife told me that a new show, *Charlie Chan*, was having script problems. I did the same thing with the same result. By the end of the year I was the regular writer on those two shows and branching out to *The Shadow* and others. The comic book days were over, but the splendid training I received in visualization, attack, dialogue and economy stayed with me forever. The imagination must come from within; no one can teach you that. The ideas must come from without, and I'd better explain that.

Usually, ideas don't just come to you out of nowhere; they require a compost heap for germination, and the compost is diligent preparation. I spent many hours a week in the reading rooms of the New York public library at 42nd Street and Fifth Avenue. I read everything and anything with magpie attention for a possible story idea; art frauds, police methods, smuggling, psychiatry, scientific research, colour dictionaries, music, demography, biography, plays . . . the list is endless. I'd been forced to develop a speed-reading technique in law school and averaged a dozen books per session. I thought that one potential idea per book was a reasonable return. All that material went into my Commonplace Book for future use. I'm still using it and still adding to it.

And so for the next five or six years I forgot comics, forgot science fiction and immersed myself in the entertainment business. It was new, colourful, challenging and – I must be honest – far more profitable. I wrote mystery, adventure, fantasy, variety, anything that was a challenge, a new experience, something I'd never done before. I even became the director on one of the shows, and that was another fascinating challenge.

I did write one straight science fiction show. It was called, I think, *Tom Corbett, Space Cadet*. It was a very low budget show and most of the action was played in bookfold sets. Even the doors weren't practical, they were painted and you had to dissolve before a character made his exit. I quit for an amusing reason. In those early days of tv there wasn't any standard form for typing scripts; each show had its own particular requirements. *Corbett*, for reasons which I never could understand, insisted that all stage directions be typed in lower case and all dialogue in caps:

	(Corbett enters office)
CORBETT:	YOU WANTED TO SEE ME, SIR?
CAPTAIN:	YES. AT EASE, CORBETT. SIT DOWN.
	(Corbett sits)
CAPTAIN:	WHAT I'M GOING TO TELL YOU IS TOP SECRET.
CORBETT:	SIR?
CAPTAIN:	IT'S MUTINY.
CORBETT:	(Leaping up in consternation) NO!
CAPTAIN:	(Quietly) KEEP YOUR VOICE DOWN.

I just couldn't stand the characters continually shouting at each other.

Eventually a very slow and insidious poison began to diminish my pleasure; it was the constraints of network censorship and client control. There were too many ideas which I was not permitted to explore. Management said they were too different, the public would never understand them. Accounting said they were too expensive to do, the budget couldn't stand it. One Chicago client wrote an angry letter to the producer of one of my shows – 'Tell Bester to stop trying to be original. All I want is ordinary scripts'. That really hurt. Originality is the essence of what the artist has to offer. One way or another we must produce a new sound.

But I must admit that the originality compulsion can often be a nuisance to myself as well as others. When a concept for a story develops, a half-dozen ideas for the working-out come to mind. These are explored and dismissed. If they came that easily they can't be worthwhile. 'Do it the hard way,' I say to myself, and so I search for the hard way, driving myself and everybody around me quite mad in the process. I pace interminably, mumbling to myself. I go for long walks. I sit in bars and drink, hoping that an overheard fragment of conversation may give me a clue. It never happens but all the same, for reasons which I don't understand, I do get ideas in saloons.

Here's an example. Recently I was struggling with the pheromone phenomenon. A pheromone is an external hormone secreted by an insect, an ant, say, when it finds a food source. The other members of the colony are impelled to follow the pheromone trail, and they find the food, too. I wanted to extrapolate that to a man and I had to do it the hard way. So I paced and I walked and at last I went to a bar where I was nailed by a dumb announcer I knew who drilled my ear with his boring monologue. As I was gazing moodily into my drink and wondering how to escape, the hard way came to me. 'He doesn't *leave* a trail,' I burst out. 'He's impelled to *follow* a trail.' While the announcer looked at me in astonishment I whipped out my notebook and wrote 'Death left a pheromone trail for him; death in fact, death in the making, death in the planning.'

So, out of frustration, I went back to science fiction in order to keep my cool. It was a safety valve, an escape hatch, therapy for me. The ideas which no show would touch could be written as science fiction stories and I could have the satisfaction of seeing them come to life. (You must have an audience for that.) I wrote perhaps a dozen and a half stories, most of them for *Fantasy & Science Fiction* whose editors, Tony Boucher and Mick McComas, were unfailingly kind and appreciative.

I wrote a few stories for *Astounding*, and out of that came my one demented meeting with the great John W. Campbell, Jr. I needn't preface this account with the reminder that I worshipped Campbell from afar. I had never met him; all my stories had been submitted by mail. I hadn't the faintest idea of what he was like, but I imagined that he was a combination of Bertrand Russell and Ernest Rutherford. So I sent off another story to Campbell, one which no show would let me tackle. The title was 'Oddy and Id' and the concept was

Freudian, that a man is not governed by his conscious mind but rather by his unconscious compulsions. Campbell telephoned me a week later to say that he liked the story but wanted to discuss a few changes with me. Would I come to his office? I was delighted to accept the invitation despite the fact that the editorial offices of *Astounding* were then the hell and gone out in the boondocks of New Jersey.

The editorial offices were in a grim factory that looked like and probably was a printing plant. The 'offices' turned out to be one small office, cramped, dingy, occupied not only by Campbell but by his assistant, Miss Tarrant. My only yardstick for comparison was the glamourous network and advertising agency offices. I was dismayed.

Campbell arose from his desk and shook hands. I'm a fairly big guy but he looked enormous to me, about the size of a defensive tackle. He was dour and seemed preoccupied by matters of great moment. He sat down behind his desk. I sat down on the visitor's chair.

'You don't know it,' Campbell said, 'you can't have any way of knowing it, but Freud is finished.'

I stared. 'If you mean the rival schools of psychiatry, Mr Campbell, I think –'

'No I don't. Psychiatry, as we know it, is dead.'

'Oh come now, Mr Campbell. Surely you're joking.'

'I have never been more serious in my life. Freud has been destroyed by one of the greatest discoveries of our time.'

'What's that?'

'Dianetics.'

'I never heard of it.'

'It was discovered by L. Ron Hubbard, and he will win the Nobel peace prize for it,' Campbell said solemnly.

'The peace prize? What for?'

'Wouldn't the man who wiped out war win the Nobel peace prize?'

'I suppose so, but how?'

'Through dianetics.'

'I honestly don't know what you're talking about, Mr Campbell.'

'Read this,' he said, and handed me a sheaf of long galley proofs. They were, I discovered later, the galleys of the very first dianetics piece to appear in *Astounding*.

'Read them here and now? This is an awful lot of copy.'

He nodded, shuffled some papers, spoke to Miss Tarrant and went about his business, ignoring me. I read the first galley carefully, the second not so carefully as I became bored by the dianetics mishmash. Finally I was just letting my eyes wander along, but was very careful to allow enough time for each galley so Campbell wouldn't know I was faking. He looked very shrewd and observant to me. After a sufficient time I stacked the galleys neatly and returned them to Campbell's desk.

'Well?' he demanded. 'Will Hubbard win the peace prize?'

'It's difficult to say. Dianetics is a most original and imaginative idea, but I've only been able to read through the piece once. If I could take a set of galleys home and – '

'No,' Campbell said. 'There's only this one set. I'm rescheduling and pushing the article into the very next issue. It's that important.' He handed the galleys to Miss Tarrant. 'You're blocking it,' he told me. 'That's all right. Most people do that when a new idea threatens to overturn their thinking.'

'That may well be,' I said, 'but I don't think it's true of myself. I'm a hyperthyroid, an intellectual monkey, curious about everything.'

'No,' Campbell said, with the assurance of a diagnostician, 'You're a hyp-O-thyroid. But it's not a question of intellect, it's one of emotion. We conceal our emotional history from ourselves although dianetics can trace our history all the way back to the womb.'

'To the womb!'

'Yes. The foetus remembers. Come and have lunch.'

Remember, I was fresh from Madison Avenue and expense-account luncheons. We didn't go to the Jersey equivalent of Sardi's, '21', or even P. J. Clark's. He led me downstairs and we entered a tacky little lunchroom crowded with printers and file clerks; an interior room with blank walls that made every sound reverberate. I got myself a liverwurst on white, no mustard, and a coke. I can't remember what Campbell ate.

We sat down at a small table while he continued to discourse on dianetics, the great salvation of the future when the world would at last be cleared of its emotional wounds. Suddenly he stood up and towered over me. 'You can drive your memory back to the womb,' he said. 'You can do it if you release every block, clear yourself and remember. Try it.'

'Now?'

'Now. Think. Think back. Clear yourself. Remember! You can remember when your mother tried to abort you with a button hook. You've never stopped hating her for it.'

Around me there were cries of 'BLT down, hold the mayo. Eighty-six on the English. Combo rye, relish. Coffee shake, pick up.' And here was this grim tackle standing over me, practising dianetics without a licence. The scene was so lunatic that I began to tremble with suppressed laughter. I prayed. 'Help me out of this, please. Don't let me laugh in his face. Show me a way out.' God showed me. I looked up at Campbell and said, 'You're absolutely right, Mr Campbell, but the emotional wounds are too much to bear. I can't go on with this.'

He was completely satisfied. 'Yes, I could see you were shaking.' He sat down again and we finished our lunch and returned to his office. It developed that the only changes he wanted in my story was the removal of all Freudian terms which dianetics had now made obsolete. I agreed, of course; they were minor and it was a great honour to appear in *Astounding* no matter what the price. I escaped at last and returned to civilization where I had three double gibsons and don't be stingy with the onions.

That was my one and only meeting with John Campbell and certainly my only story conference with him. I've had some wild ones in the entertainment business but nothing to equal that. It reinforced my private opinion that a majority of the science fiction crowd, despite their brilliance, were missing their marbles. Perhaps that's the price that must be paid for brilliance.

One day, out of the clear sky, Horace Gold telephoned to ask me to write for *Galaxy* which he had launched with tremendous success. It filled an open space in the field; *Astounding* was hard science, *Fantasy & Science Fiction* was wit and sophistication, *Galaxy* was psychiatry-orientated. I was flattered but begged off, explaining that I didn't think I was much of a science fiction author compared to the genuine greats.

'Why me?' I asked, 'you can have Sturgeon, Kornbluth, Asimov, Heinlein.'

'I've got them,' he said, 'and I want you.'

'Horace, you're an old script writer so you'll understand. I'm tied up with a bitch of a tv show starring a no-talent. I've got to write continuity for him, quiz sections for him to emcee and dramatic sketches for him to mutilate. He's driving me up the wall. His agent is driving me up the wall. I really haven't got the time.'

Horace didn't give up. He would call every so often to chat about the latest science fiction, new concepts, what authors had failed and how they'd failed. In the course of these gossips he contrived to argue that I was a better writer than I thought and to ask if I didn't have any ideas that I might be interested in working out.

All this was on the phone because Horace was trapped in his apartment. He'd had shattering experiences in both the European and Pacific Theatres during World War II and had been released from the service with complete agoraphobia. Everybody had to come to his apartment to see him, including his psychiatrist. Horace was most entertaining on the phone; witty, ironic, perceptive, making shrewd criticisms of science fiction.

I enjoyed these professional gossips with Horace so much that I began to feel beholden to him; after all, I was more or less trapped in my workshop, too. At last I submitted perhaps a dozen ideas for his judgment. Horace discussed them all, very sensibly and realistically, and suggested combining two different ideas into what ultimately became *The Demolished Man.* I remember one of the ideas only vaguely; it had something to do with extra sensory perception but I've forgotten the gimmick. The other I remember quite well. I wanted to write a mystery about a future in which the police are armed with time machines so that if a crime is committed they could trace it back to its origin. This would make crime impossible. How then, in an open story, could a clever criminal outwit the police?

I'd better explain 'open story'. The classic mystery is the closed story or whodunnit. It's a puzzle in which everything is concealed except the clues carefully scattered through the story. It's up to the audience to piece them together and solve the puzzle. I had become quite expert at that. However, I was carrying too many mystery shows and often fell behind in my deadlines, a heinous crime, so occasionally I would commit the lesser crime of stealing one of my scripts from Show A and adapting it for Show B.

I was reading a three-year-old Show A script for possible theft when it dawned on me that I had written all the wrong scenes. It was a solid story but in the attempt to keep it a closed puzzle I had been forced to omit the real drama in order to present the perplexing results of the behind-the-scenes action. So I developed for myself a style of action-mystery writing in which everything is open and known to the audience, every move and counter-move, with only the final resolution coming as a surprise. The technique is a commonplace today. This is an extremely difficult form of writing; it requires you to make your antagonists outwit each other continually with ingenuity and resourcefulness.

Horace suggested that instead of using time machines as the obstacle for the criminal I use ESP. Time travel, he said, was a pretty worn out theme, and I had to agree. ESP, Horace said, would be an even tougher obstacle to cope with, and I had to agree.

'But I don't like the idea of a mind-reading detective,' I said, 'it makes him too special.'

'No, no,' Horace said. 'You've got to create an entire Esper society.'

And so the creation began. We discussed it on the phone almost daily, each making suggestions, dismissing suggestions, adapting and revising suggestions. Horace was, at least for me, the ideal editor, always helpful, always encouraging, never losing his enthusiasm. He was opinionated, God knows, but so was I, perhaps even more than he. What saved the relationship was the fact that we both knew we respected each other; and our professional concentration on the job. For professionals the job is the boss.

The writing began in New York. When my show went off for the summer, I took the ms out to our summer cottage on Fire Island and continued there. I remember a few amusing incidents. For a while I typed on the front porch. Wolcott Gibbs, the *New Yorker* drama critic, lived up the street and every time he passed our cottage and saw me working he would denounce me. Wolcott had promised to write a biography of Harold Ross that summer and hadn't done a lick of work yet. I. F. (Izzy) Stone dropped in once and found himself in the midst of an animated discussion of political thought as reflected by science fiction. Izzy became so fascinated that he asked us to take five while he ran home to put a fresh battery in his hearing-aid.

I used to go surf-fishing every dawn and dusk. One evening I was minding my own business, casting and thinking of nothing in particular when the idea of using typeface symbols in names dropped into my mind. I reeled in so quickly that I fouled my line, rushed to the cottage and experimented on the typewriter. Then I went back through the ms and changed all the names. I remember quitting work one morning to watch an eclipse and it turned cloudy. Obviously somebody up there didn't approve of eclipse-breaks. And so, by the end of the summer, the novel was finished. My working title had been 'Demolition'. Horace changed it to *The Demolished Man*. Much better, I think.

The book was received with considerable enthusiasm by the *Galaxy* readers, which was gratifying but surprising. I hadn't had any conscious intention of breaking new trails, I was just trying to do a craftsmanlike job. Some of the fans' remarks bemused me. 'Oh, Mr Bester! How well you understand women.' I never thought I understood women. 'Who were the models for your characters?' They're surprised when I tell them that the model for one of the protagonists was a bronze statue of a Roman emperor in the Metropolitan museum. It's haunted me ever since I was a child. I read the emperor's character into the face and when it came time to write this particular fictional character I used my emperor for the mould.

The *reclame* of the novel turned me into a science fiction somebody and people were curious about me. I was invited to gatherings of the science fiction Hydra Club where I met the people I was curious about; Ted Sturgeon, Jim Blish, Tony Boucher, Ike Asimov, Avram Davidson, then a professional Jew wearing a yarmulka, and many others. They were all lunatic (So am I. It takes one to spot one.) and convinced me again that most science fiction authors have marbles missing. I can remember listening to an argument about the correct design for a robot which became so heated that for a moment I thought Judy Merril was going to punch Lester del Rey in the nose. Or maybe it was *vice versa*.

I was particularly attracted to Blish and Sturgeon. Both were soft-spoken and charming conversationalists. Jim and I would take walks in Central Park during his lunch hour (he was then working as a public relations officer for a pharmaceutical house) and we would talk shop. He was very serious. Although I was an admirer of his work I felt that it lacked the hard drive to which I'd been trained, and I constantly urged him to attack his stories with more vigour. He never seemed to resent it, or at least was too courteous to show it. His basic problem was how to hold down a PR writing job and yet write creatively on the side. I had no advice for that. It's a problem which very few people have solved.

Sturgeon and I used to meet occasionally in bars for drinks and talk. Ted's writing exactly suited my taste which is why I thought he was the finest of us all. But he had a quality which amused and exasperated me. Like Mort Sahl and a few other celebrities I've interviewed – Tony Quinn is another – Ted lived on crisis and if he wasn't in a crisis he'd create one for himself. His life was completely disorganized, so it was impossible for him to do his best work consistently. What a waste!

I'd written a contemporary novel based on my tv experiences and it had a fairly decent reprint sale and at last sold to the movies. My wife and I decided to blow the loot on a few years abroad. We put everything into storage, contracted for a little English car, stripped our luggage down to the bare minimum and took off. The only writing materials I took with me were a portable, my Commonplace Book, a thesaurus and an idea for another science fiction novel.

For some time I'd been toying with the notion of using the *Count of Monte Cristo* pattern for a story. The reason is simple; I'd always preferred the anti-hero and I'd always found high drama in compulsive types. It remained a notion until we bought our cottage on Fire Island and I found a pile of old *National Geographics*. Naturally I read them and came across a most interesting piece on the survival of torpedoed sailors at sea. The record was held by a Philippine cook's helper who lasted for something like four months on an open raft. Then came the detail that racked me up. He'd been sighted several times by passing ships which refused to change course to rescue him because it was a Nazi submarine trick to put out decoys like this. The magpie mind darted down, picked it up, and the notion was transformed into a developing story with a strong attack.

The Stars My Destination (I've forgotten what my working title was) began in a romantic white cottage down in Surrey. This accounts for the fact that so many of the names are English. When I start a story I spend days reading maps and telephone directories for help in putting together character names – I'm very fussy about names – and in this case I used English maps and directories. I'm compelled to find or invent names with varying syllables; one, two, three, and four. I'm extremely sensitive to tempo. I'm also extremely sensitive to word colour and context. For me there is no such thing as a synonym.

The book got under way very slowly and by the time we left Surrey for a flat in London I had lost momentum. I went back, took it from the top and started all over again, hoping to generate steam pressure. I write out of hysteria. I bogged down again and I didn't know why. Everything seemed to go wrong. I couldn't use a portable but the only standard machines I could rent had English keyboards. That threw me off. English ms paper was smaller than the American and that threw me off. And I was cold, cold, cold. So in November we packed and drove to the car ferry at Dover, with the fog snapping at our ass all the way, crossed the Channel and drove south to Rome.

After many adventures we finally settled into a penthouse apartment on the Piazza della Muse. My wife went to work in Italian films. I located the one (1) standard typewriter in all Rome with an American keyboard and started in again, once more taking it from the top. This time I began to build up momentum, very slowly, and was waiting for the hysteria to set in. I remember the day that it came vividly.

I was talking shop with a young Italian film director for whom my wife was working, both of us beefing about the experimental things we'd never been permitted to do. I told him about a note on synesthesia which I'd been dying to write as a tv script for years. I had to explain synesthesia – this was years before the exploration of psychedelic drugs – and while I was describing the phenomenon I suddenly thought, 'Jesus Christ! This is for the novel. It leads me into the climax'. And I realized that what had been holding me up for so many months was the fact that I didn't have a fiery finish in mind. I must have an attack and a finale. I'm like the old Hollywood gag – 'start with an earthquake and build to a climax'.

The work went well despite many agonies. Rome is no place for a writer who needs quiet. The Italians *fa rumore* (make noise) passionately. The pilot of a Piper Cub was enchanted by a girl who sunbathed on the roof of a mansion across the road and buzzed her, and me, every morning from seven to nine. There were frequent informal motorcycle rallies in our piazza and the Italians always remove the mufflers from their vehicles; it makes them feel like Tazio Nuvolare. On the other side of our penthouse a building was in construction and you haven't heard *rumore* until you've heard stonemasons talking politics.

I also had research problems. The official US library was woefully inadequate. The British Consul library was a love and we used it regularly, but none of their books was dated later than 1930, no help for a science fiction writer needing data about radiation belts. In desperation I plagued Tony Boucher and Willy Ley with letters asking for information. They always came through, bless them, Tony on the humanities – 'Dear Tony, what the hell is the name of that Russian sect that practised self-castration? Slotsky? Something like that.' – Willy on the disciplines – 'Dear Willy, how long could an unprotected man last in naked space? Ten minutes? Five minutes? How would he die?'

The book was completed about three months after the third start in Rome; the first draft of a novel usually takes me about three months. Then there's the pleasant period of revision and rewriting; I always enjoy polishing. What can I say about the material? I've told you about the attack and the climax. I've told you about the years of preparation stored in my mind and my Commonplace Book. If you want the empiric equation for my science fiction writing, for all my writing, in fact, it's:

$$\text{Concept} + \left\{ \begin{array}{l} \text{Discipline} \\ \text{Experiment} \\ \text{Experience} \\ \text{Pattern sense} \\ \text{Drama sense} \\ \text{Preparation} \\ \text{Imagination} \\ \text{Extrapolation} \\ \text{Hysteria} \end{array} \right\} = \text{Story} \leftrightarrows \text{Statement}$$

I must enlarge on this just a little. The mature science fiction author doesn't merely tell a story about Brick Malloy vs The Giant Yeastmen from Gethsemane. He makes a statement through his story. What is the statement? Himself, his own dimension and depth. His statement is seeing what everybody else sees but thinking what no one else has thought, and having the courage to say it. The hell of it is that only time will tell whether it was worth saying.

Back in London the next year I was able to meet the young English science fiction authors through Ted Carnell and my London publisher. They gathered in a pub somewhere off the Strand. They were an entertaining crowd, speaking with a rapidity and intensity that reminded me of a debating team from the Oxford Union. And they raised a question which I've never been able to answer: Why is it that the English science fiction writers, so brilliant socially, too often turn out rather dull and predictable stories? There are notable exceptions, of course, but I have the sneaky suspicion that they had American mothers.

John Wyndham and Arthur Clarke came to those gatherings. I thought Arthur rather strange, very much like John Campbell, utterly devoid of a sense of humour and I'm always ill-at-ease with humourless people. Once he pledged us all to come to the meeting the following week; he would show slides of some amazing underwater photographs he had taken. He did indeed bring a projector and slides and show them. After looking at a few I called, 'Damn it, Arthur, these aren't underwater shots. You took them in an aquarium. I can see the reflections in the plate glass'. And it degenerated into an argument about whether the photographer and his camera had to be underwater too.

It was around this time that an event took place which will answer a question often asked me: Why did I drop science fiction after my first two novels? I'll have to use a flashback, a device I despise, but I can't see any other way out. A month before I left the States my agent called me in to meet a distinguished gentleman, senior editor of *Holiday* magazine, who was in search of a feature on television. He told me that he'd tried two professional magazine writers without success, and as a last resort wanted to try me on the basis of the novel I'd written about the business.

It was an intriguing challenge. I knew television but I knew absolutely nothing about magazine piece-writing. So once again I explored, experimented and taught myself. *Holiday* liked the piece so much that they asked me to do pieces on Italian, French and English tv while I was abroad, which I did. Just when my wife and I had decided to settle in London permanently, word came from *Holiday* that they wanted me to come back to the States. They were starting a new feature called 'The Antic Arts' and wanted me to become a regular monthly contributor. Another challenge. I returned to New York.

An exciting new writing life began for me. I was no longer isolated in my workshop; I was getting out and interviewing stimulating people in interesting professions. Reality had become so colourful for me that I no longer needed the therapy of science fiction. And since the magazine imposed no constraints on me, outside of the practical requirements of professional magazine technique, I no longer needed a safety valve.

I wrote scores of pieces, and I confess that they were much easier than fiction, so perhaps I was lazy. But try to visualize the joy of being sent back to your old university to do a feature on it, going to Detroit to test-drive their new cars, covering the NASA centers, taking the very first flight of the Boeing 747, interviewing Sophia Loren in Pisa, De Sica in Rome, Peter Ustinov, Sir Laurence Olivier (they called him Sir Larry in Hollywood), Mike Todd and Elizabeth Taylor, George Balanchine. I interviewed and wrote, and wrote, and wrote, until it became cheaper for *Holiday* to hire me as Senior Editor, and here was a brand new challenge.

I didn't altogether lose touch with science fiction; I did book reviews for *Fantasy & Science Fiction* under Bob Mills' editorship and later Avram Davidson's. Unfortunately, my standards had become so high that I seemed to infuriate the fans who wanted special treatment for science fiction. My attitude was that science fiction was merely one of many forms of fiction and should be judged by the standards which apply to all. A silly story is a silly story whether written by Robert Heinlein or Norman Mailer. One enraged fan wrote in to say that I was obviously going through change of life.

Alas, all things must come to an end. *Holiday* failed after a robust twenty-five years; my eyes failed, like poor Congreve's; and here I am, here I am, back in my workshop again, immured and alone, and so turning to my first love, my original love, science fiction. I hope it's not too late to rekindle the affair. Ike Asimov once said to me 'Alfie, we broke new trails in our time but we have to face the fact that we're over the hill now.' I hope not, but if it's true I'll go down fighting for a fresh challenge.

What am I like? Here's as honest a description of myself as possible. You come to my workshop, a three-room apartment, which is a mess, filled with books, mss, typewriters, telescopes, microscopes, reams of typing paper, chemical glassware. We live in the apartment upstairs and my wife uses my downstairs kitchen for a storeroom. This annoys me; I used to use it as a laboratory. Here's an interesting sidelight. Although I'm a powerful drinker I won't permit liquor to be stored there; I won't have booze in my workshop.

You find me on a high stool at a large drafting table editing some of my pages. I'm probably wearing flimsy pyjama bottoms, an old shirt and am barefoot; my customary at-home clothes. You see a biggish guy with dark brown hair going grey, a tight beard nearly all white and the dark brown eyes of a sad spaniel. I shake hands, seat you, hoist myself on the stool again and light a cigarette, always chatting cordially about anything and everything to put you at your ease. However, it's possible that I like to sit higher than you because it gives me a psychological edge. I don't think so, but I've been accused of it.

My voice is a light tenor (except when I'm angry; then it turns harsh and strident) and is curiously inflected. In one sentence I can run up and down an octave. I have a tendency to drawl my vowels. I've spent so much time abroad that my speech pattern may seem affected, for certain European pronunciations cling to me. I don't know why. GA-rahj for garage, the French *r* in the back of the throat, and if there's a knock on the door I automatically holler, '*Avanti!*' a habit I picked up in Italy.

On the other hand my speech is larded with the customary profanity of the entertainment business, as well as Yiddish words and professional phrases. I corrupted the WASP *Holiday* office. It was a camp to have a blond junior editor from Yale come into my office and say, 'Alfie, we're having a *tsimmis* with the theater piece. That *goniff* won't rewrite'. What you don't know is that I always adapt my speech pattern to that of my vis-à-vis in an attempt to put him at his ease. It can vary anywhere from burley (burlesque) to Phi Beta Kappa.

I try to warm you by relating to you, showing interest in you, listening to you. Once I sense that you're at your ease I shut up and listen. Occasionally I'll break in to put a question, argue a point, or ask you to enlarge on one of your ideas. Now and then I'll say 'wait a minute, you're going too fast. I have to think about that.' Then I stare into nowhere and think hard. Frankly, I'm not lightning, but a novel idea can always launch me into outer space. Then I pace excitedly, exploring it out loud.

What I don't reveal is the emotional storms that rage within me. I have my fair share of frustrations and despairs, but I was raised to show a cheerful countenance to the world and suffer in private. Most people are too preoccupied with their own troubles to be much interested in yours. Do you remember Viola's lovely line in *Twelfth Night*? 'And with a green and yellow melancholy, she sat like Patience on a monument, smiling at grief.'

I have some odd mannerisms. I use the accusing finger of a prosecuting attorney as an exclamation point to express appreciation for an idea or a witticism. I'm a 'toucher', hugging and kissing men and women alike, and giving them a hard pat on the behind to show approval. Once I embarrassed my boss, the *Holiday* editor-in-chief, terribly. He'd just returned from a junket to India and, as usual, I breezed into his office and gave him a huge welcoming hug and kiss. Then I noticed he had visitors there. My boss turned red and told them 'Alfie Bester is the most affectionate straight in the world.'

I'm a faker, often forced to play the scene. In my time I've been mistaken for a fag, a hardhat, a psychiatrist, an artist, a dirty old man, a dirty young man, and I always respond in character and play the scene. Sometimes I'm compelled to play opposites – my fast to your slow, my slow to your fast – all this to the amusement and annoyance of my wife. When we get home she berates me for being a liar and all I can do is laugh helplessly while she swears she'll never trust me again.

71

I do laugh a lot, with you and at myself, and my laughter is loud and uninhibited. I'm a kind of noisy guy. But don't ever be fooled by me even when I'm clowning. That magpie mind is always looking to pick up something.

A BRIEF BIOGRAPHY

Born:	18 Dec. 1913
Height:	6 ft. 1 in.
Weight:	180 lbs.
Hair:	Brown-grey
Eyes:	Brown
Beard:	Grey-brown
Scars:	None
Tattoos:	None
I.Q. (1928):	119

Born 18 December 1913 in New York City and raised there. New York public schools and the University of Pennsylvania, class of 1935. Suffered from what later came to be known as TMA – too many aptitudes. By a fluke sold a story and dropped all the other A's. Professional writer ever since; fiction, comics, radio, tv, interviewer, editor. Not very good to start with but hopefully have improved. Never learned how to spell.

Married in 1936 and still married to the same lady, which is some sort of record these days. She is an actress who is now a swingin' vice-president of an advertising agency. No children (outside of myself). We decided never to give hostages to fortune. Also we were way ahead of Women's Lib. Little remains to be told. I have my ups and downs; big money, no money, but by some strange freak of luck my wife is earning most when I'm earning least. Perhaps we should have become professional gamblers; there's a gambler's streak in all artists. We stake our lives on everything we produce.

Ever since I became aware of writers and writing, I've been irritated by writers who claim to have been cooks, lumberjacks, and sandhogs; and whose photographs show them as unshaven persons in hairy sweaters at the tiller of a sloop. It's almost as though writers in America suffer from a terror of being thought effete ... at least that class of writers who are of the masculine persuasion.

I have never been a cook, a lumberjack, a sandhog, or even a soda-jerk. I've been a writer all my life, and I don't give a damn who knows it. If required, I can produce my favourite photograph of myself, an epicene portrait of a burly gent in Edwardian waistcoat standing on the fire escape of a tenement, brandishing a beautifully furled umbrella. This is symbolic of my background and my taste.

I come from a middle class family, was born on 'The Rock', as genuine New York locals call Manhattan Island, and was raised on The Rock where I was the worst stick-ball player on Post Avenue between Dyckman Street and 204th Street. I went to George Washington High School and, much to my regret, did not play a part in any of the sex scandals that were the gossip of the cafeteria.

I went to the University of Pennsylvania where I was the worst center in the history of Penn football squads, and where I did not discover sulfanilamide. I was given this newfangled drug for an experiment in vital staining in physiology research, and reported that sulfa was useless. I also studied music composition and orchestration, and offended my classmates by arriving stinking to high heaven from dissection work in the comparative anatomy lab. It was a triumph and vindication for me when we first visited Leopold Stokowski's studio. It stank to high heaven from cooked cauliflower.

I began writing when I graduated from college in 1935, only because I'd tried law and medicine, given them up, and was floundering around, wondering what to do with myself. I sold a few stories of the old pulp science fiction sort to *Thrilling Wonder* magazine (Ugh!), and then came the advent of comic books. This fantastic phenomenon exploded into a million dollar industry overnight, and there was a desperate search for writers who could be trained to turn out scenarios for the artists. I wrote stories for comic book heroes with unlikely names like 'the Green Lantern', 'the Star

Spangled Kid', and 'Captain Marvel'. These were the days before sex and sadism polluted the comics, and we had wonderful training in visualization, and tight, crisp, action writing.

With this preparation it was only natural for me to shift to radio script writing. For years I wrote *Charlie Chan, Nick Carter, The Shadow* and other shows. When the shift to television came, I went along with it, but rather reluctantly. Radio had been a tough, demanding craft, without room for fakers. Television was quite the opposite. It was around this time that I began writing science fiction again, solely for release from an entertainment medium which I disliked. After a few stories for *Astounding* and *Fantasy & Science Fiction* I was persuaded by Horace Gold of *Galaxy* to write *The Demolished Man* which had and still has a renown that amazes me.

After three years of tv writing I became so disgusted that I wrote a corrosive novel about the business called *Who He?* (reprinted as *The Rat Race*), took the money from the movie sale, got the hell out of the country and lived abroad for a couple of years. Some people claim I had to get out, but, alas, the book wasn't that corrosive. I only wish it had been. It must always be the mission of the writer to excite and astonish and, if possible, to infuriate.

While I was abroad I wrote another science fiction novel, *The Stars My Destination*, and did some magazine pieces for *Holiday Magazine* who insisted on bringing me back, kicking and screaming, to write their entertainment column. Since then I've been writing magazine features, occasional tv hour specials, and am in hock to my publisher for a couple of books.

I collect XIXth century scientific apparatus, am the world's worst amateur astronomer, am a trustee of my town on Fire Island where I'm also the world's worst surf-fisherman. Last year I took a refresher course in physiology at the graduate school at Washington Square and discovered that science has passed me by, so this year I'm studying bookbinding at the YWCA.

Almost everybody I know has a secret ambition to be a writer. I am a writer, and, typically, I have a secret ambition to be a scientist. I want to win the Nobel Prize for discovering something like 'Bester's Binomial' or 'Bester's Syndrome' or 'The Fissure of Bester'. I don't think I ever got over that sulfa goof.

Harry Harrison:

the beginning
of the affair

What I find interesting, something I had never considered before I began to write this particular piece of prose, is that for many years I never had any sort of strong drive to become a writer. As a child I never had much of a strong drive to 'become' any particular sort of adult, which gave me many moments of depression and guilt. My interests were many and I began far more projects than I ever completed. At some time during high school I seem to have reached the decision that my fate was in the arts, but whether in writing or painting I could not be sure. I remember a period of mental coin-flipping where art won and I slanted my plans in that direction. Not that plans could be slanted very much, other than choosing which service to enter. Mine was the draftee generation; halfway through high school when the war began – with war not college waiting upon graduation.

The war did many good things for me, though I certainly did not appreciate them at the time. First, and most important, it kicked into existence a strong sense of survival that has been of great service since. It also terminated my childhood, a fact that I was certainly not grateful for at the time since growing up can be a painful process. I also learned to drink and curse, the universal coin of military life, but, more important, I was robbed of three years of my life without satisfactory return. At least I believed so for a long time, which is the same thing, and this gave me that singular capacity for solitary work, the drive to get it done, without which the freelance cannot succeed. That I am a writer now I can blame almost completely on science fiction.

I was a single child, always solitary and bookish, reading constantly from some tender age. *Loneliness* is a word that has deepfelt meaning to me. Until the age of twelve I did not have a single friend among my classmates, nor did I belong to any gang or pack. Totally without companions I was absorbed in reading. Through the telescope of time I cannot quite make out if bookishness prevented personal relationships, or if rejection by my peer group drove me to books. I do know that I cannot remember a time when I could not read. The Queens Borough Public Library was quite a long walk from one of the apartments where we lived (these were depression days and we moved very often, dodging creditors and greedy landlords) so, in order not to waste valuable reading time, I cultivated the ability to walk and read at the same time, glancing up only when I came to a curb. But these library books, ten or twenty a week, were there to back up the gaps in my reading time when I could not read the pulps. While I would root through the shelves in the library with catholic taste, both fiction and non-fiction, my taste in the pulps was very exacting. No straight detective fiction, no westerns (and certainly no love-westerns, that awful mismatch that was poor Eisenhower's favourite reading) and no general fiction pulps. War, air war, railroad and science fiction, with science fiction heading the list as best of all. And of course the hero-centred pulps, but only when the hero was of a science fictional nature. Doc Savage, Operator 5, The Spider; wonderful stuff. And science fiction, always science fiction. As my tastes and enthusiasms changed and modified during the years sf was the single thing I was true to. John Buchan had a very long run for his money, while the works of C. S. Forester are the only ones to match the sf interest for longevity. Through everything the single unchanging pivot of my life was always science fiction. This is obvious only by hindsight; at the time I had other things to think about.

Coming out of the army was a traumatic experience and years passed before I could understand why. It seems very obvious now. I was a sergeant, I had been a gunnery instructor, a truck driver, an armourer, a power-operated turret and computing gunsight specialist, a prison guard with a loaded repeating shotgun to guard my charges when we went out in the garbage trucks, and a number of other interesting things. Though I loathed the army I was completely adjusted to it. I could not return to the only role I knew in civilian life, that of being a child.

Some months passed, lubricated alcoholically by what we called the 52–20 Club. Among the benefits received by those who survived the war was a mini-pension of $20 a week for 52 weeks while the veteran theoretically sought employment. Employment was easy to dodge and the twenty bucks was enough for beer money. Days passed easily. But in a few months the fall term was due to begin and I resolved to end the lotus eating and go to college. Despite the feeling of anger that the girls and draft dodgers I had graduated high school with would be getting their degrees soon after I entered. (The term 'draft dodger' is used here in the military sense, not the civilian one. We members of the civilian army looked with envy and applause upon anyone smart enough or sick enough to miss the draft. When on furlough we helped friends still undrafted to avoid the fate we suffered. We jeered openly at anyone sucker enough to volunteer. It might have been different in the navy or the marines – but let us not forget they were drafting marines too in those days.)

Fate, and an overburdened educational system, saw to it that I enrolled at Hunter College which, up until this point, had been for girls only. In the mythology of New York City the Hunter girls had always been known for (a) their brains and (b) their ugliness. For once rumour proved to be fact. It was a sort of horrifying and warped mirror image of the army where everyone had been male and stupid. I did not finish out the term.

Hunter did one good thing for me, for it was there I met John Blomshield. I was in John's watercolour class and he spotted some infinitesimal drop of talent in my work. When I left Hunter I continued as a private pupil of his. I must say either too much or too little about this admirable man so, sadly, it will have to be too little. He was a master painter, a mannerist five centuries late for his school, an incomparable draftsman, a great portraitist, a professional artist and a civilized man of the world. The first one I had ever met. He had studied in Paris after the First World War and knew all of the people who to me were just names on canvases or book spines. He was a man of culture and gave me a glimpse of a world I had never known. The results of this exposure were not immediate – but the seed was planted. I continued to study with him privately, went to a number of art schools, and within the year I was a hardworking comic book hack who still spent three afternoons a week drawing the antique at the Metropolitan Museum of Art.

Within a few years I became a practising and moderately successful commercial artist, eventually to have a studio of my own with three other artists who depended upon me to draw in the accounts. Illustrations, lettering, book jackets, anything, but mostly those hack comic books. This sort of operation was called a 'factory' for obvious reasons. I draw the curtain gratefully over those years. I *know* that all those hours at the drawing board have helped my visual sense in my writing; I just wish there had not been so many of them. In the end I had stopped most of the drawing and began packaging comics instead. For a fee I would assemble a complete comic book ready for the engraver. The fee was so small I had to write most of the book myself, and even ink some of the stories. Which was fine since I was building a new career. When the comic business folded I used my editorial experience to move into editing pulps, which were gasping their last at the time. Then into writing. And it was the science fiction that got me into writing as I have said before.

I had been an sf reader since the age of seven, an active fan since thirteen when I wrote my first letter to an sf magazine, and an enthusiast all of the time. We were now into the fifties, that false spring of science fiction success. New magazines were being started every day and New York was the centre of the science fiction world. Everyone was there. If they didn't live there then by God they came through town to see the editors. There was an organization called the Hydra Club, which was the focal point of professional sf activity, and I had the pleasure of being a member – eventually even attaining the heights of the presidency. (Before being hurled down and out of the club completely in a power struggle. Many pros were ex-fans and fannish ways die hard.) I was Harry the artist because I did sf book jackets and magazine illustrations. But at heart I was Harry the fan and wallowing in a fannish dream of glory. Just look at who was there.

Many of the meetings took place in Fletcher Pratt's apartment, a wonderful great place on 58th Street. He was collaborating with L. Sprague de Camp at the time. Fletcher was chess champion of the club until Fred Brown took the crown away from him. I drew a game with Fred once; he always beat me after that. It was at Fletcher's place that we all met Olaf Stapledon when he came to the city. Fred Pohl was one of the pillars of the club, as was Judy Merril. So Cyril Kornbluth came too. The list of the others reads like a history of modern science fiction. Damon Knight, Frank Belknap Long, Lester del Rey, Phil (William Tenn) Klass, H. Beam Piper, Richard Wilson, Isaac Asimov, Sam Merwin, Bruce Elliot, Jerry Bixby, Doc Lowndes, Groff Conklin, Ted Sturgeon, George O. Smith, Hans Santesson, Willy Ley, Katherine McLean, Danny Keyes. Editors too, Marty Greenberg and Dave Kyle who founded Gnome Press, Larry Shaw, Horace Gold, Sam Merwin; Tony Boucher would stop by when in town. I'm sure I have forgotten some here, I apologize in advance, but what an overabundance of riches!

While science fiction was having a fine time and going along at a great clip my personal world was getting a bit unstable. An unfortunate first marriage was breaking up and the comic book business was going on the rocks, I lost fifty pounds during a massive throat infection and Damon Knight was editing *Worlds Beyond.* Yes, they all do fit together. I was doing illustrations for Damon's magazine, some of the best I have ever done because Damon worked me very hard, and I would have illustrated almost all of the third issue if I hadn't been laid low by the infection. I was too sick to draw, but was able to write since a trembling finger on the typewriter key does not show.

Until this time I had done some comic script writing, some fillers for those same magazines, and a page or two of experimental work. I almost had to, being surrounded by writers and hearing writing talk so much. But my interest was still with the graphic arts. Bedridden, I wrote a story, and when I eventually staggered out I went to see Damon to pick up my assignments and to ask him what I should do with the story. He read it, quickly as I remember, and said that he would give me a hundred dollars for it. I was getting fifteen bucks a shot for the illos (or was it five?) so the price was certainly right. My story appeared in issue three of Damon's magazine, instead of the missing illos, and as soon as it was published the magazine promptly folded. At this time Fred Pohl had his own literary agency and he took me on as a client and my next sale was to him. He anthologized the story I had sold Damon. This sort of success was not repeated for a long time.

This first story had a terrible title ('I Walk Through Rocks', which Damon promptly changed to 'Rock Diver', a distinct improvement) but was well slanted commercially. I was a commercial artist, wasn't I? If I was going to write, I was going to write in the same way. I used a tried and true sf device, the matter penetrator, and expanded upon its possible uses. I borrowed a classic western plot, the claim jumpers, as a vehicle. I had many years to go before I attempted to practise the art of writing in addition to the craft.

Not that I intend to knock the craft. John Blomshield always said that painters should be like masons; learn to lay bricks before you build a house. I believe the same is true of writing. Since all my drawings were done on assignments by editors, ('Harrison, I want a three by four of an eight tentacled monster squashing a girl with big tits in a transparent space suit, line and none of your zip-a-tones or damn Benday, twelve bucks by tomorrow afternoon,') I went to editors to find out what kind of writing they wanted. What they wanted I wrote.

Men's adventures.

I WENT DOWN WITH MY SHIP,
I CUT OFF MY OWN ARM,
MAGRUDER – THE WOODEN CANNON
  GENERAL
Confessions.
HE THREW ACID IN MY FACE,
MY IRON LUNG BABY,
MY HUSBAND GAMBLED MY BODY AWAY

And more. I don't regret a one of them. I learned to write clearly, I learned to communicate with the reader, I learned to write to deadline, I learned a lot of things. And I stopped writing this sort of repetitive, unrewarding hack just as soon as I could.

Because I really wanted to write fiction, and particularly science fiction. I could not write it in New York because I did not have the sitting and thinking time, nor the correct atmosphere, nor the money to afford the sitting and thinking. I needed out. I also had the wife, Joan, who made everything possible, and a newborn son. She will read these words first, as she first reads everything I write. The baby, Todd, is now in college and the movie projectionist in the local fleapit and he will read them next. Moira, a very grown up fifteen, will read them about the same time. All of their lives and all of my work was made possible by fleeing New York.

Bruce Elliott, who had written commissioned stories for me when he was down and I was editing, was at this time managing editor of *Pic* and *Picture Week* and other dime pocket magazines, and said sure when I went to him for a job. I had my choice of art director or copy editor. I took the art job since I could do it in my sleep, and often did, and I wanted to save my writing energies for articles in the evenings. I worked until I had saved a bit of money; then I quit and we went to Mexico.

In those days everyone came to New York and no one left it, so everyone said I was psycho. Joan was about the only exception – and she was the only one who would suffer if I were cracked. Todd just smiled; a very happy baby. We sold our air conditioner (a New Yorker's most prized possession) and everything else we could not take with us, loaded up our Ford Anglia with cot and mattress and bags and left. We never came back. After a year in Mexico we moved to England, then to Italy. We returned for a few months to stay in Long Beach, New York, when Moira was born (I have very little good to say about the doctors in the Naples area), but left as soon as we could for Denmark. The children grew up there, a country made for children, then after a year in England we came to California where this is being written. If things go as planned we will be living in England again by the time you read this. Charles Monteith, who is, I am happy to say, my friend and editor as well as Brian's, once told me 'Harry, you are the most peripatetic fellow I know'. Perhaps he was right.

And what has this got to do with science fiction? Everything. With a few exceptions everything I wrote after going to Mexico was science fiction. Everything I sold was science fiction and every penny I earned was from science fiction. This has both a good and bad side. Good; I could write the thing I enjoyed most. Bad; until I learned my art I was a commercial writer and wrote with my market in mind at all times. This is a fine way to begin but no way to end. I wrote and sold the same novel four times before I had the nerve, pushed on reluctantly by Joan's encouragement, to write a book just for myself. But this was to come much later. At the time I was the most unliterary of writers, which also has both a good and bad side to it. The good is that I had no pretensions of art, no unattainable goals, no ambitions to make any kind of particular mark in writing. I was literarily very naive; in 1950 I took *A Passage to India* out of the library by mistake, thinking by a quick glimpse at the spine that it was by C. S. Forester. This 'mistake' was more than compensated for by the pleasure of discovering Forster's novel for myself; I still reread it at least once a year. My background of literary appreciation was only that of New York City elementary and high school, a singularly weak reed in the thirties and early forties. For me reading has always been primarily a pleasure, the reading of good fiction the greatest pleasure of all.

The bad side of this coin is that thinking myself an 'unliterary' person I took a very long time to write anything other than beginning, middle, end, action-moved, plot-supported, sexless, hardcore science fiction. But agonizing decisions about my work were still years in the future. I had yet to write my first novel. In fact I did not really think of it as a novel but rather a serial for *Astounding,* the most important magazine in the history of science fiction.

Cuautla is a market town one hundred kilometres south of Mexico City. In 1956 there were no American tourists there and only a handful of gringo residents. Our furnished house was rented for thirty dollars a month, the full time maid was just five dollars for the same month, with food and drink in the equivalent price range. Despite this the money finally vanished and for a moment there we thought that everyone in New York had been right. Patience, worrying, writing and tequila at 75¢ a litre bridged this period and some money began to come in. Soon there was enough so that I could consider writing on speculation, that is doing fiction in the hopes it would eventually sell, rather than hacking out confessions and men's adventures to order. A few years earlier I had practised writing narrative hooks, just the hooks without stories to follow. (This is a pulp writer's term – which may very well have its roots in Grub Street – for the copy on the first page of manuscripts. Something lively, fascinating or intriguing must be on this half a page to 'hook' the editor, and eventually the reader, into turning to the second page of manuscript.) I had written one that intrigued me so much that I had to write the story to find out what the hook meant. This hook forms the first four paragraphs of *The Stainless Steel Rat,* originally written as a novelette, later expanded into a novel that was eventually to have two sequels. From small acorns . . .

So I wrote the story and mailed it off to John Campbell who bought it for *Astounding.* Emboldened by this sale, while eating regularly with a little money in the bank, I outlined an idea for a novel and sent it to John. His response was warm and immediate and generous, the response he gave to all writers. He liked the idea and suggested ways of developing it that I had not considered. Buoyed up by his enthusiasm I began writing *Deathworld.*

My ambition might be said to have outrun my talent because I wanted to do more than simply sell a story for money. I felt that there was too much empty writing in *Astounding*, stories that just talked and described and never moved on any level. I wanted to bring the 'action' back into science fiction. (How times change. Today there is far too much pulp action and I lean in the opposite direction.) But I didn't want forced action, so I needed a plot where the movement was an integral part. I started the book slowly. I worked on it during the year we lived in Mexico, continued it in England and Italy, then brought it back to the United States. Still unfinished. Completely unsure of myself I sent John 30,000 words, about half the final length, and he responded with a deep editorial grumble that he thought he was reading the entire thing and looked forward to finishing it. I finished it. At that time I did not know John's habit of not writing acceptance notes since my previous sale to him had been done through an agent. (A terrible agent, given the bounce when we returned from Italy.) Off the book went to him and some days passed and a thin envelope arrived in the mail. There was no letter in it. Just a cheque for $2,100.

This was a very clear message. I could write and sell short stories and now I had sold the serialized version of my novel to the best paying and most prestigious magazine in the field. One half of the money would be a bit of financial security, the other half was spent on one way tickets for us all to Denmark.

Written so long after the fact all of this seems to have a sort of destiny to it, as though there were no other course, that this was the wisest possible decision, that money flowed in steadily to support my advancing career. Nothing could be further from the truth, everything happened by happenstance. We settled in Cuautla, Mexico because that is the town where the paved road ends. We went to England because a fan flight had been organized for the first world sf convention outside of North America. We went to Bromley because we met an English fan at the convention who lived there. We stayed there some months because money ran out and we couldn't pay our bill to leave the loathsome residential hotel where we were staying. With the bill paid we moved to a Pakistani rooming house in London because we had met Pakistani friends of Hans Santesson's. It was a very

cold winter and when an old friend wrote us he would be
going to Italy it did not take much more temptation to join
Gary. (This was Gary Davis, World Citizen Number One.) I
wrote a last true confession story to buy our way out of
England and we went to join him on Capri, the island made
famous by the song – which was about all we knew about it –
where he had friends. It was some time before Gary showed
up, followed closely by the police since he had entered the
country illegally and without a passport. But we were well
settled in by that time and could only wish him luck when he
was arrested and sent off to the concentration camp at
Frascati. But Gary had been staying in France with Dan
Barry, another American expatriate, who came to join us in
Capri a few months later. Dan is the well known artist who
had just started doing the comic strip *Flash Gordon* for King
Features. He needed a writer and since there were very few
ex-comic artist American science fiction script writers living
in Europe I got the job. Then we went back to the United
States to find a decent doctor and to bounce my agent, next
to Denmark, because we had a friend there named Preben
Zahle whom we had met in Mexico when I heard him trying
to explain his automobile problems in French to a mechanic
and I aided him with some translation. Preben was a very
fine painter who also acted as consulting art director on
Tidens Kvinder, the leading Danish woman's magazine.
Through his good offices I wrote some travel articles for the
magazine and even collaborated with Joan on an article
about travelling with children. About which we had amassed
a good bit of empirical information. We had planned only to
visit Denmark, but we liked it so much we stayed six years.

There is no way that this series of events could have been
predicted. Certainly most things were not planned in
advance. I have always felt that they just happened and,
after happening, became part of the record. But perhaps
there is more to the sequence than the blind workings of
chance. When Brian read the first draft of this memoir he
questioned my attitude. He felt that there was more than a
touch of destiny in this. He has caused me to pause and think
a bit.

I think he is right – if he will agree that we hold destiny in our hands and work to shape it. There are more ways *not* to become a freelance, self-employed author than there are ways to attain this goal. The writers who do get through the obstacle course must climb over and under some strange things and put up with a good deal of assorted miseries along the way. If they are blocked they find a new path through the maze. The path can be very long and very difficult and the reading public should be aware that when they read about authors, as they are reading about them in this volume, they are reading about the victors. Among the fallen are writers with just as much talent – occasionally more – who are victims of what Cyril Connolly called 'the enemies of promise'. The best way to irritate a freelance is to tell him how *lucky* he is to be able to lead the kind of life he does.

In this series, meeting Dan Barry was, in a way, the most fortunate event, because writing the daily and Sunday *Flash Gordon* scripts gave me a solid bit of income that almost covered basic living expenses. Up until this point we had been broke too often; my camera and Joan's gold bracelet made many trips into and out of hock shops. (I learned early *never* to hock something at anything like its true value, not that uncle will allow this to happen in any case. The camera was worth $150 so I would hock it for $15. This made it worth getting out of pawn. To be held in reserve not only for taking the occasional picture but for another rainy day of hocking.) It is hard to write when hungry, cold and broke. Even harder to write when (as happened in Italy) the only money to hand was 100 lire (7 pence) which made the decision difficult whether to buy one more air mail stamp with it to write once more to the moron agent (the one I later dumped) for some money, or to buy milk for the baby with it.

Salvation came from two directions. Joan got credit from the local grocer for food and Hans Santesson sent some money in advance against a story yet to be written. A friend in need, he bought a number of robot stories from me for *Fantastic Universe* which he edited. A good number of them were written after receipt of the money. They were later gathered into a collection titled *War With the Robots* which was published in America, England, Germany, Italy and Spain.

Too much boom and bust is hard on the writer, not to mention his wife and children. For ten years I wrote the scripts for *Flash* until I was so choked up with loathing for comics I could not type a word more. This is my hangup and not the fault of either Dan or Flash. They underwrote the slow years of getting established, until I could actually live on the income from my books and stories.

I was writing more, becoming more critical at the same time, more aware of what I was doing, aware that I was working to a pulp formula in my novels but too fearful to change a winning technique. *Deathworld* has pulp motion and plot because that was all I knew. *The Stainless Steel Rat* was clobbered together from two *Astounding* novelettes and seemed a good idea at the time to make money. *Sense of Obligation*, my next *ASF* serial, was a slightly disguised *Deathworld*. The next was *The Ethical Engineer* which appeared in paperback as *Deathworld 2* – which is certainly clear enough description. The serials were popular with *ASF* readers who always voted me a bonus, and the same for my short stories as well. The fans liked them too: *Deathworld* lost out to a Heinlein novel for a Hugo. Bantam was selling an awful lot of copies of the paperback versions. The world was quite happy with my work; I wasn't. It was a strange time to get a critical conscience. I wanted to write better and I wanted to use different material.

Salvation came through the good offices of Joseph Heller and Brian Aldiss. I read *Catch-22* which crystallized my thinking, and had met Brian a few years earlier. In addition to his friendship, which I value above all others, I appreciate his literary and critical skills. Brian is a prose stylist, one of the best writing in the English language and certainly the best in science fiction. As different as we are as writers and in background, we are in agreement on so many other things that friendship and collaboration come naturally. (It was after reading his sf literary criticism that I realized I wanted to read more like it. From this came the idea for *SF Horizons*, the first critical sf magazine, which we published and edited.) We met often, at conventions and even stranger places, and we talked a good deal – oh yes how we talked and still do!

The Beginning of the Affair

It was a little late, but my literary education had begun. Proximity to England helped because there is not as much snobbism there about sf being some kind of inferior form of fiction. For the first time in my life I met writers and critics who were not sf writers – yet who respected the sf field of literary endeavour. Brian himself, of course, was for endless years a full time literary editor who would later publish best-selling mainstream novels. Kingsley Amis, whose critical look at sf gets more than a nod in the title of this book, Bruce Montgomery, Robert Conquest and Geoff Doherty are the names that spring instantly to mind. If they were going to respect sf as part of literature I would have to look at it that way myself.

Heller and Voltaire demonstrated to me that some things are so awful that they can only be approached through the medium of humour. I had already written at least one humorous short story that was well received and anthologized, 'Captain Honario Harpplayer, RN', and I felt I could do more. All of my experimentation so far had been in the short story, since the time investment there is obviously much less than the novel. This was both good and bad because the 'experimental' did not do very well, not in these dark days of the early sixties. The quotes are around experimental there because my stories were nothing of the kind. They just fell outside the classic pulp taboos that still dominated the field.

The story of one of them 'The Streets of Ashkelon', is typical. I wrote this for a Judy Merril anthology of 'dangerous' ideas that was never published due to the publisher going broke. The story came back and went out, and returned rather quickly from all the American markets. It was too hot to handle since it had an atheist in it. This is the truth. Even my good friend, Ted Carnell, would not take it for the more liberal British *New Worlds*. I asked Brian if he had any idea what could be done with it. He had some critical remarks about the priest's characterization, which I agreed with, but said as well that he would like to use it in an anthology he was doing for Penguin. (And I must add that Carnell, once he knew the story would be anthologized, felt it would be all right to use in his magazine. This might indicate that his spine needed stiffening, but if so it indicates as well that the American editors had no spines at all.) The story has a happy ending in that it was eventually anthologized three times in the United States and translated into Swedish, Italian, Russian, Hungarian – and twice into French.

It was this sort of experience that made me hesitant to put the time into an entire novel that might not sell. At that period a novel a year was the most I could do and the thought of losing a year's book income was not to be considered. Until then all of my novels had been serialized in *ASF*, bringing in nearly three thousand dollars with the bonus, and the novel I had in mind was certainly not for Campbell.

Eventually the artist triumphed over the businessman, ears became numb to the sound of hungry children crying in the background, and I contacted Damon Knight. Damon was acting as an sf literary scout for Berkley Books and I was sure he would be *simpatico* to my needs. I sent him the first (and only) chapter I had written of an experimental novel titled *If You Can Read This You Are Too Damn Close*. With it were some one page character sketches and a few words about the kind of novel I wanted to attempt. Damon liked it and went to bat for me and extracted a $1,500 advance from Berkley. Taking a deep breath I climbed to my office in the attic, looked out across the frozen Øresund to the snowy shore of Sweden, and began writing *Bill, the Galactic Hero*.

It was a shaking experience. I was doing less than half my normal wordage every day and greatly enjoying myself – at the time. Laughter all day at the typewriter – how I *do* enjoy my own jokes – instant depression when I came down for dinner. Upon rereading, the stuff seemed awful. Or awfully way out; there had never been anything like it in sf before. Then back the next day for some more chuckling and suffering. Joan was a pillar of strength at this period, reading the copy and laughing out loud and saying it was great and get on with the job and stop muttering to yourself. I got on with it, finished it, had it typed and mailed off to Damon.

Who rejected it saying what I had here was an adventure story loused up with bad jokes. Take the jokes out and it would be OK.

The Beginning of the Affair

Although everything eventually ended happily this was one of life's low moments. Tom Dardis, the editor-in-chief at Berkley, seemed to like the book, but he did not want to go over the head of his paid adviser. It was Tim Seldes, the Doubleday sf editor, who broke the ice. He greatly enjoyed the book and said he would buy it for that firm. Cheered on by this assurance Berkley agreed to publish it as well. In England, Hilary Rubinstein was then editor for Gollancz and he read, enjoyed and bought it as well. (Thus beginning a long and enduring relationship for he is now a literary agent, the best in Britain, and mine of course.) Fred Pohl bought the serial rights for *Galaxy* and Mike Moorcock did the same in Britain for *New Worlds*, then in the first flower of its new personality after Mike had replaced Carnell as editor.

Here was a message of some kind. Sf was growing and contained within its once pulp boundaries new and different markets. *Bill* was positively not an *ASF* serial and had not even been submitted there. (In later years I discovered that my judgment had been correct in this at least. One day John Campbell asked me why I had written this book. I said I would tell him if he told me why he had asked. His answer was that he had seen my name on the paperback and bought it – as if he did not have enough sf to read! – and had hated it. I made some sort of waffling answer and worked hard to change the subject.) I felt that there must be a bigger market out there than I had imagined and perhaps I could now write for myself *and* please readers at the same time. This was a momentous discovery and marked a new period in my writing. Not that I didn't do the familiar to stay alive. *Deathworld 3* and a number of Stainless Steel Rat books were still in the future, but I found I could experiment with new ideas and forms and still hope to sell them as well. This has a happy ending in that I now usually write only the kind of novels I want to write and enjoy good serial and book sales.

There was no sudden change in my life. The work crawled out and the checks crept in. I was still earning about as much as a non-union elevator operator in New York. Except I was not living in New York. At that time the dollar went much further in Europe than it does now. We lived well and

91

enjoyed life. Each winter we would go skiing in Norway, every summer camping across the continent to Italy. We could only do this because, just ten years ago, the prices were unbelievable by present inflated standards. Norway? One person, round trip by overnight ferry with sleeping cabin from Copenhagen to Oslo, then train to the ski resort plus seven days room and full board there cost £20 for an adult. Half price for children. Camping for the four of us, in our rebuilt VW bus, formerly a Copenhagen taxi, averaged £5 a day. Including all gas, camping fees, booze, film, food – with dinner in a restaurant every night for four. Life was as pleasant as it ever can be, considering the number of dark things that are sweeping down the river towards us at all times, and I had a major book I wanted to do.

I had been working on it for some time, a total of five years of preparation in fact, just digging out the material to make an intelligent estimate of what life would be like in the year 2000 AD. At this time there were no popular nonfiction books on the dangers of overpopulation, overconsumption, pollution and allied problems. But there was a great deal of talk and speculation in the scientific journals that interested me greatly. Overpopulation had been a recurrent theme in sf for years, but the overpopulated future had always been the far future and was about as relevant to life today as E. E. Smith's Lensman.

My basic idea was a simple one : set a novel in the year 2000 just a few decades away, when the reader, and certainly the reader's children, would be around to see what the world would be like. But in setting a novel so close in time I had to extrapolate every detail of our lives and see that I got it as right as possible. I also wanted to write a more realistic novel than I had ever attempted before. I went to the specialists, the demographers and the petrologists and agronomists, and read a great number of very thick books. It took a great deal of time to write the novel, which was the longest I had ever done, since, in addition to getting my facts right, I had to write the realistic story of life in that world. I smile as I remember that I wanted to rush the book into print before the growing interest in these problems faded. As it was, *Make Room! Make Room!* came out too early and vanished with a dull whiffling sound. But it was the only novel on these topics and when the world at large became aware of these problems it was bought for movie adaptation and turned into the film *Soylent Green* – which, at times, bears a slight resemblance to the book.

If you want a neat commentary on contemporary values consider this; I discovered that MGM had been looking at this book for five years as a possible film. But they did not think the theme of overpopulation was an important enough one to shoot. However, when a cannibalism twist was added to the script they saw real possibilities and went ahead with contracts.

All of this was still in the future. What was coming next was a physical change in my life which, for better or worse, would affect my work. We left Denmark – for a number of reasons. We were tired of renting and wanted to buy – but could not in Denmark. Nor were we sure we wanted a permanent home there. There were more things like this; the children spoke more Danish than English, I had trouble talking English myself at times, a problem for a writer, there were family crises in the States. No one thing, but they all added up to a move. We weren't quite ready for the States yet and considered buying a house in England. We went there and rented for a year, but it came to nothing. It was a rather stern furnished house in a grimly middle class neighbourhood. This did not bother us, but horrified many English writer friends who had spent their life substances fleeing such a deadend place. But I shall always be fond of Banstead Road South in Sutton, Surrey. The year was fun and I wrote *The Technicolor Time Machine* in the dining room which I took over for a study.

We have a Greek friend who owns some ships and he gave us a most reasonable passage on one of his vessels. We brought the decaying VW bus along as deck cargo, or ballast, since we had been offered only $100 as a trade-in on a new car. After a stop in New York we left, pursued by a blizzard, and crossed the continent looking for a warm spot to settle. (Reverse gear fell out of the bus which was fine since we planned only a one-way trip.) California seemed the best bet, for climate and work, and we reached San Diego in a rainstorm. Next day the sun shone and we came down a hill in the boondocks near the Mexican border and saw the house for us. We bought it a few weeks later.

This memoir is being written in that same house, a number of books, stories and seven years later. But the house is on the market and within a few months we hope to be out and moved back to England. Though this piece is about writing, and the writing of science fiction at that, I feel that some explanation of a move of this sort is needed. It is not a simple thing because too many factors are involved. Part of it, surely, is dissatisfaction with life in a country that could commit the crimes of Vietnam and not be ashamed. Or living under a government headed by the man whom Harry Truman called 'a shifty-eyed goddamn liar', a man who appears to have done his best to destroy the democratic form of government. I will try not to complain and say not why I am leaving, but what I am going to. No paradise! I doubt if you will find a single Briton who claims that. It is a country we know well and respect, where life has a different pace that helps both my work and my existence, where there are many friends, where there is a fullness of things to do and see and enjoy and an entire continent of more of the same just a few miles away. A writer lives by ingesting from life and from books. I can read the same books anywhere. But when I walk out of my front door into the arid, sidewalkless streets of Southern California – or into the streets of Oxford or London, I am entering totally different worlds. Nor is the choice mine alone. Joan and the children are eager for the move.

I have never had great expectations for my work so I can truthfully say I am pleased with it and the way it is going. I keep saying that I don't enjoy editing, but I must or I would not still be doing it. Happily I do a lot of it with Brian, such as the annual best sf series, *The Astounding-Analog Reader* and others. But writing is where the real action is and I know I have good books lurking in my future. (I can't see the form or idea for any of them now, which is perhaps another reason I am going to England.) I have learned to write and am still learning to write all of the time. My books have been well received and translated into a number of languages –

eighteen at the last count – and I sell more and more of them every year. I have learned that when I put time, effort and love into a book or a story the final product is worth the effort. I hope to have more of all of these elements in England, but you will have to judge the resulting work on its own merits. I know where I have been, I know where I am, I know where I am going. I could not always say this; that I can now is a victory of sorts.

Damon Knight:

knight piece

I was born in Baker, Oregon, at midnight on 19 September 1922, the only child of Frederick Stuart Knight and Leola Damon Knight. They seem to have decided that I would be a writer even before I was born – at any rate, my father once told me he had chosen my name, Damon Francis Knight, to be a euphonious by-line on the model of 'Stuart Edward White'.

On both sides, my ancestors were middle-west Protestants. My father was taught that drinking, smoking, dancing and card-playing were all sinful; he relaxed his views on all but the first when he was grown. On my mother's side most of the men were ministers; I have a crayon portrait of her grand-father, a stern-featured man with a full beard and shoulder-length hair; and one of his wife, an even sterner crone who looks thirty years older, even allowing for the evident fact that she has lost all her teeth.

My father ran away from the South Dakota farm where he grew up when he was sixteen, went to the West Coast and put himself through college by washing dishes. He met my mother when she was an elementary schoolteacher in Bingen, Washington, and they were engaged; then he went off to teach for four years in a rural school in the Philippines.

She broke off the engagement, but when he came back they were married anyhow.

In photographs he brought back from the Philippines my father is slender, but when I knew him his paunch and deep chest made him look stocky. He was forty when I was born, and my mother was thirty-five. It was her third pregnancy; the first two children were stillborn girls.

My father was a frustrated newspaperman, and taught a journalism class in the high school whose principal he became in 1928; his heroes were Irvin S. Cobb and Will Rogers. He was a shy man who could not express his emotions. Although he had run away from the farm, he always loved farming and believed in hard physical labour; he was concerned about me because I didn't sweat enough. He owned a farm left him by his father and kept tenants on it, hoping that when I grew up I might want to go and live there. He described it as good farmland but when I went there with him as a child and tramped over it with the tenant, it was nothing to my eye but a sea of dried mud.

When I was five or six my mother had what was called a nervous breakdown, as a consequence of which she remained nervous and jumpy and one eye bulged a little. I associate this with a recollection of driving in the country with my mother and passing a field below the road where there was a wrecked car and some people were groaning. I remember imitating their noises, thinking it was funny. After that she never drove, and my parents never went out together to visit or had company in our house. I accepted this without question then, but it is a mystery to me now. Although she got a little queer when she was older, and thought the family doctor, a much younger man, was secretly in love with her, there was nothing whatever wrong with her mind when I was a child. My mother was an affectionate and demonstrative woman who laughed easily. She spent hours reading to me from the Thornton W. Burgess books, and we both laughed until we cried over the adventures of Peter Rabbit.

It may be that neither of my parents was very sociable to begin with. I never saw any sign that either of them felt the lack of company. My father had his lodge meetings, about which he was forbidden to tell us anything, my mother pretended to believe that the Masons took off all their clothes and ran around in their little aprons. Both my parents went to the Riverside Church (non-denominational) every Sunday; they took me, too, until I said I didn't want to go any more. They never reproached me for this.

In the summers, while my father took more education courses in summer schools, my mother and I went to the seaside resort town of Newport, where her stepmother kept a boarding house called the Damon House. The stepmother was a wrinkled, shrewd old woman, famous for her table. (It was wasted on me – I wouldn't eat seafood.)

Neither my mother nor I knew how to swim. I had lessons at the Natatorium, but couldn't get over my paralyzing fear of water, and although the teacher told my mother I had swum a few strokes, in order to earn me a promised reward, it was a lie.

We spent the long afternoons on the beach. There were dunes of golden sand that broke away in chunks, nascent sandstone, and I pretended that it was gold and that I was rich. At low tide there were cratered rocks covered with barnacles that closed and squirted if you touched them. There were miles of flat sand on which to run trailing a stick or a long strand of kelp. A little farther up the coast there was another beach, accessible only at low tide, where the sand was covered with the polished shells of periwinkles. And somewhere there must have been crabs, for I remember bringing home a bucket of them, and waking up later to find them all over the walls.

I loved this place, and looked forward to it all year with longing and disbelief. There was a little library shaped like a lighthouse; on the boardwalk I remember on one side a jewellery shop whose windows were filled with polished pieces of moss agate and jasper; on the other, a candy shop in whose window the taffy machine endlessly revolved its shining arms. The taffy was hard and brittle; you bought it in porous chunks broken off with a hammer, and it crunched and melted sublimely in the mouth.

Knight Piece

Although both my parents were teachers, neither one had any great habit of reading, and there were few books in the house. There was a copy of *Anthony Adverse*, which my father had abstracted from the school library as too racy (but if so, I could never find the good parts), and a volume of Philippine fairy tales which I still own, and that was nearly all. We had a little illustrated dictionary, not Webster's, with fascinating colour plates of fruits and national flags. I remember my father reading a historical novel which had something in it about Greek fire, and my mother reading a modern novel called *if i have four apples*. In each case the event was memorable because it was unparalleled. Both of them had great respect for writing, however, or for any creative work, and often said that I was going to be an artist. I drew pictures from the time I could hold a pencil, and in my teens made some clumsy attempts at painting without any instruction.

Hood River, Oregon where my father was principal of the high school for twelve years, is a little town on the confluence of the Hood River and the Columbia. The climate is mild and wet. Two snow-capped mountains are visible from Hood River – Mt Hood and Mt Adams. The town is built on a hillside as steep as San Francisco's, and from walking up and down it to and from school, I could go as fast uphill as I could on level ground.

Although toward the end I longed to get away, looking back I can see that Hood River was not a bad place for children to grow up. The streets were ours for bicycling and skating; we even skated down Creamery Hill, reaching a velocity that would have crushed us to bits if we had run into anything, but we never did. In the summer evenings we gathered in a group of ten or twenty to play hide-and-seek or king of the hill or red-light. I remember the purple twilights and the scent of lilacs and the lonesome sound of 'Allee-allee-all's-in-free'. We played until it was too dark to see, and after; we hated to go in to bed.

Because of my slow physical development I began losing touch with my contemporaries when I was about eight, and got most of my ideas about life out of books. When I tried to apply these to the world around me, I was usually disappointed. *Boy's Life*, for example, published a series of stories about a bunch of boys who had a secret club, with mysterious hailing signs and so on. I organized one like it on my block, but when I chalked the assembly symbol on the sidewalk, the other members went on riding their tricycles. Later I tried to organize another club which would assemble model airplanes and sell them for profit, but when I tried my first kit, I put it together wrong. In shop, I could not plane a board smooth or wash the paint out of a brush. I continued to read novels, especially English novels, because England was a long way away and I could believe that life was different there.

We had our local halfwit, a man named Warren Chaffee who could not talk without slobbering but was good at mechanical things and could fix toys for children; he had a hauling service and once turned in a bill to my parents that read: '2 kums 2 goes @ 50¢ a went'. There was a retarded child across the street, a boy named Petie, on whom cruel jokes were played and who was brutal to others. Next door to him lived a girl named Zella Hendricks and her little brother, with both of whom I practised what we called 'doing naughty things' – feeling each other's bodies inexpertly under our clothes – until their mother caught me with my hand down the brother's shirt, looking for God knows what. When she came over to talk to my mother about it I tried to hold the door shut.

Our house in Hood River was one of two identical white frame cottages on adjoining lots in a neighbourhood of much older houses. It had a living room and dining room symbolically separated by a false beam; two bedrooms, bath and kitchen. When I grew too old to sleep in my mother's room my father hired a carpenter to help him and built on another room beside the back porch. The walls were made of Fir-Tex, a thick felt-like substance made of compacted wood fibres, and the floor and woodwork, at my request, were painted black. The living room and bedrooms had kalsomined walls which my father renewed every year or two, using an enormous brush. There was no central heating; the kitchen was kept warm by the old wood-burning range, and the living room first by a potbellied stove and later by an oil-burning space heater that was not much bigger. On cold nights we took hot-water bottles to bed with us.

Our street was just outside a respectable residential area and was not far from being a slum, although that never occurred to me then. Up the hill, separated from our house by their back garden and ours, was the elegant home of Mr Breckinridge, the school superintendent, whose daughter Ada May was my playmate up until the time she started wearing high heels and lipstick. Around us were old two-storey houses in various stages of decay; the one next door even had a barn, weathered grey like the house. The children who lived there were barefoot and ragged and had the grey-brown faces of the poor, but they were active, alert and good humoured. The oldest, a boy of sixteen or so, drew cartoons that were better than mine – and I was not modest about my drawing – then dropped them on the ground; I never could understand why he valued them so little. I kept everything, and counted my possessions like a miser. I knew and cherished every marble; when a boy cozened me into playing 'for keeps' and took four of mine, I wept. I was inconsolable when a tree surgeon cut off the low horizontal limb of the cherry tree in the front yard, the one I had used to climb on.

As I grew older I played with younger children, sometimes joined by another outcast, a boy even older than myself. As time advanced I lost even these playmates and fell back on solitary pleasures entirely. I attacked the Hood River library in various ways, by authors – all of Dickens, all of Dumas – then by subject – all the pirate books – and finally, at random. One of my pleasant memories is of some illness when the librarian sent me out a pile of books, all by authors new to me. I read children's books and fairy tales, but I also read romantic novels and novels of manners that I only half understood. I read a novel called *V.V.'s Eyes* which had belonged to an uncle of mine, and found that he had written in the margin encouraging comments such as 'Go it, V.V!' This was my first experience with the defacers of books. For years I could not bring myself to make any mark in a book, even when I had it for review; now I do it, but always with a feeling of guilt, and I use a soft pencil in case anyone should want to erase what I write.

In the thirties I became aware that there were such things as pulp magazines. There were *Spicy Adventure* and *Spicy Mystery*, which I did not dare buy, even in the dingy little second-hand store at the bottom of a side street in town. There were air-war magazines which I did buy and devoured. One story concerned a squadron leader who was having headaches and whose hair was falling out; it turned out that a German agent had been concealing a capsule of radium under his pillow.

Then I saw and bought an issue of something called *Amazing Stories*. It was bigger than other pulps, about 8½ × 11, and the cover, in sick pastels, showed two helmetted and white-suited men aiming rifles at a bunch of golliwogs. This was the August-September 1933 issue, and the cover story was 'Meteor-Men of Plaa' by Henry J. Kostkos. That was the beginning.

The illustrations in *Amazing*, the work of a man named Leo Morey, were sketchy, grey, and ill-defined, but that somehow increased the mysterious and alien feeling. In Gernsback's magazines, especially the back issues, I admired the work of Frank R. Paul in other ways, but I got from it much the same satisfaction. Paul's drawings look a little quaint now, because of the knee-breeches and the statuesque poses, but he was endlessly fertile at inventing strange land-scapes and filling them with the flora and fauna of strange worlds. These cover paintings and illustrations served as focal points for daydreaming. They supplied the visual information which the stories, as a rule, did not give, and they helped an adolescent reader dream himself into the world of the story.

Not all the science fiction magazines were available in Hood River, and I could not always afford to buy them, but when we made our annual family trip to Portland it was not only Jantzen's Beach (the amusement park) that drew me, it was the second-hand stores with their stacks of *Science Wonders* and *Amazings*.

On one visit I found a new magazine on the news-stands, one I had never even heard of before – *Astounding Stories*.

Knight Piece

Back in our hotel room I developed a fever; it turned out that I had the measles and we were all quarantined. My parents must have been chagrined, but I was blissful, lying there reading 'The Son of Old Faithful' by Raymond Z. Gallun.

At home, along one wall over my bed, I had shelves put up, and presently these shelves were filled with science fiction magazines. I read and reread every story, including those I didn't understand. I read the editorials and the readers' letters; I read the ads. I read the stories believing that something like them must be true. I yearned to go to Barsoom, and I spread my arms to the red planet, but nothing happened. I tried to calculate if I was likely to live to see the year 2000. I haunted libraries and bookshops, and seized on any book whose title made it sound as if it might be science fiction. See me as a desperate limpet, sucking my nourishment out of books.

In the mid-thirties *Wonder Stories* was being edited by Charles Hornig, under whom the magazine displayed a marked interest in sadism. I did not know the word, but could not help noticing that the stories emphasized torture.

Sex and sadism were the formula of a string of pulp magazines published at that time, with titles such as *Terror Tales* and *Horror Stories*. The *Spicy* magazines (*Spicy Mystery, Spicy Adventure,* etc.) used this formula in a much milder form, along with conventional titillation, and the editor of two sf magazines, *Dynamic* and *Marvel,* tried it briefly.

I also sampled several of the series-hero pulps, such as *The Spider, Doc Savage* and *The Shadow*. Images from these stories have stayed with me all my life. In an issue of *Operator #5,* the villain used a sinister drug, graphically described and depicted on the cover, to destroy his victims' will. The stuff looked like viscous green ink; I can still see and taste it. These pulps did not satisfy my thirst for fantastic adventures; the stories were too muddled to let me identify with their heroes, and I always dropped them after one or two tries. But I read with fascination all the *Saint* novels of Leslie Charteris. The Saint was precisely everything I was not and longed to be – grown up, strong, handsome, fearless, cool in the presence of women. I yearned after

Leslie Howard in *The Scarlet Pimpernel*, too, and I read my way through eight or ten of Raphael Sabatini's novels. These were particularly satisfying, because the heroine always misunderstood the hero and had to apologize later.

Presently I invented a scheme whereby my father would subscribe to the science fiction magazines in my name, and I would pay him back monthly out of my allowance. *Wonder Stories* promptly dwindled and expired, and *Astounding* began to trim its edges, changed illustrators, and became inferior to its old self in every way. I read it faithfully, all the same.

In high school I became the cartoonist for the school paper, the *Guide*. It was a mimeographed paper, well produced under my father's direction, and it won some state prizes. My cartoons appeared weekly for nearly three years, and by the time I graduated I was an expert in an art that turned out to be dying.

In the late thirties science fiction magazines began to pick up again after a few years in the doldrums. *Astounding* became livelier under a new editor, John W. Campbell Jr. *Wonder* had been converted into *Thrilling Wonder* and was bad but interesting because novel. There was a rash of new magazines. Campbell brought out *Unknown*, which instantly enthralled me. Among the other new magazines were two called *Super Science* and *Astonishing*, both edited by Frederik Pohl, and in one or the other was a regular listing of magazines published by fans. I sent for some, and got into correspondence with Bob Tucker, the editor of *Le Zombie*. I did some cartoons for him. I published my own fanzine, *Snide*. From this other correspondence followed, including some with Richard Wilson, Donald A. Wollheim and Robert W. Lowndes, all New York fans, members of a group that called itself the Futurian Society.

I wrote and illustrated *Snide* myself, and manufactured a hundred copies or so on a tray hektograph I had been given for Christmas. The cover of the first issue showed a man with a briefcase running after a rocket ship which had just taken off; he was shouting, 'Hey, wait!'

Knight Piece

When *Astounding* came into full flower in the late thirties, with stories in every issue by Robert A. Heinlein and L. Sprague de Camp, and beautifully realistic brush-drawn illustrations by Hubert Rogers, I would have given anything to be Campbell, or Heinlein, or Rogers. I sent Campbell stories, and he sent them back with letters of rejection on grey stationery, signed with his looping scrawl. I now know how much more this was than I had any right to expect, but I was frustrated because I couldn't sell the stories and had no idea how to make them better. I drew cartoons and inked them in, and *Amazing* bought one for three dollars. (A spacesuited man has found a robot in a cavern, and is about to push one of the buttons on its chest; the robot is waving a huge mallet behind its back. Caption: *Wonder what this one does.*) This success elated me, and I sent *Amazing* more cartoons and proposals, but they never bought another. Years later, walking down a street in Queens, I saw a copy of *Amazing* in the gutter, open to my cartoon.

During this time I wrote several short pieces that were published in fanzines, including an article called 'Unite or Fie!' which urged the formation of a national fan organization. That was the extent of my contribution; a fan named Art Widner took up the idea, published correspondence about it, drew up a set of by-laws and saw it into being. This was the National Fantasy Fan Foundation, which later became notorious for its lack of accomplishment.

I kept trying to write science fiction stories, spurred on by one of John W. Campbell's periodic announcements that he would pay $60 for a short story (inconceivable wealth). I could start stories but could not finish them; baffled, I gave the manuscripts to my father with a covering letter to myself and asked him to put them in his safe deposit box. Later I did succeed in finishing two or three new stories and sent them to Robert A. ('Doc') Lowndes, who was then trying to set himself up as an agent. Lowndes sent most of them back with patronizing letters about plot and characterization; then he wrote me that Donald A. Wollheim was putting together the first issue of a new magazine and would print my story 'Resilience' if I would donate it. (Wollheim had no editorial budget for the magazine, and had to fill the whole issue this way.) I of course agreed.

One of my unfinished stories was about a young man who had duplicated himself seven or eight times by means of a matter-duplicator; I was going to have him/them set out in a spaceship of his design to explore the universe, but after the first few pages I didn't know what to write. The story had narcissistic overtones, like David Gerrold's recent novel *The Man Who Folded Himself*.

I kept running into incomprehensible responses in other people around me, as when I criticized the new comic strip *Flash Gordon* because the natives of Mongo spoke English, and a friend of mine said. 'What else would they talk?' I came to believe that somewhere in the outside world, probably in New York, things were altogether different, and Hood River became hateful to me because I couldn't get out of it.

My last year in high school was a nightmare of boredom. When it was over, my father offered to send me to college, but that was the last thing I wanted. We agreed that I would go to Salem for a year and attend the WPA Art Center there. I lived in a boarding house at first, run by an insurance man and his fat, comely, cheerful wife. At her table I ate my first steak and found it unchewable; it was not until years later that I discovered steak did not have to be tough.

While I was in Salem Don Wollheim's first issue of *Stirring Science Stories* appeared, with my story in it. The printers had changed 'Brittle People' to 'Little People' in the first sentence, rendering the story unintelligible, but I was proud of it anyway.

In Salem I met another science fiction reader – found him working in a second-hand bookstore. He was a blond, moon-faced, blue-spectacled young man named Bill Evans, and we agreed to publish the next issue of *Snide* together, since he had access to a Ditto machine at school. We did so, and announced payment for stories (½¢ a word) beginning with the next issue, but it never appeared. Bill finished school and went into the Bureau of Standards because that was where Richard Seaton, the hero of E. E. Smith's *Skylark* series, worked. The last I heard, he was still there.

Knight Piece

I began to feel that I had no vocation as an artist, or any desire to go on to school, and when the Futurians invited me to come to New York and live with them, my parents agreed to let me go. The World Science Fiction Convention that year was in Denver, and they drove me there over precipitous mountain roads. It was late at night when they dropped me in front of the hotel, but I found a few fans standing around in the convention room. Sick with embarrassment, I goosestepped toward them and raised my hand in a Nazi salute. They asked me who I was and I told them. 'Ah, Damon Knight,' said Forry Ackerman kindly.

The Futurians, when I met them later, were an odd-looking group. Wollheim was the oldest and least beautiful (Kornbluth once introduced him as 'this gargoyle on my right'). He was, I learned later, almost pathologically shy, but he was the unquestioned leader of the group, and John Michel, who worshipped him, later informed me that Donald's personality was such that he could have any woman he wanted. Lowndes was ungainly and flatfooted; he had buck teeth which made him lisp and sputter, and a hectic glare like a cockatoo's. Michel was slender and looked so much more normal than the rest that he seemed handsome by contrast, although he was pockmarked and balding. He had a high voice and stammered painfully. Cyril Kornbluth, the youngest (a few months younger than I) was plump, pale and sullen. He had narrow Tartar eyes and spoke in a rumbling monotone; he looked ten years older than he was. He liked to play the ogre; at the art auction that weekend he bid fifty cents for a Cartier illustration, got it, and tore it in half. Chester Cohen was about my age, and although he was neurotic and jumpy, a nail-picker (not enough left to bite), he was able to freeze on command and hold a pose indefinitely; once Michel pretended to hypnotize him in the elevator and left him there, to the consternation of the hotel employees. They had to find out who he was and carry him up to his room, where he lay like a corpse until Michel arrived and snapped his fingers.

Heinlein, a handsome man in his thirties, was the guest of

honour at the convention, and we glimpsed him and his slender brown wife Leslyn occasionally.

After the convention we divided into two groups; Kornbluth, who had been on a trip to Los Angeles with Cohen, got into one car with Wollheim, Michel and me, leaving Chet to go home with Lowndes. 'I've seen a lot of Chester Cohen', Cyril said. We were travelling by 'wildcat bus' – sharing expenses with a goodnatured man named Jack Inskeep who was driving to Cleveland. On the way, Wollheim expanded on an idea of his that the surface of the earth was composed of strips of solid material about two miles across, with roads running down the middle, the rest being hollow. Kornbluth played up to this, thinking of feeble objections which Wollheim demolished one by one.

In Hill City, Kansas, the car broke down. Hill City was a slight rise in the road, not more than a foot and a half in elevation. The whole town could have been covered by a single good-sized aircraft hangar. The garage where the car was worked on had a calendar on the wall depicting a bosomy young woman who was not Rita Hayworth, although that was the name printed under the picture. The one movie theatre was upstairs in a ramshackle building, reached by an outside stairway; locusts leapt in the tall weeds nearby. Down a side street, we came upon a house behind a white picket fence; in the lawn was a neat sign that read: 'Dr ——, Physian and Surgon'.

Near Columbus, our driver obligingly stopped so that Cyril could meet his girl, Mary Byers, who lived on a farm with several fierce uncles. We went to a bar, and Inskeep played the pinball machines while Cyril and Mary stared into each other's eyes. In Cleveland he left us and Wollheim took a train, while the rest of us went on by bus.

The Futurians at that time lived in a railroad apartment on 103rd Street. It had four rooms in a row: first the kitchen/ bathroom (the tub was under the drainboard), then two small bedrooms for Michel and me, then the living room which was also Lowndes's bedroom. It was bare but sunny and clean. I paid my share of the rent (I don't remember how much, but probably about $7), and was expected to keep my room clean and wash the dishes. Lowndes did the cooking;

his speciality was Futurian Chop Suey – noodles, hamburger, and a can of cream of mushroom soup; it was better when it had rotted a day in the refrigerator. I don't now remember what Michel's contribution was.

We had wall newspapers, in which Lowndes published communiques about our campaign against the Enemy (bedbugs). We squirted the mattresses with kerosene, and eventually vanquished them.

All the Futurian apartments, then and later, had names; this one was the Futurian Embassy. Kornbluth stayed over on weekends; he lived with his parents, and so did Wollheim. None of us had any money; for amusement in the evenings, we played poker for stakes of 15¢ each, and drank California wine at 50¢ a gallon. Once or twice when Chet and I were sent out for wine, we bought the cheaper stuff at 35¢ and pocketed the difference. When the game broke up at midnight, we would walk down to Times Square to look at the advertising signs, have a cup of coffee in the Times Square Cafeteria, and walk back.

I adopted all the Futurians' attitudes. They looked down on fannish activity, and so did I. They said they were communists; I said I was a communist. They expressed contempt for Campbell and his stable of writers; I lost interest in *Astounding* and stopped reading it. They were nearly all native New Yorkers who would have died rather than get on a sightseeing bus; I lived in Manhattan for ten years, and never saw the sights.

My ambition now was to be published among the Futurian writers in their magazines, but except for two sales to Lowndes, I couldn't even do that.

Wollheim's *Stirring Science* and *Cosmic* had folded shortly after I got to New York, but Lowndes was editing *Future Fiction* and *Science Fiction* (later *The Original Science Fiction*, as if it were a tavern) while Fred Pohl, still technically a Futurian although he did not have much to do with us, was the editor of *Super Science* and *Astonishing*.

Kornbluth organized something called the Inwood Hills Literary Society, which met once a week either at his house or at ours. It was a forerunner of the Milford Conference; each writer was expected to produce a story every week for criticism. When the group met in the Embassy, everybody there but me was a member, and I had to leave the room. I thought this was a bit thick, since I lived there. When the group met at Cyril's, however, I used the time to write, and gradually my work got a little better.

Kornbluth was writing stories under various pseudonyms for all the Futurian magazines. He was nineteen. One of his unfinished stories, which I found lying around at the Embassy, began with a flashback in the stream of consciousness of an intelligent mouse during intercourse. Another, called 'The Ten-G Pussies' (about cats, raised under ten gravities in a centrifuge, that became so muscular that if they pounced at you they would go right through you), began with a philosophical dialogue about the nature of cuteness.

The Futurians had a written set of by-laws which declared that the club was in session whenever two or more members were present. The Futurians seldom troubled with elections but on one occasion when there was an election, Fred Pohl running against Wollheim for president, we prepared for it the night before by making posters setting forth various drawbacks in Fred's character. I drew a skull-face and a pointing finger, with the legend, 'Uncle Freddie Wants YOU!' I also made a linoleum block print and with it printed dark-blue skull faces on several yards of the roll of toilet paper in the bathroom. Fred came over for the balloting, was magnificently cool, and lost the election.

Shortly after this I painted a pentacle on the floor of one of the rooms, with Greek characters around the rim and in the centre (Kornbluth's idea) the Hebrew characters Resh Sin Vau Pe (RSVP). I also painted a mural depicting three sinister supernatural characters, the central one with his hand thrust suggestively under his robe; we called them Stinky, Shorty, and the Holy Ghost.

Kornbluth played the ogre seldom; his humour was sardonic and sometimes cruel, but he was the least malicious of the Futurians. He told us stories about his relatives. Once, a female cousin stepped into the bathroom after him, locked the door, and said, 'Well?' Cyril replied, 'I'll be through in a moment,' finished washing his hands, and left. He played at being grown-up. One fall day he came in wearing a hat, solemnly explaining that in cold weather a man needed head-wear in order to balance the bulkier silhouette of his overcoat. When drunk, he was playful.

Michel was a posturer and poseur; he affected corduroy jackets and trousers, smoked a pipe, talked about his dates. He had had several operations for bone tuberculosis, and had ugly craters in his legs to show for it. He took me on an Elevated tour of New York, borrowed a dollar, and said, 'Don't tell Donald'. He had had three or four stories published, and managed to give the impression that he was the most professional writer of us all.

Lowndes was the one we always found ourselves talking about when he was not there. Often when we were going somewhere together, for no evident reason he would cross the street and walk by himself. Except for me, he was the only gentile in the group. His parents had been funda-mentalists who thought even the Sunday comics were sinful, and Lowndes as a small boy had had to crawl under the porch to read them. In his youth he had been in the Civilian Conservation Corps, and his arms and legs remained muscu-lar although the rest of him was flabby. When drunk he lurched hideously, and sometimes passed out with his eyes open.

Wollheim did not drink at all, and his remote brown eyes were always watchful.

I myself looked like the ghost of a blond Charlie Chase. We were a gallery of grotesques, but we were all talented to one degree or another, and we counted on that to save us.

We were anything but a close-knit group, and yet we stood together against the outside world. A Futurian crest, designed by I forget who, had a large flat-headed screw with the legend, *Omnes qui non Futurianes sunt.*

I first saw Dick Wilson on the beach at Far Rockaway; he had just been in the water and was red, white and blue. He was a gentle, spade-jawed man with a high and very quiet voice, something like Liberace's. Also at the beach that day were Jessica Gould, Dick's plump, pretty and flirtatious girl friend, and Hannes Bok, who was leaping athletically about.

111

There were two groups of Futurians, the ones I was living with, and the others whom we called the Compatible People (this referred to a party to which our group had not been invited).

The CP were Frederik Pohl, Richard Wilson and Harry Dockweiler and their wives. They differed from us basically in having money, and jobs and being married.

The Futurians had their own official religion, invented by Wollheim; it was called GhuGhuism, and began with the cracking of the Cosmic Egg. It had Vestal Virgins, whose virginity was perpetually renewed, and other features I have forgotten. Wollheim also invented a private language to write the Gholy Ghible in, but he was the only one who could read it.

None of us knew any girls, or had any way of meeting them, except Wollheim, whose girl-friend, Elsie Balter, was part of our circle. Wollheim's courtship was slow. Elsie, who was older than Donald, was a decidedly plain but beautifully good-natured and kind woman. Wollheim gave Elsie a friendship ring after about two years, and after another year or so they were married. (Telling me about the friendship ring, Elsie said, 'And then, do you know what Donald did? He *kissed* me.')

I see now that if any of the rest of us had gone to work, or to school, we would have met girls in any desired numbers, but this did not occur to us. We once got dressed up and went to a Trotskyist meeting because we had heard the Trotskyists had a lot of horny girls. There were a couple of girls, but they wanted no part of us. Another time we went down to Greenwich Village to Anton Romatka's poetry circle, because Donald said we were the real writers and would command instant respect, but it did not work out that way. I put an orange scarf around my neck and read a sonnet which was received in absolute silence.

The Trotskyists called themselves Trotskyists but we called them Trotskyites, because we were Reds. Actually, the Futurians were very mild parlour radicals who had never even joined the YCL (the Young Communist League). In those days, nearly every educated young person in New York was a red-hot radical, in words if not in deeds. With the

Futurians, this took the form of occasional doctrinaire articles in fanzines, and that was all. Our bunch knew very well that if they joined any communist organization they would be put to work, and work was what they were trying to avoid. They showed their solidarity, however, by going to Russian movies occasionally and by listening intently to Shostakovich.

We were too poor to go to movies often, or buy books, or travel, or eat at restaurants, but we were used to that and did not mind it. Our recreation was talking. We played endless word-games – *People* (a form of Twenty Questions) and *Tsohg* (Ghost backwards).

When on rare occasions we did have money enough to go out, it was usually to the Dragon Inn in Greenwich Village, where I ate fried rice because it was the only Chinese food I could stomach. Years later, in the throes of an unhappy love affair, I went to a Chinese restaurant and ordered shrimp chow mein in order to distract my mind.

Wollheim had two parlour tricks. One was to put one arm behind his back, bring the hand up all the way around his face and lay it on his opposite cheek. The other was to put a small flashlight up his nose and turn it on; his whole nose would then light up like a pink cucumber.

Once when we walked him to the subway late at night he gestured me to follow him through the turnstile and then onto the train; we rode in silence to his stop. There I got up to follow him off, but he gestured me, with a grin, to remain. The door closed between us.

We moved so many times that I can't remember the sequence. It was a renter's market then; if we wanted to move we just hired a truck and went, usually owing the last month's rent. On one occasion we had to pay up, though, because Lowndes wrote two letters, one to the landlord wishing him bad luck in the hereafter, and one to Elsie giving our new address, and put them in the wrong envelopes.

Lowndes and Michel and I shared another apartment after the Embassy; it was in Chelsea and was called the Futurian Fortress. At various times Lowndes and Michel, Lowndes and Jim Blish, Michel and Larry Shaw briefly shared apartments.

The Blish/Lowndes place was called 'Blowndsh'. While he lived there, Lowndes had a cat named Charles that hid all his pencils under the bedclothes, and another named Blackout that thought Lowndes was God: whenever it rained and he couldn't go out on the fire escape, he walked over and bit Lowndes.

New York excited me, and I wrote a long free-verse poem which included the line, 'I have known hunger and loneness' (for the metre) and sent it to my mother, and she wrote back in some anxiety that she did not want me to go hungry, and wasn't the money they were sending enough? In fact, I was stretching my monthly allowance to pay for Chet Cohen's existence as well as mine (we were sharing an apartment), and some days what we had for dinner was a can of Campbell's pork and beans; but we never felt poor. When we had money we spent it, and when we were broke we waited till we had money. If we couldn't afford cigarettes, we rolled new ones out of butts.

Lowndes got tired of his unsuccessful agency and turned it over to me. I dutifully trudged around to various editorial offices with my unsaleable manuscripts. In the anteroom of Campbell's office one day I met Hannes Bok, who showed me a cheque for a thousand dollars, then a huge sum: he had just sold Campbell a novel for *Unknown*. Campbell was a portly, bristled-haired blond man with a challenging stare, who told me that he wasn't sure how much longer he would edit *Astounding*. He might quit and go into science. 'I'm a nuclear physicist, you know,' he said, looking me right in the eye.

Fred Pohl had persuaded Popular Publications to publish *Super Science* and *Astonishing* in 1940 and had edited both magazines for a year or two; then he had been asked to step down, but had remained as an assistant editor to Alden H. Norton, to whose group at Popular the magazines were added. In 1943 there was a vacancy under Norton, and Fred recommended me to fill it; he also lent me a white shirt to appear in when I applied for the job. I was hired at $25 a week.

Norton was a large, bald, amiable man in his forties, who was responsible for half a dozen pulp magazines. He had two sports magazines, the two science fiction pulps, a detective magazine, and *G-8 and His Battle Aces*. As was customary at Popular, he read all the manuscripts, bought stories and scheduled them; the rest of the work – copy-editing, proof-reading, and so on – was done by his assistants: Fred, a young woman named Olga Quadland and me. Each of us had two or three magazines for which he was responsible every month, but *G-8*, because it was so awful, was rotated among us.

G-8 and His Battle Aces was written entirely by one man, Robert J. Hogan. He wrote the lead 'novel', the short stories, and the departments, and brought in every other month a huge stack of manuscripts which then had to be gone over line by line. A *G-8* manuscript edited by Fred, which they showed me, had no word of the original text unchanged. The one I did concerned a plot by the Germans in World War I to make their soldiers incredibly fierce by injecting them with rhinoceros juice.

After I had been at Popular a month or so I was trans-ferred to Mike Tilden's department and felt at home there immediately. He was a sloppy, beer-bellied man with a quiet, rumbling voice; he was one of the kindest people I ever knew. He always looked unlaundered. He had troubles at home, financial and otherwise, and was always borrowing small sums from other editors, but never from people who worked for him. Once I passed his door and looked in, to find him sitting with his feet up and his hands in his pockets. 'I'm just sitting here saying shit,' he said.

My number came up, and I went down to the Induction Center in Grand Central Station. Lines of men dressed only in undershorts, socks and shoes moped back and forth across a huge hall. Every expression given by the Creator to the idea 'Man' was there. The whole tour took hours, and by the time I got toward the end of it I was numbed and apathetic. Three psychiatrists interviewed me; the first was intelligent and evidently trained, and wrote on my papers, 'Schizoid. Does not think he would do well in the army, and I am inclined to think he is right'. The second man wrote down 'Split Personality', and the third followed his lead. When I handed my papers to the colonel in charge, he read them and said the magic words, 'Oh, well, he's underweight anyway. Four-F'.

Popular Publications at that time had forty titles and was the largest pulp publisher, followed by Better Publications under various corporate names, then Street and Smith, then a straggle of little companies with eight or ten magazines apiece. A year or so before I started work there, Popular had bought up the assets of the Frank A. Munsey company, including a number of pulp titles. The pulps were still the principal enterprise of the company, and there was no hint that they were coming to the end of their time.

Our offices were roomy and airy, on the next-to-the-top floor of a large office building on East 42nd Street. Each department head ran his own magazines with very little interference, and our work relationships were relaxed and easy.

There were three large editorial departments, run by Norton, Tilden, and Harry Widmer, each employing a secretary and one or two assistant editors, plus two editors who ran a couple of magazines each with a secretary – these were love magazines in both cases, for some reason.

Harry Widmer was a pear-shaped little man with a rum-blossom and a dainty way of moving and speaking. He had a young and pretty wife. There was a story told about him, that he had taken the entire contents of a magazine home to work on over the weekend, as we often did, and had stopped for a few drinks before and after dinner with a friend. When he got home with the friend, barely able to stand, he decided to put the manuscript envelope in the safest place he could think of, which at that moment was the refrigerator. When he woke up the next day, he went to the refrigerator; the envelope was not there. He could not account for this until he realized that next to the refrigerator door there was another, very similar in appearance – the door of the incinerator.

I met Harry Harrison and his wife Evelyn in their vast, dim uptown apartment. Harry was short and at that time

116

slender, a voluble, sputtering little chipmunk of a man whom I liked at once; his wife was taller, intense, rodent-toothed and intelligent. Harry was a commercial artist doing comic-book work at that time and I was told that Evelyn was writing the continuities. Later, Harry surprised me by becoming a writer, and I had the pleasure of buying his first story, which I called 'Rock Diver', for *Worlds Beyond*. Still later he became the editor of *Space* and *Science Fiction Adventures*, succeeding Lester del Rey, and he bought stories from me. We have been on the same merry-go-round ever since.

When Fred Pohl went into the army, his place was taken by Ejler Jakobsson, a Finn who had come to this country as a boy and who had been on the Columbia track team. He gave me advice about my love life. I told him about a girl named Sally Green who came to see me occasionally and always borrowed a book when she left. (She later told me she had given these books to the Armed Services.) We necked a lot, but I couldn't get any farther. 'Tell her you love her,' said Jake. I tried this, but she didn't believe me.

New people began coming into our circle. Virginia Kidd was from Baltimore; she was fat but shapely (had an hour-glass figure, like a John Held drawing). Her face was soft and pretty. She had had polio as a child and had spent years in bed, having her bad leg rubbed by her parents with cocoa butter. She had been a bar girl in Baltimore, and was a science fiction fan; *Wonder Stories* had printed some of her letters. James Blish had been in the army and was still in uniform when I met him in a bar; he spent the whole time talking about James Joyce. He was dark-haired and thin, and had a disability pension. Larry Shaw was from a Catholic family in Rochester, which he hated. He was a funny-looking little man with upstanding hair and bottle-thick glasses; he spoke with difficulty, his face writhing.

At a party one afternoon I was introduced to Judith Zissman, a quiet, intense young woman who had just moved to New York from Philadelphia. She was eager to know science fiction people, and carried me off to dinner in her cluttered Greenwich Village apartment. Here I met a stocky blonde girl named Edith Liebert, who set out to seduce me. (She told me later that she thought it would be nice to have an affair with someone innocent.) She made overtures which would have been enough for anyone else, but not for me, and it was weeks before we finally got to bed in my apartment. I was so inexpert that I left her unsatisfied, and refused her invitations the next morning when we woke up because I had to go to work.

In the spring of that year I had grown increasingly restless at Popular. I sat with a thick manuscript on my lapboard, a Western novelette by Harry Olmsted, and found that I absolutely could not penetrate it. Olmsted always needed heavy editing, but in order to edit him you first had to find out what he meant, and I couldn't. When this had gone on for some weeks, I gave notice and quit.

I went job-hunting. I tried all the conventional things, read the ads in the *New York Times* on Sunday, typed up resumés, went to agencies, was sent on interviews. One of the jobs I applied for was on the *Police Gazette*, where I was interviewed in a crowded room near a table spread with glossy $8\frac{1}{2} \times 11$ photographs of ladies in various costumes. I was asked if I knew anything about the *Gazette*, and replied that I believed it was the sort of thing that was read in barber shops. I didn't get the job. (I wrote about this in 'On the Wheel'.) I applied for a job as a mimeographer, but was turned down because I was overtrained. I left some of these unsuccessful interviews with a feeling of relief; I wanted and yet didn't want the jobs.

At one point Chester and I were reduced to typing envelopes at a penny each for an addressing service. We quit after two back-breaking hours.

We went down to the Merchant Marine office to apply as yeomen and took the typing test. The standard was forty words a minute; I barely made it. Chester and Larry Shaw actually shipped out later, but I never did; the Merchant Marine ID card came in handy, though, and got me into the Museum of Modern Art at half price. Larry made one trip as a steward's mate, or whatever they call waiters on ships; on the way back he broke his glasses and was relieved of duty.

I met Phil Klass, who was nonviolent but excitable; his voice would begin rather softly and then at a certain point, as if he had shifted gears, would begin to blare as he warmed to his subject. He had a set of comic Jewish gestures and grimaces which through habituation had become almost second nature. When I first knew him he had fallen under the spell of Scott Meredith and was writing a series of commercial sf stories which he published under the name of William Tenn. He was saving his own name for the *New Yorker* pieces he meant to write later. His brother Mort told me it was hard to get him up in the morning because he could carry on a perfectly rational conversation while sound asleep. Mathematics was the one thing he could not handle in this way, Mort said: if you asked him, 'How much is two and two, Phil?' he would reply, 'Well, now, that's a very interesting question. The Babylonians – '

Still at loose ends, I had signed up for a free class in radio writing and had attended the first session, at which the instructor had told us how he felt about the expression, 'But first – ' when I was notified that my father had had a heart attack. My mother wired money and I flew home.

I found my father convalescing, and stayed a week in the familiar house now grown intolerably small. To stave off boredom, I wrote part of a story called 'The Third Little Green Man', which Ree Dragonette later admired for its action scenes. When the time came to go, my father broke down. My mother nodded me out, and I went.

I sold 'The Third Little Green Man' to Malcolm Reiss of *Planet Stories,* an editor who is remembered with affection. I sold one or two other stories to the same magazine, but by then Wilbur S. Peacock was the editor. I got into the habit of buying him lunch whenever he bought a story of mine, but I don't know why; I didn't like him much.

I also met Ray Cummings, a really frightful-looking man, cadaverous, grey-faced, dressed all in black with a turned-around collar. He was a survivor from the Gernsback days; he had been a secretary to Thomas Edison, and had filled the early *Wonder Stories* and *Astoundings* with long stories such as 'Wandl, the Invader' and 'Brigands of the Moon'. Lowndes had been reprinting these, and I was given the task of illustrating a couple. I also illustrated a long novelette by F. Orlin Tremaine, in which a young man blundered into a lost civilization and became its dictator. I was so indignant over this that I drew the hero in a black leather uniform with jackboots, wearing insignia that I made as close to swastikas as I dared, against a background in which little people were dying in the stench of factories and under the whips of overseers. Nobody noticed.

Theodore Sturgeon came back from the Virgin Islands and took up residence in the Village with L. Jerome Stanton and Rita Dragonette. Jay was a popeyed, dark-haired man with a quiet, slow voice that never stopped; Rita, called Ree, was a tiny brown woman, attractive in spite of some missing molars, who later turned out to have several personality quirks. Sturgeon was my agent for a while; he expressed the belief that since Jay was working for Campbell, manuscripts submitted by him would have the inside track, but it did not work out that way.

Lowndes had remained at Columbia Publications, where he edited all the magazines (including one ingenuously called *Complete Cowboy*) with the exception of the two love pulps, which were edited by a large woman named Marie Park who later appeared in reducing-salon advertisements headlined, 'I looked like a water buffalo.' She was a southern lady, and went into hysterics one day when she discovered that a Negro illustrator had sat in her chair.

Judy Zissman (born Juliet Grossman) was then in her twenties, a strong, rather shapely and good-looking woman with dark skin and hair. Her teeth were bad; later she had them replaced. She was so full of energy that she could not abide sloth and indifference around her, and she soon stirred us up. She and her husband Danny were Trotskyists, and Judy in a political argument was a juggernaut. Danny was in the navy, serving aboard a submarine, and Judy struck up a friendship with Johnny Michel. This displeased Wollheim, and presently Judy came to tell us that Wollheim had forbidden Johnny to have anything more to do with her (because she was a Trotskyist) or Jim Blish (because he was thought to be a fascist). Our indignation was acute, and we sat up half the night composing a document in which we read Wollheim, Elsie and Michel out of the Futurian Society. We mimeographed and mailed this out to a fanzine mailing list. Wollheim then filed suit for libel in the state supreme court, naming the seven of us who had signed the document: Judy, Blish, Lowndes, Virginia, Chet, Larry and me. The suit was thrown out of court, with costs charged to Wollheim, but it cost us $100 apiece in legal fees.

Blish and I were rivals at first, and I sniped at him in a mimeographed magazine called '   ', whose missing title was supposed to satirize the meaninglessness of all titles; but his ability to absorb criticism without anger disarmed me and we became friends.

In these magazines Blish and Judy Zissman had a rivalry which was much more bitter and long-lasting. Blish and Virginia Kidd were married in the late forties. Jim, who had been trying to make a living as a freelance writer, went to work as a reader for the Scott Meredith Literary Agency. Presently he got me a job there too.

Scott Meredith, born Feldman, was a small, slight man who as a young writer in Brooklyn had been so poor that he had walked across the bridge to hand-deliver his manuscripts. He and Kornbluth had lived on the same block as children. He had saved his money in the air force, and after the war, in partnership with his brother Sid, had opened the agency, which at first did such a feeble business that the partners had to sweep the place out themselves. This stage did not last long.

Sid's role in the agency was not clear. He had an office of his own and stayed in it most of the time, emerging only to distribute manuscripts and collect finished work, and to deliver an occasional homily about the resemblance of the agency to a shoe factory: 'They have the raw materials, the *leather,* you know, and they take that and put it through the machines just like we do here, and make *shoes.*'

Meredith also had a list of professional clients, including P. G. Wodehouse, whom he had acquired by writing him a fan letter, but this end of the business was kept separate from the reading-fee operation, and Scott managed it himself. Later, as the agency grew, he handled only the most important clients personally and the rest were turned over to an employee at what was called the 'pro desk'.

Meredith took full page, back-cover ads each month in *Writers' Digest;* these ads, which were lively and ingenious, encouraged amateur writers to send us their mss for evaluation at $5 for a short story and $25 for a novel. When the manuscripts came in the morning mail, they were distributed to us, and it was our job to read them and write letters of comment, for which we got $1 out of the $5, and $5 out of the $25. The first letter to a new client always began by explaining that his story was unsaleable because it did not follow the Plot Skeleton. The letter went on to enumerate the parts of the Plot Skeleton, viz: 1 A sympathetic and believable *lead character;* 2 an urgent and vital *problem;* 3 *complications* caused by the lead character's unsuccessful attempts to solve the problem; 4 the *crisis* (this element was added by Blish); 5 the *resolution,* in which the lead character solves the problem by means of his own courage and resourcefulness.

In a concluding paragraph the letter pointed out which of the elements were missing (ordinarily all of them were) and invited the client to try again. Subsequent letters grew more detailed. We really tried to help the clients, and in one or two cases I think we succeeded.

We had considerable latitude. The introductory letter always used the formula, 'I'm sorry I can't give you a better report, but – ' and then the news about the plot skeleton. Blish once got a manuscript that was so awful that he ended the sentence 'it stinks', and then wrote 'Sincerely yours'. Meredith laughed and signed it.

The fact that we were a shifting population and that all the letters were signed by Meredith (or by Sid, imitating Scott's handwriting) sometimes led to anomalies. Jim got into a lengthy correspondence about modern music with one client, then quit, and the client was turned over to Lester del Rey, another Meredith employee. The client, who had been hearing from Jim about Bartók and Hindemith, now began getting letters about Ravel's *'Bolero'*.

My contribution to these letters was the term 'paper

Robert Silverberg
(photo credit:
William Rotsler)

Alfred Bester (photo
credit: *Jay Garfield)*

Harry Harrison *(left)* and Brian Aldiss (photo credit: *Chris Love)*

Damon Knight
(photo credit:
Kate Wilhelm)

Frederik Pohl
(photo credit:
Jay Kay Klein)

dragon plot', meaning the frequent plot in which the ending discloses that there never was a problem. The work was exhausting and challenging, and I liked it. We were certainly exploited, but the training we got was invaluable. A long line of Meredith employees went on to become editors. Meredith encouraged this, on the theory that such people would be inclined to buy from the agency, and in most cases he was right.

The office was in the middle of the entertainment district, and at lunch time, when we had finished eating what we had brought (Jim once complained that Virginia had given him a potato-chip sandwich), we walked down the street to a penny arcade and spent the rest of our lunch hour there. Our favourite was the hockey game, on which I developed a bank shot that exasperated Jim by going through the space between the opposing player's stick and his cast-iron body.

A new office girl called Trudy Werndl joined us, just out of high school, blonde, plump and pretty, and seemed to be impressed with Jim and me because we were writers. We took her out for a beer after work, and I invited her to come and see me that weekend. One thing led to another, and when I asked her to come and live with me she agreed, but her girl-friends were shocked when she told them that, and with some misgivings I married her instead. Just at this point the Blishes had taken a house in Staten Island and asked us to come and share it. Trudy and I were married in the Little Church Around the Corner (chosen by one of the girl-friends) during the worst snow-storm of the decade.

As soon as the novelty wore off it became evident that our marriage was a mistake. We were not well suited, sexually or in any other way. Commuting to work from Staten Island, half an hour on the ferry alone, was exhausting for me and staying home all day was boring for Trudy. I was promoted to the pro desk, which had a huge backlog of work. After a month or so I became ill with cerebrospinal meningitis and was carted off to the Staten Island Hospital, a few blocks away, where in my delirium I read phantom manuscripts. Shortly after I came out, Trudy got appendicitis and went in. Meanwhile we and the Blishes were getting on each other's nerves a little; Trudy and I decided to try to improve our relationship by moving back into Manhattan. This was at the height of the wartime apartment shortage, and we were able to move into a Greenwich Village studio apartment (so called because it had a little skylight in the living room) only by buying the previous tenant's furniture with $700 put up by my mother.

Now began the most miserable and boring time of my life. My relations with Trudy deteriorated. We acquired a large circle of new friends, mostly musicians who met once a week at Julian Goodenough's apartment. He lived alone, in the apartment over his silversmith shop and in his little bedroom, under a pink light, he kept a row of high-heeled patent leather shoes in an assortment of sizes. At his weekly jam sessions, he sometimes played the bass, sometimes thumped on the piano, grinning around his cigar. He could not drink – one highball made his face flush red.

In the Village I met Stewart Kerby, a former sf fan who had published a limited edition of one of David H. Keller's stories. A friend of his, Kenneth Koch, sometimes hunted Stew up and brought him to my apartment to compose tunes to his poems on the piano.

Needing money, I returned to Meredith's, where I found myself in company with Don Fine and James A. Bryans, a slow, gangling man who later became editor in chief of Popular Library. Still later Fine became the head of his own publishing house. I trained myself to pot either of them with a wad of paper, sitting or standing.

When Ejler Jakobsson invited me to go back to Popular as his assistant, I was pleased, particularly since Jake had inherited Al Norton's department, which included the two science fiction magazines. (Norton was now associate publisher.) This was the reason Jake wanted me, anticipating my help in a field unfamiliar to him, but in this we were both disappointed. Jake rejected stories I recommended with enthusiasm, including two early Charles Harness stories, and filled the book with other things that I thought barely publishable. We disagreed about the merits of the pulp-style covers, and he was not amused when I traced one of them, putting football uniforms on the figures instead of spacesuits.

Wollheim married Elsie at last; they moved out to Queens,

to an apartment with a sunken living room that featured a photo-mural. Kornbluth married Mary Byers and they went to live in Levittown. Lowndes' was living in Westchester, married to a woman whose name suddenly changed. Pohl told me that he had called Lowndes on the phone and had said casually, 'How's Dorothy?' The following conversation ensued:

LOWNDES: Who?

POHL: Dorothy.

LOWNDES: *Who?*

POHL: Dorothy, your wife.

LOWNDES: (with great emphasis): She who *was* Dorothy is *now* Bar-bar-a.

Pohl married Judy Zissman. They went househunting in Red Bank, New Jersey, and because they were wearing old clothes the house agent assumed they were rich and showed them a huge three-storey house. They bought it and Fred still lives there.

I omit the details of my breakup with Trudy. Because the marriage was less than a year old and there were no children, it turned out to be possible to get an annulment rather than a divorce. She stayed with Julian for about a year, lost a lot of weight, bought new clothes and became svelte and elegant.

I did not have to appear at the annulment hearing; I had appeared earlier, however, in Judy Zissman's divorce action against Danny, in which I testified that Dan and a girl not his wife had spent some time in a bedroom in my apartment. The divorce referee was an old man named, appropriately, Schmuck. He asked me, 'What were you running, a whorehouse?' and muttered frequently, 'There'll be no divorce in this case, no divorce'. He granted it, all the same, and Judy at her request became legally Judith Merril.

I was fascinated by the permutations of Judy's names, and once when we were in a restaurant together wrote a poem about them on a napkin:

Juliet Grossman Zissman Pohl
Hated her name from the bottom of her soul:
Went to court in imminent peril;
Changed her name to Judith Merril.

At a party I had met Lester del Rey's wife Helen and later had learned that their marriage was breaking up. I took her out to a Chinese movie, and again one thing led to another. I turned the studio apartment over to Dick Wilson and moved in with Helen. Later we were married.

Lester del Rey signed his early letters to *Astounding* R. (for Ramon) Alvarez, and he had four or five other given names; the whole thing went something like Ramon Felippe Maria something something Alvarez-del Rey. He explained that his father was descended from a royalist branch of the Alvarez family, and so on. In conversation he liked to defend unlikely propositions. If he tossed out some assertion that aroused his hearer's incredulity he would immediately repeat it with more emphasis, and even if he had only thought of it a moment before, he would be prepared to defend it all afternoon, quoting sources which might or might not be imaginary: all this with a goblin grin and such evident enjoyment that it was hard to dislike him. I described this aspect of Lester among others in 'A Likely Story', in which he appeared as Ray Alvarez.

In the introduction to one of his stories I once called Lester one of the most contentious men alive. His wife Evelyn later told me that when he read this Lester shouted, 'I am *not* contentious!'

I was tired of Popular again, and wished I had my own science fiction magazine to edit. I asked Fred Pohl if he knew of any publisher who might be interested; he suggested I try Alex Hillman of Hillman Publications. I sent Hillman a written proposal and was called in for an interview. Hillman, who looked something like Charles Coburn, hired me in ten minutes. When he asked about salary, I said I was getting $75 at Popular (an exaggeration) but would like to do better than that; we settled on $85 a week, the most I had ever earned in my life. I paid off some debts and bought two new suits for the first time in my life. I had never owned more than one suit, mostly second-hand, before.

I wanted to call the magazine *Science-Fantasy*, but the firm's lawyers, after a haphazard search, advised against it because both words were in use in the titles of other magazines. We finally settled on *Worlds Beyond*, swiped from the title of a symposium edited by Lloyd Arthur Eshback, *Of Worlds Beyond*. My handshake agreement with Hillman was so hasty that I discovered afterward I didn't even know if the magazine was to be a monthly. I was too green to ask for a contract guaranteeing a minimum number of issues, or to settle details of production and format. Hillman was leaving on a vacation, and told me to have a cover ready for him when he got back.

Fred, now an agent, laughed with delighted disbelief when I told him I had sold Hillman the magazine. I bought several stories for the first issue from his clients, and one or two others from Meredith. From a young writer named Richard Matheson, then almost unknown, I bought a story called 'Clothes Make the Man', a deft little satire about a suit of clothes that takes over its owner's personality. This was the story I chose to illustrate on the cover. I called in an artist named Herman Bischoff and gave him the commission; he turned out a fine spooky painting of an empty suit of clothes waving its arms at a startled girl. When he came back, Hillman rejected the painting and would not be dissuaded, even though a vice-president took my side. I discovered that I had only thought I had authority to order the painting made; what Hillman had meant was for me to get a sketch made for his approval. Bischoff was never paid. I turned to Paul Callé, who I knew had a painting that had been turned down by Popular, and we bought it for $100.

The atmosphere at Hillman Publications was utterly unlike that at Popular. I had an office to myself for a week or two, then was put in with the staff of Hillman's fact detective magazines, headed by an irascible, popeyed man whose name I have forgotten. Every editor seemed alone at his little desk, even though several of us worked in the same room. There was no camaraderie and no fraternization. Meeting Hillman in the hall was an unnerving experience. Smoking a cigar, he lumbered down the hall staring straight ahead, hands clasped behind his back. When I said good morning, he continued to stare and lumber. (I used him as the Boss of Colorado in my novel *A for Anything*.)

I had the tiniest of budgets, but since I was using about half reprint material I could afford to pay the going rate for new stories. Fred sent me an elegant satire by Phil Klass which I retitled 'Null-P'. I got stories from Poul Anderson, Fred Brown and Mack Reynolds, John Cristopher and others. I wrote a book review department, which I called 'The Dissecting Table'.

The first issue appeared, with a dumb headline sticker contrived by one of Hillman's lieutenants (something about FLYING SAUCER MEN). It was printed on the poorest grade of newsprint I had ever seen, worse even than Lowndes's magazines. When the first sales report came in three weeks later, it was so bad that Hillman cancelled the project at once. Two more issues were in preparation by then and appeared. The cover for the fourth had been painted. The firm did not want to pay the artist for this, either, but this time I stood by him (his sketch had been approved), and he got his money.

In the forties nearly every science fiction magazine had a book review department, but these were mostly of what I later called the shopping guide type; the reviews were about an inch long, and always ended 'A must for every science fiction fan'. Besides the *Worlds Beyond* reviews, I had already written one long critical essay about the works of A. E. van Vogt, which Larry Shaw had published in one of his amateur magazines *Destiny's Child*. When Lester started two new magazines, *Space Science Fiction* and *Science Fiction Adventures*, I was able to talk him into letting me do the book department in one of them. He paid me, if I remember, $15 a column.

After a year or so Lowndes also offered to run any reviews I sent him, no matter what the length, and to pay his usual rates, i.e. half a cent a word. At various times I also published reviews in Harlan Ellison's huge sloppy fanzine *Dimensions* (where my column was called 'Gardy-loo', a call formerly used when throwing the contents of chamber pots out of windows), in Walt Willis's *Hyphen,* in *Infinity,* and finally in the *Magazine of Fantasy & Science Fiction.* When I quit, in a dispute over a review *F&SF* refused to print, I had been reviewing books for nine years.

These reviews were generally successful, even with the authors. (Bob Tucker told me he had been present when

Jerry Sohl read my review of *Point Ultimate*, and that Jerry had laughed and cried at the same time.) There were a few exceptions, however. Someone wrote a virulent letter to *Infinity* under a pseudonym objecting to my review of a book of stories by Richard Matheson. (He called me, I think, 'one of the great frustrates of our time'.) *Infinity* published the letter. I noticed that the address was the same as that of Charles McNutt, a one-time fan who had, not quite incomprehensibly, changed his name to Charles Beaumont. I wrote to ask him if he was the author of the letter, and he replied that he was not but that he knew who was. He wouldn't tell me who, and could not explain why his address had been used. I said I would not duel with anybody who fired from ambush, and that was the end of that.

Horace Gold, the editor of the new magazine *Galaxy*, had bought a story of mine called 'To Serve Man', and I wrote him another story. He bought that, and a third story, and a fourth. I wrote them one after another sitting on the sofabed Lester had given us, with my typewriter on a kitchen chair between my knees. When I sold Horace still another story I realized that, as a successful author, I was no longer tied to New York. Helen and I stored our furniture and bought air tickets to California.

We rented a cottage on the side of a mountain in La Sierra. The view across the valley was magnificent, and there was a little garden. I put my typewriter on a chair under the pepper tree in the yard and finished 'Double Meaning', the novelette I had started before we left New York.

My relationship with Helen was affectionate and companionable rather than romantic. As long as we were poor we got along beautifully and were very happy together. If we were down to a dollar and a half, we spent it on a movie, knowing that something would turn up in a day or two. We invented balloon-ball, played with a string for a net: whoever let the balloon touch the floor on his side lost a point. I worked out a way of simulating computer-written stories, called it 'logogenetics', and we spent hours at that.

Gold rejected 'Double Meaning', my first clue that all was not well in the writers' paradise. (Sam Merwin later bought it

129

and published it in *Startling*.) I wrote another story and Gold rejected that one too.

Feeling too isolated in La Sierra, we moved to Santa Monica, where we met Richard Matheson and his girlfriend. We lived in a garage apartment owned by a tv actress. Broke, I went to work in an aircraft plant as a file clerk. They fired me after six weeks, to my relief.

We decided we had had enough of southern California, with its eight months of sunshine and four months of rain. We went back to New York and stayed temporarily in Lester's apartment again. (He was living elsewhere.)

I went back to Popular one more time when Mike Tilden needed someone to fill in for a month or so. He said gruffly that I could keep the job if I wanted it, but I didn't. By then it was routine; I could do it without thinking about it, and didn't like it anymore.

Within a year Popular folded all its pulps and let the editors go. Later I found Mike and Ejler Jakobsson working in the same office with Larry Shaw on a series of porn novels published by Universal Publishing & Distributing Co. Mike's wife had died and his son had committed suicide; he died himself a few years later, broke, unlaundered and patient to the end.

Looking at a map, Helen and I saw names we liked in the Poconos and took a bus there. We found a four-room cabin in the woods and rented it from the owner, a bartender named Diebold and his wife. (I used him in *A for Anything*.) It was about a mile from Canadensis, itself nothing but a crossroads with a post office and a few stores. There was a good-sized lawn which I had to cut with a scythe. Behind us in the woods was a tiny shed, not much bigger than a phone booth, in which a halfwit lived. I found an old desk in a shed and dragged it into the house; it was fragrant with barnyard odours and had great gaps between the boards of its top. We acquired kittens; one of them fell into the well and another was caught in a trap set by the halfwit. In August of that year our first child was born; we named her Valerie. I began writing again, and finished a long story, 'Natural State', which Gold bought.

This was my first editorial collaboration with Horace, and

it left me with mixed feelings. Previously I had just written the stories and he had either bought or rejected them; this time I went to him with an idea and we talked it over. The idea was for a story to be called 'Cannon Fodder', which was to take the form of an epic journey by some soldiers and their 'cannon' – a living creature biologically engineered to be a weapon. Gold turned this around and produced the idea of a whole culture based on biological engineering rather than machines; he also contributed some of the most telling details, such as the knife-bushes. Beyond doubt, this was a much better story than the one I had had in mind, but I could not help feeling that I would rather have written my story. I bore this in mind when I next became an editor.

I wrote another long story, 'Rule Golden', but Gold bounced it and I had to get rid of it to *Science Fiction Adventures*, then edited by Harry Harrison. Even so, we had money again, and bought another car, an imposing green sedan. Helen's father, who was dying, came to live with us; he was patient and quiet in his pain, made no trouble, scarcely disturbed the air.

I wrote 'Special Delivery', a story about an unborn superman, based on Helen's pregnancy and on a remark of hers, 'Give him one for me'.

I wrote a long story intended for *Beyond*, called 'Be My Guest', finishing it just before Christmas, but Gold bounced that one and it was years before I sold it to Hans Santesson for *Fantastic Universe*. One of the characters in this story was modelled after a disturbed girl whom Chester had gone to bed with once, and who for months afterward came around and left little tokens for him – poems, Christmas cards, crushed eggshells.

I had first met Horace Gold in 1950, shortly after the first issue of *Galaxy* appeared. He was a bald, stocky man, restless and energetic, boastful, innovative, brilliant – all the things that *Galaxy* was. Under all this there was a hard core of despair. Once when he reached for some small object on his desk it toppled and broke. 'Gold touched it,' he said glumly. After the war Gold had developed an extreme case of agoraphobia, and now never left the East Side apartment where he lived with his wife and young son. There were frequent parties there, and he spent hours in telephone conversations. I was always uneasy around Gold because he was the only editor who was buying my stuff with any regularity and because I wanted to like him better than I did. I have since felt the vibrations of similar feelings from writers I have published. It's easier to like someone who is dependent on your favours than it is for him to like you.

Once I called Horace to ask how the magazine was doing, and he asked me as a favour to write to the publishers praising the first issue. I thought this was an odd request, but said I would, and wrote a letter beginning, 'At H. L. Gold's suggestion, I write to tell you what a great job I think he is doing as editor of *Galaxy*'. They showed this letter to Gold, and he told me his wife thought I was knifing him, but he realized I was merely naive. After that, every time something went wrong at *Galaxy*, Evelyn said, 'Oh, well, Damon can always take over'.

Gold had an incurable habit of overediting stories; as Lester once said, he turned mediocre stories into good ones, and excellent stories into good ones. He bought Edgar Pangborn's beautiful 'Angel's Egg' and showed it to several writers in manuscript, then rewrote some of its best phrases. He changed the description of the 'angel' (a visitor from another planet) riding on the back of a hawk 'with her speaking hands on his terrible head' to 'with her telepathic hands on his predatory head'. According to Ted Sturgeon, when the issue came out and the story was read in the printed version, three pairs of heels hit the floor at that point and three people tried to phone Gold to curse him for a meddler. Sturgeon got in the habit of marking out certain phrases in his manuscripts and writing them in again above the line in ink. Gold asked him why he did that, pointing out that it made it difficult for him to write in corrections. 'That's why I do it,' Sturgeon replied.

Gold was certainly one of the best idea men in the business, and contributed more to the stories published in *Galaxy* than will ever be known. Blish complained that his invariable response to an author's idea was to turn it on its head, but in fact sometimes he merely turned it sidewise, to its great benefit.

Once Horace called me up in Canadensis and proposed that I become what he called a utility writer for *Galaxy*, writing stories to order on whatever themes Horace needed at the moment, and under various pseudonyms – 'maybe even under women's names'. I wanted to say no but didn't dare, and agreed with such faint enthusiasm that Horace knew what I meant, and was disappointed twice – once for my refusal and once for my failure to come out with it. I know now that editors are constantly disappointed by authors' unwillingness to fight, and would often rather have a forthright 'no' than a weak-kneed 'yes'.

I had been disappointed in my early ambition to become an *Astounding* writer; Campbell returned my submissions via Sturgeon with scrawled comments such as 'early 1930' or 'so what?' which hurt my feelings without teaching me anything. I managed to sell him one-half of a story (a collaboration with Blish called 'Tiger Ride'), and that was all until 1952 when I sold him one story of my own, 'The Analogues', which had a touch of Dianetics in it. In 1964 I sold him another, 'Semper Fi', which he retitled 'Satisfaction'. (My title, which I prefer, is Marine slang for 'Fuck you, Jack. I've got mine'.)

I heard about the four-page letters other people got from Campbell, and I felt left out. Eventually I wrote to him asking for more guidance, and he wrote back inviting me to lunch, but I was about to leave for California and had to decline. No doubt I could have got myself invited to lunch long before, but Campbell's lecture-room manner was so unpleasant to me that I was unwilling to face it. Campbell talked a great deal more than he listened, and he liked to say outrageous things; I could not cope with this, and if my patience gave out, my only response was anger.

Now I saw *Galaxy* as the longed-for ideal science fiction market, and the fact that Horace was buying nearly everything I wrote made it easy to overlook any defects in it. My stories were consistently appearing in first place in the readers' ballots as long as Gold ran them. (Gold insisted, by the way, that Campbell had told him on the phone that he threw away readers' letters and made up the percentages in his 'AnLab' department.)

When Gold began rejecting my stories and I had to look for other markets, I felt betrayed. It's true that these were not the sort of stories he was used to buying from me, but I felt that ought not to matter, and that the whole point of a magazine like *Galaxy* was that it should buy, if it could, the best work of the best writers no matter what kind it was.

When I came to edit *Orbit* I tried to live up to this ideal and found that I couldn't. I bought five or six stories in a row from Gardner Dozois and Gene Wolfe and other writers, and then rejected other stories which they must have had every reason to think I would buy. So it goes.

Helen and I wanted a bigger house, and found one for rent in Canadensis, but the owner's eyes narrowed when I said I was a writer. Finding nothing else nearer, we went house-hunting in Milford, with Judy Merril's energetic help.

The first Milford colonists had been the Blishes, who had answered an ad in the *Times* and had signed an agreement by which they would buy a house in installments and would not get the deed until it was all paid for. This kept them out of the mortgage mill – they had no money for a down payment anyhow – but it made them nervous for years lest they lose the house and all their investment. Their house was a charming two-storey cottage with a sundeck overlooking a long sweep of lawn down to the Sawkill (which later flooded them out).

Judy came next, rented a cold Victorian house on Broad Street, reassembled her family and set out to be a mother. Both children had been living with their fathers and both came to Judy voluntarily, but in taking them she violated custody agreements and that led to trouble later. Fred sued her to regain custody of their daughter Ann, and there was a messy court hearing at which nearly everybody we knew was drawn in to testify on one side or the other.

Milford is a quiet little town on the Delaware. The permanent population then was about a thousand. The streets are lined with old maples, and are beautiful in the fall. Most of the houses are white-painted frame, many of them Victorian houses, with gingerbread, gables and slate roofs. The town has a high society composed of old residents, second and third generation; newcomers are never admitted to this, but anybody who stays one winter will thereafter be treated as human. Tourism keeps Milford alive; to the north of it there are towns like Hawley which are shockingly decayed. The town has always been known for its restaurants, among them the Fauchère, which serves an old-fashioned menu and requires its guests to be decently dressed.

We found a cottage on Ann Street at $35 a month and moved in. The house was painted white inside and out, had sagging wood floors and a bow window with window-seats. The front room was unheated except for a fireplace and in the winter we found that we had to close it off or we couldn't heat the rest of the house. The front room was where we kept the television, however, and there was no convenient place for it in the middle room. Our solution was to tack a blanket across the open doorway and watch the tv over it.

I had been writing longer and longer things, and I thought I was due for a novel, but I still shrank from the idea of doing all that work from scratch. Instead, I thought of a sequel to a story of mine called 'The Analogues'. The sequel, 'Turncoat', was a little over twenty thousand words, and then I had enough to offer with an outline of the rest to Walter Fultz of Lion Books. He gave me a contract, and I finished the book as *Hell's Pavement*. The novel was about the consequences of an invention, and it was more or less legitimate for it to be broken down into a short section (the original story) introducing the invention, then a longer one showing its early development, and a still longer section winding up the plot.

I thought I would try this again with another gadget, and this time I chose the matter duplicator, because I thought previous writers had handled it badly. George O. Smith, in 'Pandora's Box', had preserved civilization by introducing coins made of an unduplicable substance. I thought this was a rabbit out of a hat, and that the thing to do was to let civilization collapse and then see what happened. (Later an Alaskan writer, Ralph Williams, took exception to my version and wrote a lovely story called 'Business as Usual, During Alterations', in which he argued persuasively that civilization would not even shudder.) I wrote the first part and sold it to *F&SF* as 'A for Anything', then, with that and an outline, got a contract from Fultz for the novel. My thesis was that following the collapse of industrial civilization a new slave-holding society would arise, and that the new masters would necessarily take over the only existing houses big and isolated enough for their purposes, like resort hotels. I put my hero in a real place called Buck Hill, not far from Canadensis; the description of the grounds and the exterior of the house is from observation.

I got to within about ten thousand words of the end of this novel and then hit a block – I knew what was to happen next, but just couldn't write it. Fultz by this time had left Lion, to be replaced by his former secretary; the firm had gone into liquidation and its assets had been acquired by a new corporation doing business as Zenith Books. In order to finish the book I plunged in and wrote it as best I could. The treatment of the rebel leader in the last chapters was perfunctory, but otherwise the ending seemed all right to me. I delivered the ms. to Zenith and asked Fultz's successor to hold off. publication for a few months so that I could sell serial rights; she refused, saying that she needed the book right away, and since I was late with it, I gulped and agreed. The book was not published until nearly twelve months later.

Zenith's emblem was a V-shaped thing, and the fact that it pointed downward made me suggest to the editor that the company ought to call itself Nadir Books; but she didn't get it. I was right, though.

In 1955 the partners in a new fan publishing house called Advent approached me with the idea of making a collection of my book reviews. They gave me a contract under which I was to get half the profits after the costs of production had been met. I put the collection together from tearsheets and carbons, although my agent would have no part of it, and said I would never see a nickel. Anthony Boucher contributed an introduction, and I insisted that he get a percentage too. The collection was published in 1956. A revised and enlarged edition was published in 1967, and the book has brought in a few hundred dollars every year since it was first published, for a total of about $2,000.

In 1958 James L. Quinn, the publisher of *If*, asked me to

become the editor of the magazine. Larry Shaw had been the editor in the early fifties, when he published the original novelette version of Blish's 'A Case of Conscience'; but when Larry returned a story of Judith Merril's because he thought she could sell it elsewhere for more money, Quinn took this as disloyalty and fired him. At this time Quinn had been editing the magazine himself for several years, and its circulation had been going down. He was faced with the choice of folding it or trying another editor. He did the layouts for *If* himself and was good at it, but his tastes in fiction ran to conventional satires about automobiles and computers. I edited three issues of *If*, and gave it my best, but the circulation did not go up and Quinn sold the magazine to *Galaxy*.

Among the stories I inherited when I began editing the magazine was one called 'The Founding of Fishdollar Five' (I shortened this to 'The Fishdollar Affair') by Richard McKenna. Quinn had promised McKenna he would buy this story if he would cut it in half. McKenna has told how he did this and how important it was to him in his 'Journey With a Little Man'. The story was cut to the bone, and Quinn said he had not expected to be taken literally, but he bought it. I was impressed with McKenna and invited him to the Milford Conference. I also invited a writer named Kate Wilhelm, from whom I hadn't bought anything but whose stories had caught my eye. These were fateful decisions.

I had visualized Kate Wilhelm as a middle-aged woman with iron-gray hair and flat heels; instead, she turned out to be young, slender and pretty. That year we had also invited an MIT student called Shag, who was not a professional writer and really should not have been there; he was hopelessly smitten with Katie. We sat up all night in the Blishes' living room, the last night of the Conference, and in the morning A. J. Budrys and I took Kate to the train, where AJ kissed her and she shook hands with me. When we got back to the Blishes', AJ said to Shag, with a twinkle in his eye, 'She was incredibly passionate,' and Shag said, 'You bastard'.

In 1959 I got a copy of the French magazine *Fiction*, which had translated one of my stories. *Fiction* was founded as the French edition of *F&SF*, but almost from the beginning had been using the work of native writers, and at this time the contents were about half and half. It was then an attractive little magazine, with covers by Jean-Claude Forest, the artist who created *Barbarella*.

In the forties I had taught myself a little French with the intention of trying to puzzle out the text of sexy French magazines and books. (I had an exaggerated idea of the naughtiness of *La Vie Parisienne*, from references to that magazine in early science fiction stories.) I was disappointed in the texts I found, but kept at it anyhow and got as far as reading all the way through a novel of Andre Maurois', *Climats*. This was by no means enough to qualify me as a translator, but I got out my French-English dictionary and sat down at the dining room table with the first story in the magazine, 'Au Pilote Aveugle' by Charles Henneberg (really a collaboration between Henneberg and his wife Nathalie, who continued writing stories much like this one after his death). The story went smoothly into English, happened to be very good, and I sold the translation to *F&SF*. Then it was easy to do more. The work of translation, and even more the correspondence with the authors, improved my French enormously, although I still can't understand spoken French well enough to carry on a conversation. The only time I ever had the courage to try it was with José Sanz, the organizer of the film festival in Rio, who wouldn't talk to us because he was ashamed of his English. After two or three shots of my French, he gave in and began talking in perfect and almost accentless English.

In 1960 Robert P. Mills, who had been the editor of *F&SF*, went into the agency business, first as an associate of Rogers Terrill, then with Ashley Famous Agency, and finally on his own. I was his first client, and the first thing he said to me was, 'I think you ought to be in hard-cover'. He sent a collection of my stories over to Simon & Schuster, and Clayton Rawson bought it. My original title was *Stop the World* but Clayt, who had never heard the phrase, vetoed it; I proposed *Far Out*, and the book was published under that title.

Rawson came out to the Milford Conference next year and

proposed to me that I should edit a large retrospective collection of science fiction, an idea that had occurred to him because one morning he had two proposals for sf books on his desk, one about old-time science fiction and another from a very young writer; and it struck him that there must be many young people who had never heard of the older sf.

I had always been convinced that I could edit a superior anthology, but had never found out how you convinced an editor of that unless you had already done one. (I still don't know.) I attacked this assignment with enthusiasm, dragged out all my favourite old stories, and Clayt sent several of them back with sounds of pained displeasure. I looked them over again more carefully and realized with dismay that they were junk which had impressed me in my ignorance when I was twelve and thirteen. In spite of this I managed to put together a collection that pleased both Clayt and me (the excerpt from *Twenty Thousand Leagues Under the Sea* was included at his suggestion), then found that the second anthology was no trouble to sell. As my production of fiction diminished and my responsibilities increased I turned more and more to anthologies as a way of making a living.

Thomas A. Dardis of Berkley Books asked in 1960 if I would be interested in becoming their science fiction consultant. He had approached Groff Conklin first; Groff had suggested me. I served in this capacity for six years, reading manuscripts and writing reports for Dardis, and also did some freelance copy-editing. In 1963 I persuaded Dardis to let me edit four books a year, working directly with the authors and giving contracts on the basis of outlines. In this way I got first novels from Keith Laumer, Thomas M. Disch and others, and brought Gordon R. Dickson and Poul Anderson into the Berkley list.

In 1961, after my mother died and left me some money, my relationship with Helen began to deteriorate, as if wealth had done us in. We owned property and had money in the bank (most of the time), but we no longer enjoyed each other's company. Later Helen explained it as cabin fever: in my presence she would think, 'Ugh, he's breathing'. We tried this and that, but nothing worked, and eventually I went to an upstairs bedroom.

Helen moved out with the children, first to a little house near the river and then to Port Jervis, where she still lives. We were divorced after the degrading, grotesque and cruel preliminaries then required by the Commonwealth of Pennsylvania.

Next year at the Conference, Katie and I approached each other hesitantly; neither of us knew quite how to begin, but we finally managed. We agreed that Katie would get a divorce, bring her two boys to Milford and live there for a year; then if all went well we would be married. She stayed with Judy for a week or two, then rented a little house on the Dingmans road. Kate's sons, Dusty and Dickie, were then thirteen and nine, and they circled me like strange dogs. Dickie, who wore paratrooper's boots, tried to kick me in the kneecap, but I caught his foot and dumped him. After that things went a little better, and eventually very well.

When I told Judy that Kate and I were going to be married, her jaw dropped. I had read about this in fiction, but it was the first time I had ever seen it happen.

We wanted a real wedding but not a minister, and on finding out that Pennsylvania law permits a couple to stand up before witnesses and declare themselves married, we asked Ted Thomas to perform a ceremony which we devised, basing it on a Unitarian service Ted got for us and altering it here and there. Mac McKenna gave the bride away; Avram Davidson was my best man and Carol Emshwiller was the matron of honour.

In 1963 when I was working on a short novel called *The Other Foot,* which is still my favourite, and was having difficulty with it, I turned for relaxation to another novel which I made up as I went along; I called it *The Tree of Time.* It was a wild vanVogtian adventure involving an amnesiac superman from the future and a search for a monster which turned out to be the hero in disguise, etc. I enjoyed writing it, especially the sequences that took place in a zero-G satellite of the future (a nasty little scientist I introduced here was modelled partly after J. R. Pierce). All my friends and well-wishers hated it, but I sold it every-where – *F&SF*, Doubleday, book club, paperback.

The Tocks Island Dam and Recreation Project was threatening to inundate the Delaware Valley, and the condemnation line ran down the middle of the highway in front of our house. It was evident to us that if we stayed, eventually we would be surrounded by hot-dog stands. Worse, we were getting air pollution from New York for the first time. We made up our minds to sell the Anchorage and move to Florida.

We found a twelve-year-old house for sale on the bay; the waterfront was narrow and at the end of an inlet, and the house was not as spacious as we had wanted, but it would do and we bought it. In our little back yard there is an ear tree (something like a jacaranda), and from this tree we have hung a bird-feeder, and wild budgerigars cluster on this bird-feeder, along with sparrows, doves, and occasional jays and cardinals. Herons perch on our dock. The bay is polluted, but not as much as it was before the experimental sewage plant nearby was turned into a pumping station, and I swim there nearly every day. Kate's son Dick and my son Kris, who had been living with their father and mother respectively, are now living with us, and our son Jon, who ignored the ocean when we first brought him down here, has had swimming lessons at the Bath Club and swims like a blond seal now. Pinellas County has the highest growth rate in the country, and we know pollution and crowding will force us to move on in three or four years, but for the present we are all right.

In 1969 the Brazilian government held a film festival in an effort to put Rio de Janeiro on the map, and José Sanz, a science fiction buff, talked them into holding an sf seminar in conjunction with it. Sanz invited sf writers wholesale, and the writers suggested other writers.

Rio is the only beautiful city I have ever seen. From the mountains around the city you can look out over the blue ocean and see only one ship. We were quartered in one of the hotels along the ocean front, and were ferried every day to the French cultural centre to listen to one of our number make a speech. This was idiocy, but we attended faithfully in order to show our gratitude, and refrained from making any speeches ourselves.

Van Vogt said that the universe to him was a tree with golden balls on its branches, and the next day all the Brazilian papers faithfully reported that van Vogt had said the universe was a tree with golden balls on its branches.

Brian was in our hotel and we saw him several times, but most of the others were in three other hotels farther down the avenue. Katie and I moved in a euphoric glow for the ten days we were there. I can't explain it, but there is an ambience of sexuality and romance on the Copacabana – it is in the air, you breathe it.

The beach at Copacabana is for the people, and you see them there sunning themselves, playing volley ball, the children flying tiny homemade kites that continually flutter down, swoop up, flutter. The sand looks and feels like brown sugar. The surf is strong, and the undertow so swift that if you try to swim in water three feet deep, you find yourself stranded as the water goes out.

A Brazilian writer, André Carneiro, was the chairman of the symposium, and several others hung around the lobby of our meeting place, but they had no part in the proceedings. I tried to organize a meeting of American and Brazilian writers, through Carneiro, but instead it was a meeting of American writers and Brazilian publishers.

At a party we met some of the American embassy people, who appeared to think that the world and their relations to it were all fantasy. The servants were Brazilians; the guests, with two or three exceptions, were North Americans. According to Harlan Ellison, the hostess slipped into the bathroom after him and remarked, 'What happens now is up to you.' (Why are people always trying to seduce Jewish men in the bathroom?)

Once, walking down the Copacabana, we came upon John Brunner sitting in his misery. All Latin-American cities were very depressive, he said. Harlan Ellison, who had brought a large good-looking girl and was not getting along with her, made a scene because the symposium did not want to pay for his long-distance phone calls.

We have been drinking dark-roast coffee ever since. I

brought home some *cachaça* (the local firewater), but it was soon gone, and I can't get any more. José Sanz wrote a letter of apology to Harlan Ellison, and said he hoped there would be another symposium; but nothing has come of it. The postman doesn't knock twice.

I was fifty-one in September of this year (1973) and have been half-expecting a menopausal crisis like the ones I had in my early thirties and forties, but it hasn't come.

The Milford Conference is in its seventeenth year; SFWA is eight years old; *Orbit 14* will be published in the spring.

I learned to swim in the Delaware in my forties, and lost my fear of water for good when I found out how hard it is to stay underwater. Living with the bay in our back yard and the Gulf two blocks away, I have been swimming nearly every day and am smaller in the waist, bigger in chest and shoulders than I was when we came down here.

Today there was only one other person swimming in the Gulf as far as I could see in both directions. About a dozen terns were on the nearest groin, more than I have seen this year, and on the beach farther down there was a crowd of other birds, gulls and little sandpipers. Sky and water were the improbable Mediterranean colours we see every day (remembering how dingy New York looked when we first went back) – sky a luminous dark blue with puffs of white cloud, water a golden green. (Not bad.)

Frederik Pohl:

ragged claws

How do you describe what constitutes excellence in science fiction over the long-distance phone, when it's one o'clock in the morning, your coffee is cold in the cup, you've been on the phone for two hours and you have to go to the bathroom? He wasn't a bad person. He had his doctorate in English letters, he was earnestly attempting to say everything that could be said of science fiction in 2,000 words for his newspaper syndicate and he was morally determined that every word would be right. And so I prowled around the 18-foot perimeter of the telephone cord, listening to *him* tell *me* why a certain story, by a writer whose name I withhold was better than anything by Bradbury or Arthur Clarke and far superior to the overrated novels of Samuel R. Delany. And from time to time I would try to correct some error of fact or suggest a misinterpretation. The connection must have been bad, I never got through.

I understand you, O telephone pal on Mountain Standard Time. I only wish I could make you understand me. 'What breadth of imagination,' you kept saying, 'what a dazzle of conceptualization and thought.' The thing is, you hadn't ever read any science fiction at all, until your managing editor handed you the assignment. You came to it with your pores all open and receptive, and you were overcome by the combined creation of hundreds of intelligent people writing over a period of a century or so ... all wrapped up in one schlocky fourth-generation retread.

But you didn't know that was what it was, because it was all new and astonishing to you. In your longlashed virgin gaze This was It. I know how you feel, because I was once you, a far younger and more ignorant version of you.

That was a long time ago. 1930. The world was numb under the great depression. I remember the cold city streets, gloveless relief workers shovelling snow outside the second-hand magazine store where I browsed through the old copies of *Amazing Stories* before selecting the one in which I would invest my dime. I remember a hot summer in my uncle's attic, smelling of salt and curing tobacco, where I found treasure trove, twenty back years of *Argosy* and *Weird Tales*. I opened the pages of an *Amazing Stories Annual* and Mars smote me, four-armed green warriors riding six-legged steeds across the ochre plains of the evaporated seas.

No one could have suggested to me then that Edgar Rice Burroughs did not far outshine Sir Walter Scott, that David H. Keller had not a wryer view of humanity than Huxley or that Stanton A. Coblentz was not a wittier satirist than Swift or Voltaire. One might have pointed out that my judgment could have been flawed because I had not read Scott, Huxley or Swift, and only *Candide* of Voltaire. (Which my mother had given me for my eighth birthday, under the impression it was a fairy tale.) No matter. I imprinted when it was imprinting time. A year or two later I discovered I was not alone in the world, when I joined a magazine's circulation-promotion scheme called The Science Fiction League, attended meetings of its Brooklyn chapter and met people like Donald Wollheim, John Michel and others. Fandom was born: we began starting our own clubs, publishing our own mimeographed magazines, writing our bad little stories. As time went by, they got somewhat better and a few of them got published. By the time I was twenty, which was in 1940, I was editor of two ill-paying but professional sf magazines, and so was Wollheim, and so was Robert Lowndes, and we fans who called ourselves Futurians were now collectively a sizeable part of the professional mainstream of science fiction.

Well, that was quite a long time ago, but I would like to dwell on that time for a moment, the decade or a little more from the late twenties to the end of the thirties. What was it that we imprinted to, so adhesively that so many of us elected to devote our lives to it?

It wasn't world esteem. Mostly we carried our copies of science fiction magazines around with the covers folded over. It certainly wasn't literary excellence. The major authors of the sf magazines of the time – the Kellers and Joe W. Skidmores and Ed Earl Repps – were hamhanded and tone deaf to the point of pain.

And yet Keller in particular was acclaimed by persons in all other ways apparently of normal intelligence as a literary master. I suppose his most famous work was a short story called 'The Revolt of the Pedestrians'. I need hardly describe the story. The title tells it all: in the story's future age, humans have become so used to driving everywhere that they have lost the use of their legs, and their legs have consequently atrophied to stubby stumps ... until along comes a young man, a throwback, with limbs like Nureyev, who preaches the joys of walking and leads the world back to perambulatory purity. Knocks you cold, doesn't it? Would you believe that, not far from half a century ago, it in fact did strike thousands of readers as revelatory and brilliant?

And yet, although the plot is pretty trivial and the style a botch, justice demands a fairer appraisal of 'The Revolt of the Pedestrians'. It *was* satire. Swift or Voltaire would have done it better, but neither Swift nor Voltaire happened to be commenting on the current American scene at that time, and those who were limited themselves to japes about prohibition and flappers. What Keller did he surely did badly, but he was one of the very few doing it at all.

Another who ploughed those same furrows was Stanton A. Coblentz. He poked furious fun at money-hunger in *The Blue Barbarians*, at over-specialization in *After 12,000 Years*, at all of the foibles of early twentieth-century America in a score of stories. If his style was somewhat more gracious than Keller's (Coblentz is a poet as well as an sf author), his comedy was still on the pratfall level.

Nevertheless Keller, Coblentz and others were opening up a new vantage point from which to observe the human race : that dislocation in space, or in time, which permits what Harlow Shapley calls 'the view from a distant star'. How enlightening that view is! How much more clearly we can see the folly and arbitrariness and transience of our own ways when we look at them from Barsoom or from the end of time.

So that was there, in those ragged pulp magazines of four or five decades ago : social satire. It made a whole generation of us both cynics and dreamers : cynics, because we could see the shoddiness of the now, dreamers, because at the same time other writers were offering us Utopias and magnificent challenges.

The greatest challenge of all, of course, was space. Barsoom. Osnome. Persephone, and the planets of Arcturus and Altair. Where the fantasy life of the normal pre-pubescent male involved strutting into a Texas town, throwing a silver dollar on the bar and shooting it out with a sheriff, ours involved chopping squat, evil Fenachrone into hamburger with shimmering spheres of force. Where the normal fantasy life of the post-pubescent male involved girls, ours also involved girls – but pink-skinned, oviparous little angels like Dejah Thoris, or the doomed, possessed princesses who haunted the waterside bars of ancient Venus in the stories of Northwest Smith.

And all this was going on, remember, in a world that was gradually putting itself together after the cataclysm of the 1929 crash, en route to the catastrophe of World War II. Out of work veterans were being burned out of their shacks on Anacostia Flats because they were demanding a bonus and the government could find no money to give them. Hungry men sold apples in the streets. Not everyone was broke and despairing in those times, but everyone had seen what happened to a brother or a friend, and everyone was afraid. So we suffered from culture shock. Not from encountering Martians or Plutonians, but from looking up from the pages of *Science Wonder Stories* or *Amazing* and seeing the insanity outside our windows that we were told was 'real'.

As quickly as we could, we fled back to Barsoom.

Need I make a parenthesis to explain the meaning of the word 'Barsoom'? Probably not; Edgar Rice Burroughs's invented Mars still lives on; just the other day I saw the covers for a whole new reprinting of the saga, nearly a dozen books, going out in hundreds of thousands to an audience that must still somehow find them as enchanting as we did forty years ago. John Carter was the founder of the house. A veteran of the Civil War (on the rebel side) he happened to find himself trapped in a western cave with a horde of howling Apaches just outside, urging him to come out so they could torture him to death. If Zane Grey had been writing the story, Carter would have come out in a burst of unexpected action, seized a chief, stolen a horse and made his escape. Burroughs got his man out of that spot in a more inventive way, if not a perceptibly more believable one: Carter steals out when the Apaches aren't looking, gazes upward longingly at the planet Mars, holds out his hands to it ... and somehow, Burroughs did not feel obliged to explain exactly how, is drawn to it, and awakens to find himself on Mars itself, with a four-armed green warrior holding a sword to his throat.

Well, so much for that: the rest of the story is swordplay and rescued princesses. I honestly would not care to relate the plot of any of the Mars books to even the friendliest of audiences.

But plot is only a detail. There is more to the Mars books than that. I do not speak of literary style – Burroughs was a pulpster, hitting his typewriter keyboard with clenched fists. I speak of morality, and perception, and thought. Burroughs used Mars to comment on Earth, just as Swift used Lilliput and Laputa. In *The Master Mind of Mars* he ridiculed religion, an act not without courage. In all the books he jabbed at prudery (the Barsoomians ornamented their bodies instead of concealing them). The 'stately formal dances' of the Barsoomian nobles no doubt reflect his displeasure with the Charleston and the Bunny Hug. And so on; I will not labour the point, but if the man was writing adventure it was not *just* adventure.

It was even scientifically accurate. That, I admit, is a claim for Burroughs not often heard, but I think it is defensible. True, Burroughs's Barsoom is not much like the Mars of the Mariner photographs. But it is very like the Mars of Percival Lowell, and that was all that science knew of Mars at the time. Low gravity: Carter leaps over a Barsoomian building with a single bound. (I write it that way because it is how Burroughs wrote it; but how, I wonder, do you leap over anything with a double bound?) Thin air: Burroughs fixes that, by building great 'atmosphere factories' which constantly replenish the molecules that dance out into space. It is even possible to suppose that, in some way, he has anticipated the 'atmosphere factories' that a scientist like Krafft Ehricke would now build on the Moon if he could, because the Barsoomian factories use as raw material what Burroughs calls the 'eighth ray', while Ehricke would use what current science calls the 'solar wind', also a flux of charged particles. We cannot fault Burroughs for his ignorance without faulting all of *fin de siècle* astronomy. When he wrote *A Princess of Mars* the question of Mars's habitability was about an even bet. Lowell put his money on the side of Martian life; in fact, he and others were less interested in the question of whether life *did* exist on Mars, than in solutions of the problem of communicating with the putative Martian astronomers to let them know that life also existed on Earth. (The favourite proposal was to dig great trenches in the Sahara, illustrating geometric propositions like the Pythagorean theorem, fill them with oil and set them ablaze so that Martian telescopes could reveal that Terrestrials knew that $a^2 + b^2 = c^2$.) In extrapolating, if some of Burroughs's guesses were bad, a few were extraordinarily good: Ras Thavas, the brilliant and tyrannical surgeon, was doing organ transplants on Barsoom long before anyone transplanted a heart in South Africa or Texas.

Like Burroughs, Edward Elmer Smith Ph.D. wrote stories so big that a single book could not hold them. His Lensman stories run to half a dozen volumes; the Skylark books ran to three, plus a fourth afterthought written decades later, just before his death. Smith wrote *The Skylark of Space* in 1919, but there was no one to publish it; it languished in a desk drawer until *Amazing Stories* appeared in 1926 and Smith discovered its existence and submitted his novel to it a couple of years later. Smith did not write the first *Skylark* by himself. He was unsure of his ability to deal with 'the love part', and so he invited the collaboration of a lady named Mrs Lee Hawkins Garby. In later books he discovered that he could be sufficiently saccharine on his own.

The Skylark of Space is the story of a National Bureau of Standards chemist named Richard Ballinger Seaton who, fiddling with some unidentified chemicals in solution one day, drips some of them onto a piece of copper, puts an electric charge through it and sees it zap out of sight, through a wall, off into space. He has liberated atomic energy.

Corporate baddies in the employ of 'Steel' attempt to rob him of his work so that they can further loot the economy. Seaton foils them, building a spaceship and planning a pleasure cruise, which becomes a rescue mission when the Steel people build a spaceship of their own, kidnap his sweetheart in it and get trapped many light-years from Earth in the gravity field of an enormous dark star. (If only he had thought to call it a 'black hole'!) By the end of the first book Seaton has rescued his sweetheart, encountered a race of disembodied intelligences and discovered a multi-sunned system of green stars where, on a planet named Osnome, he wins a war, accumulates incredible riches and becomes the overlord of two solar systems.

Now, that, I submit, is *exciting*. It certainly excited me. Not only me; a current chief chemist for the National Bureau of Standards admitted in *Scientific American* a few years ago that *The Skylark of Space* was what had turned him on to working for the Bureau in the first place: Seaton's job looked so interesting he wanted it for himself, and ultimately got it. (He has not, however, as yet liberated the atomic energy in copper.)

Of course, that is not all there was to *The Skylark of Space*.

There was more. Much more. And it pains me, really physically pains me, to have to note that much of that much more was ludicrously bad. Science? Doc Smith did have a doctorate in chemistry, and one would think he would be pretty reliable on fundamental scientific laws; but he gave no evidence of having heard ever of, say, relativistic effects; Seaton gets in the ship and steps on the gas and before you know it he's going ninety light-years a minute, and so what? Style? Oh, not bad, in a functional, adrenal-stimulating way, but not what you'd call literature, maybe. Human relationships? Don't ask. I'm glad you asked, but don't ask. 'The love part' would make a cow blush.

There exists a passage in *The Skylark of Space* which I must quote to you, at whatever cost to my case for the defence. Seaton's sweetheart, Dorothy Vaneman, has been heard singing, along with another girl named Margaret Spencer who happened to be kidnapped at the same time. Seaton is impressed with Margaret's voice and says so to Dorothy.

'I'll say she can sing!' Dorothy exclaimed. 'I didn't know it 'til just now, but she's soprano soloist in the First Episcopal, no less!'
'Whee!' Seaton whistled.

Unfortunately there is a great deal more in the same vein. In the second volume in the series, *Skylark Three*, a whole planet of the wisest and most cultured beings in the universe stops still to listen to our intrepid explorers harmonizing on *The Bulldog on the Bank . . . und so weiter.*

And yet –

None of this greatly matters. It turns many readers off, and that is a pity; but there are few novels that don't turn a good many readers off for one reason or another, and to close one's mind to Doc Smith because of his conspicuous flaws is to miss his conspicuous virtues. One might as well reject *Moby Dick* because of Melville's really pathetic inability to write the sounds of Chinese dialect, or because of his gross misstatements of the natural history of cetaceans.

What Smith set out to do he did, and he did it superlatively well, and he taught a hundred other writers how to do it. Richard Ballinger Seaton is not a foil, he is a *person*. He does not submit to circumstance, he changes it. He is not afraid of science or technology, he uses it; and if it doesn't do what he wants it to do first time around, he works until he finds the way to make it right. All of the things Doc Smith did badly fade in comparison with the one thing he did well. He taught a whole generation how to dream on a cosmic scale.

In the bestiary of science fiction, Doc Smith was a fiddler crab. The male fiddler has one huge claw. It is so big and clumsy that he can't use it to fight, defend or eat, he can only use it to brandish in a sexy, provocative way, impressing the hell out of the dewy-eyed female fiddler crabs.

Smith is not sf's only fiddler crab, they run rampant over the pages of the early *Amazings* and they are with us today: Harlan Ellison is one, so is A. E. van Vogt, so is Ray Bradbury. They are characterized by such extreme hypertrophy of one aspect of their writing that we forgive them conspicuous lacks in others.

What Doc Smith, and Edgar Rice Burroughs, and a dozen others gave us was a new way of looking at the world, at all the worlds. In the grimy, chill early thirties the vision was revelatory. It is revelatory today. To someone coming to science fiction for the first time the experience can be overwhelming; O telephone pal, I see myself in thee.

How splendid it would be if we could build a super-crab! How fine to take the warmth and love of Bradbury and Sturgeon and the boldness of van Vogt and Smith and the word-play of Delany and Zelazny and the scientific insights of Niven, the encyclopedic invention of Heinlein, the unexpected insights of Cordwainer Smith – if we could take all the admirable organs from all the crab herd and assemble one perfect specimen!

As a matter of fact, it happens all the time.

That's where my friend from Mountain Standard Time went wrong; he confused borrowed parts, swiped from a hundred other writers, and reassembled with creation.

Science fiction calls itself a literature of ideas, and in a sense it is; but there is no copyright office to protect ideas, and we all borrowed them from each other. None of us pay royalties to H. G. Wells for using his time machine, or to Murray Leinster for borrowing his notion of alternate worlds. Consider a story about a huge derelict spaceship whose passengers have lost sight of their goal and control over their course: what does it make you think of? Heinlein? Brian Aldiss? The current tv botch, *Starlost*? It could be any of them.

Not long ago I wrote a story called 'We Purchased People' and showed it to a friend whom I will call 'X'. 'Fine story,' he said, 'but it's *awfully* like Y, by Z.' 'Bastard,' I replied to him, 'you are only right insofar as Y is awfully like *A Plague of Pythons*, which as you know I wrote myself five years before Z wrote Y.' But the more I thought of it, the more I saw antecedents to *A Plague of Pythons*, too.

It has happened to me a hundred times; it has happened to all of us. It is not unique to science fiction. Poetry grows in the same way.

I don't object to it . . . much . . . but those who are not a part of the process are sometimes confused by it, like my telephone friend, mistaking borrowing for innovation. And some of them are not a bit confused, but use it to do us harm.

These are the creatures who lurk in the entertainment industry. Directors, producers, 'writers' – I remember once visiting an indepedendent Hollywood producer at his studio, viewing his latest Technicolor disaster and chatting with him in his office. 'I used to use writers for my sci-fi flicks,' he said amiably enough. 'I don't any more. I write them myself. If I ever find myself running out of ideas, well – ' he gestured at the walls of his office, lined with *Galaxys* and *Analogs* and paper-backs – 'there's always plenty of inspiration there.'

If I were half the man I should be I would have cut his *papier-maché* throat, or at least gone straight to a lawyer and begun a class-action suit against him for theft and vandalism. I didn't. I let him live.

It is not just a question of monetary harm, it is that these creatures do not even steal well. There are a hundred fine science fiction stories that will never be filmed because some cheapjack operator has skimmed off the surface thrills, neglected the thought behind them and ruled out any proper treatment of the story by a more talented producer later on.

In the pulps of the thirties, we all learned to write by borrowing notions from our betters. Most of us could not do more; we were too young and too raw in the world to have much of our own to say. We needed the practice of putting words on paper and bouncing them off each other, off editors, off readers, to teach us our skills, and only then did most of us stop to reflect on what it was we wanted to use those skills to say.

It was rather easy for an amateur to get published and thus become an instant professional in the thirties. Especially in the latter part of that time, just before World War II, there were dozens of magazines hungry for material, and only a handful of the editors had enough taste and wisdom to distinguish good from bad. Some of us – I was one – found an end-run around even that obstacle by becoming editors ourselves. Of the Futurians – Wollheim, Lowndes, Cyril Kornbluth, Richard Wilson, Isaac Asimov, Damon Knight *et al* – I was the first to manage that.

I had formed the habit of visiting editors in their offices, trying to sell them stories. I did not often succeed, but for reasons I cannot guess they were pretty hospitable on the whole. Perhaps they thought that from me they might learn what your average teenage reader really liked in an sf magazine. Perhaps they just enjoyed being revered. F. Orlin Tremaine even bought me a lunch two or three times when he was editing *Astounding;* I don't remember what I talked about, I suppose I mostly listened. When John Campbell replaced him my supply of free lunches disappeared, but John was if anything even more receptive to my visits (and quite as unreceptive to my stories) than Tremaine; he would admit me to his office and sit me down next to his rolltop desk and fit a cigarette into a holder and explain to me why commercial television would never succeed, or how Bell Telephone was the best-run company in the world. After a while I noticed that the subject we talked about in any given month would appear on the stands as his editorial two months later, and realized what he was doing. He started out each month with some polemical notion, tried it on everybody who dropped by, shored up weaknesses and sharpened his arguments on them and by the end of the month had his

editorial written. *Amazing* was then edited by an ancient
named T. O'Connor Sloane, Ph.D, with the white beard of a
George Bernard Shaw; he never talked to me much, but he
did something Campbell never did: he bought something I
wrote and published it. It was a poem. I was like seventeen:
it was my first sale for actual money – two dollars – and I
would have framed the cheque if I hadn't wanted the money
more than I wanted the trophy.

Among the editors I favoured with my company was a
man named Robert O. Erisman; I don't remember the names
of his magazines, but I remember deciding that I knew as
much about science fiction as he did and so I asked him if he
would like to hire me as his assistant. He politely declined
the offer, but instead of throwing me out of his office he sent
me across town to see Rogers Terrill, managing editor of the
Popular Publications chain. Popular had just started a cut-
rate half-cent-a-word line of magazines and seemed to be in
the market for additional titles; Terrill offered me a job, and
at nineteen I found myself editor of two science fiction
magazines. One was *Astonishing Stories*. It sold for a dime,
ran to 112 pulp-sized pages, used about 45,000 words of
material an issue, and had a budget of $405. That was not
just for stories; that was for stories *and* black-and-white art
and an oil painting to be used for a cover.

Of course, at that kind of money I couldn't get the real top
writers in the field. I had to be content with Kornbluth and
Asimov and Heinlein and Bradbury and Kuttner and ...
well, they weren't bad, for amateurs. Some of them turned
out rather well.

For the first six months I was there Popular paid me ten
dollars a week. (Comparatively speaking it was not all that
bad. The same week I came aboard they hired another
editor, and he had to work three months for nothing before
they *raised* him to ten dollars a week.) I should have paid
them. I loved every second of it. Not only was it pure
pleasure, but I learned the facts of life in that office. I
learned that writers are human beings. I learned that it is
impossible to publish any story so good that someone won't
loathe it, or so bad that someone won't hail it as a masterpiece. I learned that even famous and widely published

writers can desperately need a sale, even a tiny sale, to buy the next day's groceries. I learned what applause feels like – and criticism, too; I've had both, and applause is better. I learned that readers, particularly science fiction readers, are often astonishingly perceptive, both for good and for ill: quick to perceive a writer's meaning even when he elects to express it elliptically, quick to detect fraud when the writer tries to get away with shoddy work. I learned that nearly all readers would rather like you than hate you; once they have bought your work it is their intention to enjoy it, otherwise they would not have bought it, and it takes a serious fault on your part to turn them against you. I learned that it is impossible to tell from a writer's conversation or appearance whether his stories are going to be any good. I learned the mechanics of preparing a manuscript for the printed page, the complexities of dealing with artists and the inflexibility of deadlines; and I learned that ten dollars a week didn't go very far. Not even in 1939.

The godlike figures who owned and operated Popular Publications knew that perfectly well. They expected us to supplement our pitiful salaries by writing for ourselves and each other – at our pitiful word rates. Popular published fifty or sixty magazines: nearly half of them Westerns, the rest a mix of detective, horror, sports, air-war, love, general adventure. I never could bring myself to write a Western, but I wrote for all the others. Even the love pulps. I'm glad I did it. I don't suppose I would have missed any important lesson about writing if I had not had the pulp experience . . . but I might have missed some important eating.

And then, along about 1942 or early 1943, I began to notice that something was missing. I was an old hand by then, all of twenty-three, considerably more prosperous; and somehow I began to perceive most of what I had written was crap. Most of what I had published was crap. Some of it was commercially pretty good – I was selling to outside markets by then, usually for better rates than I could pay myself. But, by and large, there was not much justification for pride. In four years I had managed to publish a few good stories in my magazines, shopping for bargains in the reject pile from *Astounding*; but in little more time than that John Campbell had revolutionized the science fiction field. A reasonable proportion of my own writing had become competent, but very little of it *said* anything.

So I began playing little games with myself, trying to trick myself into something worth being vain about. I knew how to write for editors. I began writing stories that I didn't think any editor would buy, experimenting with different forms, trying to find ways of using words that were not imitations of someone else. And at the same time, I began typing out manuscript copies of stories that had impressed me, seeking to see what the tactile sensation was that went with putting words like that through the typewriter keyboard. I had trained myself to sell my first drafts, beginning a story with clean white paper and a carbon in the machine; to break that habit, I began to write my first drafts on scratch paper, lined paper, the back of old correspondence – anything that would take typewriting, but that I could not possibly submit without retyping, and thus revision.

I was trying to make a break with bad habits. As it happened, I was helped to make the break. There was a war going on. I was deferred, but I didn't have to stay deferred if I didn't want to, so I went down to the draft board, asked to be reclassified and spent the next couple of years in places like Oklahoma and Colorado and Italy and France as a sergeant in the US Army Air Force.

I will not trouble you with my wartime reminiscences, but there is one event that pertains to what I am talking about. There was a time, when I was with the 456th Bomb Group in a ploughed-under potato patch south of Foggia, when I had some time to spare. As I was also faintly homesick for New York City I thought I would deal with both by writing a novel about life in New York. Because it seemed sexy and exciting to me, I elected to write about life in the advertising business; and one way or another I managed to put together two or three hundred pages of copy on the subject by the time I got back to civilian life.

At this point it occurred to me that as long as I was writing a novel about advertising, it might help if I knew something about it. So I bought a Sunday *Times*, applied for three advertising copywriter jobs listed in the Help Wanted section, got one of them and spent the next three or four years writing ads.

That novel never did work out. I had a summer home with a big fireplace one year, and I spent one whole night reading that novel manuscript in front of the fire. And page by page, as I read it, I threw it in the fire. It was awful. Not ludicrously awful, or hopelessly unpublishably awful. Just why-are-you-bothering-to-tell-me-all-this awful. But if the novel was a bust, the advertising experience wasn't; a couple of years later I began writing a science fiction novel about advertising, decided I needed help about a third of the way through, showed it to my old friend and former occasional collaborator Cyril Kornbluth, and came out with *The Space Merchants*, which probably isn't the most successful sf novel ever written but, with somewhere over ten million copies in print in about forty languages, hasn't done really badly either.

Why-am-I-bothering-to-tell-you-all-this?

Because I think one reason *The Space Merchants* succeeded was that I bloody well knew a lot about what I was writing about, not because I had read it in somebody else's book, but because I had spent several years of my life learning it. I don't think those years in advertising were wasted. I don't think any time I've ever spent that taught me something I didn't know was wasted, not the six months I spent fascinated with the theory of numbers, or the decade as a part-time political party official, or the year I spent playing chess four hours a day. I haven't used all of them yet. I don't know if I ever need to 'use' them, but they're there.

John Campbell once said the same thing to me, when I was maybe seventeen and he was well, J*O*H*N C*A*M*P*B*E*L*L, pushing thirty and secret ruler of the universe. John got out of college in the pit of the depression, no jobs, had to scratch. When he finished prepping that month's editorial with me that day, he began to reminisce. Jobs he had had. I said resolutely it was a waste for a mind like his to be doing things like that, and he put another cigarette in the holder and said I didn't understand, all those things were *part* of him, without them he would be lesser, they were components of what he thought and did and wrote. I think he was right. Can you find anything in, say, the Don A. Stuart stories that reflects his six months as a used-car dealer? Neither can I, but that doesn't mean that, in some mutated and transmogrified way, it isn't there.

It is not much good copying science out of a textbook onto your manuscript page. The bare bones show. It is not much good transcribing part of your autobiography into your story either, it seldom fits, the ends don't mesh; but what you have read and what you have done and what you have felt and what you know, are, after all, the only things you as a writer have to sell, and in some way they gurgle through the sloshy pipes of the brain, losing an amino acid here and picking up an enzyme there, and what emerges is part of you. Probably the best part of you. The best part of all of us is in what we write.

My grandfather died when I was sixteen and, for one of the few times in my life, I saw my mother cry. I was hurting, too, because I liked the deaf, bent, bald-headed old Irishman, in the aloof and self-interested way a teenager likes any drastically older person, but I discovered something. One part of my mind was trying to respond to my mother's pain and feeling pain of my own. Another part was taking notes: this is how grief is shown, here is how a chair looks when someone who sat in it has died; how can one write down the sound of a sob?

All is grist to a writer's mill. Every experience, even the worst, is in some way a deposit to that bank account we all draw on every time we put words on paper.

One of the things that has helped me write science fiction is that I am a fan of that greatest of spectator sports, science. I take no credit for knowing what goes on in science, it is fun for me; I subscribe to about a dozen journals and other periodicals, read a lot of books, spend a fair amount of time, when the opportunity presents, with people who are working at science. The result is that with not enough formal education to qualify me as a mailman I know about as much about, say, astronomy as any biochemist, as much mathematics as most physicists and so on. I don't do it because I am researching stories. I do it because it is more fun than playing bridge. (Although I also like to play bridge.)

Most of us are like that: we like to learn things. Not always science, for some of the best of us are allergic to science, hate it or fear it or simply don't include it in our lives. But we like to learn, and to share what we have learned. Among us we have produced poems and plays and journals as well as science fiction stories; works about history and biography and politics and travel and model-building and salesmanship and bicycle repair. We are all risk-taking and inquisitive by nature, and if there is a Renaissance man alive I think he is a science fiction writer.

Having come this far, I would like to tell you what science fiction writers *are*.

Probably you already have some notions of your own. Perhaps they are the world's notions: the archetypal science fiction writer as a gnomish little creature who sits in his attic and spins dreams about imaginary worlds, as uninvolved in the real world outside his windows as Proust in his cork-lined room; a little odd in his manner; a little strange in his attitudes; more prone than the rest of the population to fall apart and have to be put away.

These notions aren't wrong. There are science fiction writers like that. But they also aren't right, because there are other science fiction writers who are extroverted, gregarious, athletic and even stable. The first general statement that can be made about science fiction writers is that there are few general statements that can be made about all of them.

There are somewhere between 750 and a thousand of us, I think, scattered all over the globe. Perhaps 300 or more are in the United States, another 75 or so in Great Britain, as many as 150 (no outsider really knows for sure) in the Soviet Union. There are colonies in Germany, Japan, France and Italy; small groups or individuals, some of them world-renowned, in Poland, Brazil, Mexico, the Scandinavian countries, Australia and almost everywhere. I don't suppose there is a country in the world (possibly excepting mainland China)

Ragged Claws

literate enough to support a publishing industry at all that
has not at least one or two local sf writers. I once received a
manuscript from a man who described himself as the second-
best science fiction writer in Iran, and for all I know perhaps
he was.

There was a time when all the world was islands and a
science fiction writer in Paraguay would hardly know of the
existence of another in Brazil, although both would probably
read English novels and American magazines. The barriers
are no longer high. Now we all compete with each other, and
learn from each other, and from time to time we meet. How
we meet! In Tokyo and Trieste, Montreal and Moscow,
London and L.A. The streets outside the hotel windows look
different, but inside there are the same familiar faces. If I
ever find myself marooned on an Alp or lost in the Sahara I
have an infallible system for getting help. I will simply
announce the existence of a science fiction symposium, and
in half an hour Brian Aldiss and Arthur Clarke will be
there.

Most science fiction writers do other things than write sf.
Many are scientists: the astronomers (Fred Hoyle, R. S.
Richardson), the biochemist (Isaac Asimov), the mathemati-
cians (Chandler Davis, Eric Temple Bell alias 'John Taine'),
the medical doctors (David H. Keller, T. J. Bass), the
electronics experts (John R. Pierce, Ben Bova). A number
(Ray Bradbury, Harlan Ellison, Robert Bloch, Leigh
Brackett) double as film and television writers. An even
larger number (Jack Williamson, James E. Gunn, Richard
Wilson) are in the faculty or administration of universities.
Squads are or have been in advertising and public relations
(Bob Shaw, Algis Budrys, James Blish, Theodore Sturgeon).
L. J. Stecher was captain of the US Navy's guided-missile
cruiser *Columbus*; A. Bertram Chandler commands a cargo
vessel in the South Pacific. Keith Laumer was a captain
in the US Air Force. Wilson Tucker was a movie projectionist. Roger Zelazny works for the Civil Service. J. F. Bone
is a veterinarian. There are even a few (Larry Niven) whose
grandparents were kind enough to leave them fortunes so
they don't have to work at all – but they do, at writing sf.

The sf writer may be of any age from early literacy to

advanced decay. I once invited some of my writers to join me for cocktails at my hotel in Los Angeles; one, whom I hadn't met before, respectfully had to decline. As he was only fourteen, he wasn't allowed to stay out that late. But Wilmar Shiras was a grandmother before she wrote her first story, and E. Everett Evans only began to be successful in his sixties.

Once started, few ever stop. A few years ago *Time* did a story on science fiction and attempted to write a 'where are they now' sidebar on the great writers of the past. After a great deal of research they found that those who were not dead were all still writing.

What keeps us at it? A few years ago two sf fans named Bill Bowers and Bill Mallardi asked about ninety-four of us that question, among others. Some of the answers:

> Damon Knight: '... to tell the truth, I've never been interested in anything else.'
> John W. Campbell: 'There's room to think and move!'
> Isaac Asimov: 'Because science fiction, in these times, is the most significant literature one can write.'
> Brian W. Aldiss: 'I am a surrealist at heart; that is, I'm none too sure whether the reality of the world agrees with its appearance. Only in sf, or near-sf, can you express this feeling in words.'
> Philip K. Dick: '... it's the broadest field of fiction, permitting the most far-ranging and advanced concepts of every possible type; no variety of idea can be excluded from sf; everything is its property.'
> Theodore Sturgeon: 'It gives me almost complete freedom of speech, and absolute freedom of thought.'
> Arthur C. Clarke: 'Because most other literature isn't concerned with reality.'*

'Freedom'. 'Significance'. 'Reality'.... Does anyone remember the McCarthy years in the United States? The pipsqueak senator from Wisconsin had a nation terrorized, and while presidents and newspaper publishers were running for the storm cellars there was one surviving area of free speech in the country: the science fiction magazines. I have met

* *The DOUBLE : BILL Symposium*, D.B. Press, Akron, Ohio, 1969.

Ragged Claws

ministers who used to put the current issue of *Galaxy* on sale in their churches in those years, because nowhere else could their parishioners read anything else but the straightest of orthodoxy. I wish Horace Gold and John Campbell could have known that whole congregations were praying for their continued well-being in those days. It would have cheered – and surprised – them both.

Science fiction writers, by and large, are stubborn, smart, unconventional, independent makers-and-shakers. This is an opinion I have formed over forty years of living among them, and is supported by the only scientific study I know of, conducted by psychologists on a representative batch of us. The psychologists, John E. Drevdahl and Raymond B. Cattell, sent out questionnaires to 356 individuals, divided into three categories: general writers, artists, and science fiction writers. From the questionnaires they developed psychological profiles for each subject, averaged them out and published the numbers for a variety of traits for each group.

I'll give you some of the numbers. I should explain what the numbers mean. The average of all Americans is taken as 100% for each trait. The scores published give the departures from the average. If sf writers score 10% higher on something than the average, the score is given as +10. If 6% lower, −6. They scored in tendencies towards one or another of opposing pairs of traits (e.g., 'intelligence vs defective ability'), and plus score indicates movement in the direction of the first trait – in this case, higher intelligence. A minus score, as you no doubt already have deduced, means the direction is towards the opposed one.

Here are some of the results:

Factors	*General Writers*	*Artists*	*SF Writers*
Intelligence vs defective ability ..	+10.9	+8.4	+14.9
Ego strength vs general emotionality	+4.8	+4.0	+5.3
Dominance vs submission	+4.7	+4.0	+8.7
Super Ego, identification with group standards vs lack of identification with group standards	−8.4	−6.9	−9.5
Adventurous cyclothymia vs withdrawn	+5.7	+4.7	+25.4

(Of course, you know that 'cyclothymia' is a mild manic-depressive state. It doesn't mean that sf writers are manic-depressives. It only means that, to the extent they are, they are highly likely to do something about whatever troubles them, and hardly likely at all passively to endure.)

Science fiction writers also scored significantly above the norm on traits like 'Bohemian unconcern' and 'radicalism' – not any particular brand of radicalism, either left-wing or right. Just unwillingness to accept conventional wisdom. Altogether, the picture the profiles display is of a bunch of stubborn, intelligent individualists. Visiting any science fiction convention gives much the same picture. It may be that persons of other sorts simply could not write science fiction at all. As Drevdahl and Cattell say, we 'appear to possess what Mathew Arnold and other great writers have described as "the divine discontent".'*

And, you know? they're right. We do.

If this 'divine discontent' is real and not some flattery our private mirrors whisper to us, I wonder how it comes about.

I think one thing that happened to most of us, somehow, is that as children we were loners. I know I was. I was an only child, and we moved too often for me to make long-term friends until I was in my teens.

I was born in New York City – 26 November 1919 – but I left the city early. I spent my first Christmas at sea, and by the time I was six weeks old I was living in Gatun, where my father had got work as a machinist for the Panama Canal. I spent the first few years of my life in places like Panama and Texas and New Mexico, following my father's work; and even when we returned to New York City to stay we seldom remained in one house, or one neighbourhood, for more than a few months. My father had his own discontent. He did not much like being a machinist. Wall Street was where his rainbow came to earth, and he desperately wanted part of that action. So through all of my childhood we alternated between wealth and want as his bubbles grew and burst.

* *Personality and Creativity in Artists and Writers,* John E. Drevdahl and Raymond B. Cattell, *Journal of Clinical Psychology,* Vol. XIV, No. 2, 107–11, April, 1958.

Sometimes we lived in luxury hotels. Once or twice we lived nowhere at all, and I found myself thrust on relatives for brief periods (I suppose no more than a week or so, though they seemed terribly long) while my parents tried to locate a landlord trusting enough to take them in. It did not seem an unusual way of life to me. It was the only one I knew, and somehow or other I was always clothed, housed and fed.

My mother had quirks of her own. She took me to school at the usual time, five or six years old, and I promptly came down with whooping cough; she tried again when I was well, and I developed scarlet fever. These were pre-antibiotic days. Scarlet fever, for instance, entailed a Board of Health quarantine sign on the door and everything I owned baked two hours in an oven or thrown away. So after I had kept on doing that for a full year (during which I was present in class maybe a dozen times, few of them consecutive) she opted out of the system (red-haired, half Irish, very sure of her own mind). And for the next years I stayed home, and we sometimes dodged, sometimes debated with, the truant officer. My mother had a teaching degree, though she never taught in a school; she sometimes was able to persuade the authorities that she was tutoring me suitably at home.

Well, I think she was. What she did teach me was to read. I don't know when; I can't remember a time when I couldn't read.

The first book I owned was, grotesquely, Emerson's essays, leather binding with a silk marking ribbon. I cannot remember what prankster gave it to me, or guess at with what motives. I certainly never finished reading it; but I appreciated the thought.

Of course there had been other books long before that – I had to have been eight, at least, before encountering Voltaire – but I do not remember them as individuals, only a general recollection of kid's books by Percy Keese Fitzhugh and Leo Edwards, plus Tom Swift and even the Bobbsey Twins. Fitzhugh did make an impression. His books were about scouting. Reading them, I was desperate to reach the age of twelve so that I could become a fully-fledged Boy Scout and participate in octagonal hikes and tie knots and wear a sleeve full of merit badges. Being a Cub was beneath my dignity. A few years later I was in fact old enough to join, but by then I had long lost the impulse. (Later on I went through the identical experience with the Presbyterian church, and again with the Communist Party after that.)

The effect of it all was that I made few friends and kept them not very long, as a young child. My best friends were books.

I don't mean that I did nothing but read. I was passably good at some sports, particularly on and in the water, and I spent a good deal of time exploring the world I lived in. When I was seven or eight I discovered that I need not do my exploring on foot. It was possible to climb a subway embankment, step gingerly over the charged third rail and emerge on the platform of a BMT station, which meant that by means of carefully learned interchanges I could travel almost anywhere in the city of New York free of charge. Getting back was more problematical unless I happened to have a nickel for the turnstile, but there were ways: an ill-fitting exit I could slip through, or a fence I could climb. I was caught at one of these unauthorized excursions once or twice, when I visited an old neighbourhood and was recognized and reported to my parents. But there was no way they could stop me if I did not choose to be stopped.

For shorter distances it was also possible to hitch rides on moving vehicles. Trolley cars were available. The reel that held the cable to the trolley was just meant to be used as a handhold; the skirt that extended out at the back was sloping and slippery, but if the wind was not too sharp or the rain too intense one could ride for half a mile at a time that way. In practice one didn't, because of police. The proper thing to do was to ride a few blocks to a major intersection, drop off, walk across and pick up another hitch on the far side. Trucks and even private cars were also possible, but more danger-ous. I fell off one once, at about twenty miles an hour, and that discouraged me from that particular sport. But all in all there was free transport to cover a whole city, and I used it dedicatedly.

Roaming and reading: I suppose I've spent a major frac-tion of my waking hours in one or the other. When I was old enough to own a card in the public library the world opened up totally to me. I read everything I could put my hands on, out of the limitless resources of one of the largest library systems in the world. At twelve and thirteen it was mostly fiction: all of H. G. Wells, all of Kipling, enormous doses of O. Henry and Anatole France, of Voltaire and of Mark Twain. Around fifteen it was mostly plays: a little Shakespeare, every word of Shaw, Elmer Rice, Eugene O'Neill. By seventeen it was politics, a nibbling of history, a great deal of biography and non-fiction of one kind or another. The library filed its non-fiction according to the Dewey Decimal System, which was a convenience. Long before I learned to use catalogues I discovered that if I went back to the place on the shelves where I had found a book on an interesting subject, the books nearby were likely to be on related ones. And I read authors: William Beebe's wonderful books of undersea exploration, *Half Mile Down* and *Beneath Tropic Seas;* Richard Halliburton's sentimentalized and hyperbolic travel books. It helped that I was a rapid reader. Counting professional stints, I imagine I have averaged something better than a book a day for every day of my life. So it was no great loss if any particular book wasn't much good. I read it anyway. Because the library prissily filed O. Henry under his real name, William Sidney Porter, I read half a dozen novels by Gene Stratton Porter before realizing it wasn't the same man. It didn't much matter.

There was no science fiction to speak of in our library, or apart from Wells and Verne, in any library of that era, so there was a sharp line between my library sources and my private sources of reading. While I was cropping the library I was also reading every word of sf I could find, all the back issues of *Amazing* and *Wonder* and *Astounding,* the Carl H. Claudy juveniles, S. Fowler Wright and W. Olaf Stapledon. *Et al.* And I discovered bridges between sf and mainstream. Somehow I got turned on to James Branch Cabell and read every volume of the 'Biography of Manuel' before I was seventeen, as well as *Shirt-Smith-Smire* and a wonderful jape called *Special Delivery.* This was a volume of fan letters and

167

the wickedly witty replies he should have made (but didn't make) to them. Great discoveries came from this kind of reading. I learned that writers were human from Cabell, and that connective tissue existed linking *Amazing Stories* to the library shelves. Wells was of course in both; but *Back to Methusaleh* put Shaw firmly into science fiction for me; *With the Night Mail* and *As Easy as ABC* gave us Kipling; Cabell and Wright and others seemed to live happily in both worlds. And also I found myself reading poetry of all kinds: the sonnets, rather than the plays, of Shakespeare; Omar Khayyam (I think I can still recite at least half the Rubaiyat); Coleridge; Eliot. I think that came from my mother. I don't remember her ever telling me a bedtime story, but she used to recite poems for me when I was small.

It was so easy and natural for me to pass from reader into writer that I don't quite know when it happened. The first poem I remember writing was when I was ten. I still remember it, though I will not for anything recite it aloud. The first story I remember completing was when I was twelve, in an idle hour in an English class. I had already read the textbook and I had no interest in whatever the teacher was gabbing about, so I wrote out a six or seven-page story about Atlantis. It was of course a thoroughly hopeless story, and it is a blessing to all of us that it is lost or I might have published it somewhere along the way.

Sometimes I am asked what writers influenced my development. There are two answers. One is, 'I don't know.' The other is, 'All of them.'

I can't think of anything I learned, or borrowed, from the French decadents, for instance, but I spent so much time with Proust and Huysmans that I cannot believe I remained untouched. (There was a time around the age of twenty when I found myself reading so much science fiction professionally – I had begun editing magazines, and had every day's slushpile to contend with – that the only recreational reading I could stand was the previous Frenchmen, and the brooding Russians. I can't really find any traces of Tolstoi or Gogol or Merejkowski in my work either.) I know I owed a lot to Lewis Carroll and the *transition* stable, mostly James

Joyce, at one time, when I pleasured myself with coinages and nonsense rhymes and plays on words. And in science fiction I am sure I owe much to many writers; but we all do, we build on each other as a way of life.

The word that comes to me when I think of my teens is 'disorder'. I planned nothing. I was palping the world at random. Where it gave, I pushed a little harder; where it resisted, I turned away. I suppose if I had had a proper school background that might have imposed at least some skeletal suggestion of structure, but I gave up on school early on. At the age of twelve I entered high school. I had no real notion of what I wanted to learn but some glimmering that 'science' and 'fiction' were somehow involved. I had never heard that one might study the craft of writing (I still don't wholly believe it; most writing courses are preposterous frauds, and most of the good writers I know have had little formal learning in letters), but 'science' was a possibility. And so I applied to Brooklyn Technical High School. One needed to pass a special examination to get in, and maybe that appealed to my snob sense, too. Once in I was confronted almost at once with the necessity of making a lifetime career decision. At *twelve*. Brooklyn Tech offered only specialized courses. I could specialize in electronics or civil engineering or aeronautics or a dozen others, but I had to make up my mind which. 'Chemical engineering' sounded least unpleasant of them, and so I began to be a chemical engineer. By the age of fourteen I knew that wasn't for me, but it would have been troublesome to replace my steps and anyway I had lost interest. So I quit school with a mixed bag of failures and certificates of excellence as soon as I could – at seventeen. My entire school career was less than a decade, from beginning to end, and I begrudge most of that.

I married at twenty.

I married again at twenty-four, and at twenty-eight, and at thirty-two; for a while there it seemed that in every Leap Year of my life I was destined to get married to someone different.

There are companies in which I find this admission a little embarrassing (although the present company of this volume does not happen to be one of them); but there was no malice involved on anyone's part. All three of my ex-wives were excellent women, who simply never should have married me, or I them. The first time we were both unweaned adolescents. The second and third time we confused attraction and some common interests with an ability to live together permanently, which did not turn out to exist. All of my ex-wives achieved interesting and rewarding lives – we became friends again, after the marriages were over – and so did I, because on the fourth try practice made perfect, and Carol and I have now been married for better than twenty years. I would not have it any other way. We have had so many joys together, and so many tragedies – our first son died before he was a month old, and if there is a worse pain than that I pray to be spared it – that I do not imagine either of us has any very objective view of the other; but I know she is a beautiful and joy-giving person. Further than that I cannot say. What I know of her I cannot convey to you, and what I can convey would not do her justice.

It has not always been interesting and rewarding. When I turned fifty there was a bad time when I thought I was going to die, and actually rather preferred it that way. Everything was bad at once, in more ways than I can count. It seemed to me that, although there was some possibility I could survive, and even surmount most of the lacks and harassments in my life, and go on living, and perhaps even experience considerable joys and triumphs, it was nevertheless unlikely that anything would happen that hadn't happened at least once before. I might earn a great deal of money, or receive some honours, or discover a new city to roam, or publish a story that won praise, or experience any of a hundred sensory pleasures, or learn a thousand exciting new things. All of these were great joy; but I had *had* all these joys at one time or another. Nothing new seemed likely to happen, and a repeat performance did not seem worth going to any great trouble to achieve. So, for a time, I think it must have lasted two or three months, I waited to die. By and by it occurred to me that I was still living, and as I had nothing better to do I might as well work at it. So I began taking cautious steps towards rebirth. I began writing again, and discovered that I could actually write about as well as I ever had, even write a few stories – *The Gold at the Starbow's End, The Merchants of Venus* and *Shaffery Among the Immortals* among them – which (I speak wholly without modesty) seemed to be written about as well as it was possible to write those particular stories. I palped the world again for soft spots and pushed where it gave . . . and most of it gave.

Was this what is sometimes called the male menopause? I don't know. I only know that it seems to me that I had a complete lifetime that ended when I was fifty, and now I am several years into a bonus life which has expanded into places where I had never been before. It is almost as though that other Frederik Pohl had bequeathed me a fair estate, which I can draw on as I choose but which I do not have to earn.

I am not quite sure what I will do with this new life. You see, at this moment I am only about four years old.

One thing I am likely to do with it, as long as I can manage to put words on paper, is write science fiction. And edit it, when convenient. And lecture about it, and about the future in general, and about those tactics for shaping the future we call 'politics' and 'sociology'. There is a great good thing about my life which makes up for almost any loss, and that is that I don't have to do anything to earn a living. I spend my time doing the things I like to do for their own sake – writing and editing and lecturing – and people are kind enough to give me money for that.

. . . It is hard for me to write openly and honestly about myself. It is hard for any writer. We tend to confuse autobiography with hagiography, and we waver between twin terrors. There is Scylla on one hand, which is the peril of untruth, and over there is Charybdis, equally dreadful, whose other name is tedium. There is no easy course between bad morality and bad art, and I doubt that I have found the right one. But one tries to keep one's promises. We have collectively promised to tell not only what we know about science fiction but what we know about ourselves. And there it is.

We do the best we can.

We do not so much to please you the reader – not even so

171

much to please one another – as to please some perfect model in our own minds : to try to capture some thought no one has ever thought before, to try to suggest some new way of looking at the world, to build a temporary world as plausible as the one outside the window, and more interesting. We fail a hundred times for every success; but now and then there is a success. Stubborn, difficult, divinely discontented if you will – we do keep trying.

So I despair of telling my long-distance friend what matters in science fiction. I despair of convincing him that Stapledon and Smith and Weinbaum are great while the novel that turned him on is a multiply plagiarized potboiler. It's no use persuading him to read the originals. He would only look up from them and exclaim, 'Why, these are no great writers, they are only fiddler crabs'.

But when these stubborn and difficult people are doing the things they do best, it is the fiddler crabs among them, not the bland syncretists or the popularizers, who show the others how. They are the innovators. They blaze the trail. After them come the pulp hacks, the tv adapters and the Michael Crichtons. The proper measure of the stature of a science fiction writer isn't the size of his bank balance or his audience, it is the degree to which other writers copy him.

And so we go, divinely discontented, snapping our one gross claw; it is not the most perfect way of life one could imagine but where, in this chill and gritty real world we live in, is there another as good?

Brian Aldiss:

magic and
bare boards

The difference between fiction and non-fiction is the difference between magic and bare boards.

Imagine you're going to the theatre. The auditorium fills,
the orchestra plays, the lights dim, the curtain goes up . . . .

The stage is bare, or cluttered with old and dusty props.
Flats lie shuffled at the rear. A light dimly burns. Something
has gone wrong. There will be no play tonight, no magic.

A man appears left, looking awkward and vulnerable, as
people do when they walk unrehearsed on a stage. He says,
' "Poets are born not made." Nevertheless, a writer can look
back over his life. . . . '

There's an uneasy hush in the stalls.

Well, that's the difference between fiction and non-fiction.
Tonight, the stage is bare and lit by one naked bulb. I come
on, looking awkward and vulnerable.

'Poets are born not made.' Nevertheless a writer can look
back over his life and calculate the steps he took that made
him the kind of writer he is. Many of those important steps
are taken in childhood. As F. L. Lucas says, in childhood,

fate determines character – after which, character determines fate.

So what I intend to do is give some account of my childhood – 'edited highlights', as tv commentators say of the day's sport – and then go on to discuss what may be called my writing career; from which we can move to the subject of writing in general. It is no use talking in a vacuum. If you have some notion of what the man is like, you can make some estimate of the value of his ideas.

My father had a great physical gift: he remained thin and neat however well he ate. To the end of his life he could refer to himself self-deprecatingly as a dapper little man.

My mother's mother was the daughter of a farmer. She taught my mother the art of cooking, so that my childhood recollections include eating well. Norfolk was overrun with rabbits in those days, and rabbit made an excellent dish. Mother would serve them cooked whole in casserole, when the tongue was regarded as a great delicacy; or in pies, with whole small onions and chunks of ham. Her pies were beautiful, crowned with splendid patterned pastry. One of her specialities was salmon pudding, a noble edifice served with parsley sauce and new potatoes. Pickled mackerel were another speciality; they used to stand overnight to soak in a jug of vinegar, their skins shining with beautiful subdued colours.

Mother's pudding courses were also splendid. Summer would bring summer puddings, which disgorged lashings of gooseberries and black and red currants. She was expert at cake-making. Maids of Honour made regular appearances on the tea-table, together with Melting Moments and Surprise Buns (which had jam inside them, though you could not tell from the outside). Our cooking was done in a huge oven heated by three paraffin burners underneath.

Mother made music in that oven. Each Christmas, she excelled herself. What cascades of mince pies, what mountains of sausage rolls, appeared under her hands! And she would create, on those occasions, exquisite little marzipan titbits in beautiful colours. Young Hoggins, peering over the edge of the kitchen table, would be allowed to pinch a morsel now and then.

In short, my mother had a natural sensibility for British cooking. We were innocent of garlic, yet I never enjoyed food as much as in childhood, often washed down with lemonade made from real lemons, which slopped like skeletal millstones in our huge bone china jug. No doubt of it, all that generous eating stood the family in fine stead for the war years which were to follow. If you learn to eat well young enough, you will have a strong appetite for other pleasures.

While mother was upstairs doing the cooking, father was working downstairs in the section of the shop over which he held sway. I shall have to say something about the shop, it was so much a part of my childhood.

We lived over a part of H. H. Aldiss and Sons in what seemed to me an enormous flat. It had a long corridor, along which I could pedal like mad on my three-wheeler; once I broke the speed record (Sir Malcolm Campbell was my idol, even from an early age) and pedalled right down the stairs.

This was in East Dereham, a prosperous little market town in the rustic heart of Norfolk, where I was born in August, 1925. My mother loved giving my sister and me treats; one of the great yearly treats was when she took us to the fair. Fairs in Dereham in the thirties were really something. The whole of the market square was taken up with cake-walks, dodge'ems, coconut-shies, boxing booths, big and small roundabouts, and all the other stalls. The big roundabout had splendid cockerels with high heads, and dragons that seated three, as well as galloping horses. Mother was always lucky at the stalls; perhaps the gipsies recognized the psychic element in her. Most years, we would come away triumphantly with a goldfish or a Norwich canary, yellow and trim. One canary lived for many years, laying an egg every month. It was given brandy on a feather when it was ill.

What a pleasure it was to go to bed at night and listen to the high piping music of the organ on the big roundabout. We were near enough to the market square for it to be clearly audible. The other excitement was to go to school through the fair booths. At that time in the morning, men and women would be coming out of their travelling wagons and caravans which filled the back streets, washing themselves, singing, arguing, perhaps blowing their noses into the gutter with two fingers squeezing the bridge of the nose. How I admired that gesture – and could soon copy it accurately.

When the fair arrived in Dereham, trade in our shop was brisk. The fair people would all come to H. H. Aldiss for new clothes. So would the countryfolk, who arrived from out of town to enjoy the traditional jollifications of harvest-time, the season at which the fair was held.

When the excitement was over and the market square again deserted, my sister and I would be stood in the bath and our clothes removed, garment by garment, as mother searched us for fleas; they too rode into East Dereham with the fair.

Gypsies were never far from Dereham. On the outskirts of the town lies a tract of wild heathland called the Netherd, on which travelling wagons were often to be seen. The Netherd was ever-mysterious, ever attractive, and seemingly boundless. The gorse bushes were so tall to a boy that one could stalk and be stalked, like a small animal. In the winter, the Netherd pond used to freeze, whereupon we would skate and slide on it. Once I went to the pond with my cousins during a summer drought, to see the fish dying in the mud. We 'saved' one or two fish in jam jars full of water, but they died after we got them home.

The Netherd was a reminder that George Borrow was born in Dereham, at Dumpling Green. Borrow was a strange elusive man, and a tremendous writer. How little his works are read now! It is oddly appropriate that the only quote from him in familiar usage is 'There's a wind on the heath; life is very sweet, brother; who would wish to die?' Though the *Oxford Dictionary of Quotations* also grants him 'every dog has his day': 'Youth will be served, every dog has his day, and mine has been a fine one'.

Borrow's *The Bible in Spain*, despite its off-putting title, is one of the best and most living of travel books, to be set on the honoured shelf beside Kinglake's *Eothen*.

The other writer associated with Dereham is the poet,

William Cowper. Borrow was born there, Cowper died there. The Aldiss family, devout or pretence-devout Congregationalists – they defended their faith to the last child – went to worship every Sunday at the Cowper Memorial Church. And moreover were forbidden to take even a glance at the stills outside the Exchange Cinema on their way home to the Sunday joint. Time was when I used to read all of Cowper's poems (I actually liked 'The Sofa'), and his letters too; these days I haven't the patience. But the letters show a good English style. He went gently mad. His poem which begins 'I was a stricken deer that left the herd . . .' is moving in its eighteenth-century way.

My mother's relations lived in Peterborough, a city now ruined by industrialization. There, I had three splendid uncles, two of whom were architects, and a grandmother. Grandmother was the farmer's daughter. Her house was run on purely Victorian lines with, as I first remember it, two daily maids, a washerwoman who appeared on Mondays and wielded a ferocious dolly-tub, and a boot-boy. Every room in her house astonished me. The windows sported venetian blinds with wooden slats. The doorknobs and light-switches were enormous brass affairs. A stuffed fox snarled over the drawing-room door. All the furniture was huge and intricate, forever breaking out in animals, foliage, and faces. The breakfast-room had a vast grate which glowed angrily behind its bars and had to be black-leaded regularly for the sake of its complexion. The drawing-room held lace antimacassars and spindly glass cases containing collections of china; one was forbidden to play ball in there.

In grandmother's delicious dank cellar, which always comes to mind when I read Edgar Allan Poe, next year's Christmas puddings dangled from hooks overhead. They had to mature for eighteen months before being ripe for eating. In that house, huge hams were cured and huge pork-pies made. Huge trifles were consumed. For breakfast, one ate porridge or those gritty little Grape Nuts; the silver sugar sprinkler was magnificent; and one looked at the adventures of Pip, Squeak, and Wilfred in the *Daily Graphic*, then a *respectable* paper. Although the strip was aimed at children, it must have had some political significance, for one of the

177

minor characters, I seem to recall, was a terrible old anarchist-bolshevist called Boskofski, who dashed about with a smouldering bomb in his pocket.

My grandmother was a tiny woman with white hair and ivory-coloured skin who outlived her husband by twenty years. She always wore black for mourning with a little white lace frill of collar. Although she died in 1945, when I was in Sumatra, I recall her with absolute clarity. Yet how I *felt* about her remains a mystery. She was never other than extremely kind to me, and I never remember when she was not smiling, even when a canine friend and I were busy wrecking all that scrupulously kept house; but some reserve in her kept me ever from loving her.

On the other hand, I unreservedly loved that monster, my grandfather. That was Granpa Aldiss, H. H. Aldiss of Dereham, J.P. My father went in awe of him until his last days, and always called him 'the Guv'ner'.

The Guv'ner not only governed, but could be seen to govern. He dominated what would now be called a department store, employing some fifty staff. There were three main departments, the ladies' drapery and millinery, ruled directly by the Guv'ner, the gents' outfitting, and the household goods and furnishing, ruled by the Guv'ner through my father and my uncle. Behind these departments were 'factories' and warehouses where carpets, beds, rolls of linoleum, and many other items were stored, and workshops where men sat cross-legged and made up suits or women chattered endlessly and created dresses or hats. H. H. Aldiss also did removals and funerals. I can just recollect the glass hearse pulled by two enormous black horses wearing black plumes, and driven by Nelson Monument in his black silk topper. Then a motor-hearse was bought and the old hearse stood in one of the back yards to rot. Soon the stables were empty, although kittens – and once a brood of startingly ugly barn-owl chicks – were raised by their feral parents in lofts above the stables.

The whole complex of buildings was a playground for me and my cousins. The various departments were connected by long, often dark, corridors; below them were 'stoke-holes', where the terrifying business of keeping the departments warm went on. Established in various nooks throughout this loose assemblage of buildings were little knots of people going about their different trades. A small boy's relationship with adults is always precarious. In some nooks, one would be accepted as a welcome diversion, in some rejected as a tiresome nuisance; one might be made much of or teased; and the reception could change as the predominant character of the workroom changed.

The millinery department was established upstairs, in what had once been a dwelling house. Behind the scenes, old bedrooms with striped bedroomy wallpaper did duty as boxrooms, scruffy corridors retained the dignity of ancient gas-brackets. To this department I would advance with a fluttering heart, provoked by hope and trepidation. Yes, and love! For one of the young girls in the millinery was very beautiful. She had dark hair, blue Norfolk eyes, a pale complexion, some freckles, and a lovely red mouth. She was known to get me in one of the old bedrooms, to take me on her knee and cuddle me, to kiss me. But she also teased me. That teasing I could not bear; nevertheless, I did bear it for the sake of those wonderful kisses.

Long after we had left Dereham, I would dream of that face, and those lips, and scheme to go back and give a more grown-up account of myself.

Among the rambling buildings were nooks numberless in which to hide and ambush assistants – who sometimes retaliated by hauntings and ghostly noises from places of concealment. There were many opportunities to annoy old Monument, who would come rushing out of his harness-room swearing as his chimney was blocked from outside by a sack, and smoke poured into his little reeking room. There were endless chances to go ratting with the terriers, or to climb over and along walls, endless chances for disappearing.

Occasionally, the Guv'ner would appear in his wrath and give us the yard-stick about the legs or bottom. Or he would send father to do the same. Father would do as he was told, but he had his own fun, even in shop hours. The outfitting department was frequently convulsed with laughter at some prank of which my father was prime mover. He sometimes eluded reps ('commercial travellers' they were in those days) by dressing up in one of his own fitting-rooms and sweeping past the man with a polite lifting of his top hat, sporting a false moustache the while.

In his youth, father took part in amateur theatricals. We had a photo of him in pierrot costume, looking droll. East Dereham inflicted respectability on him, but he still enjoyed an absurd prank; he would enforce silence on us at meal-times, then sit eating with his napkin-ring screwed into his eye like a monocle. Wars of thrown dusters were covertly conducted among the serious business of his shop. He could do conjuring tricks, tell jokes, and sketch beautifully. We regularly went to the swimming pool to see him win tortoise-shell clocks and other prizes in local events.

Everyone worked tremendously hard in father's shop, enduring long hours and low pay. On late nights, a tray of tea would be brought down to father in his office. Sometimes it would stand untouched for an hour, until the tea stewed and I snaffled the buns.

Over all, the Guv'ner presided. He was short and stocky. He had small neat jowls, and a mysterious little lump on one cheek. The Guv'ner was always well-dressed. He had a sharp tongue. Everyone respected him. He took his annual holi-days in Torquay or Gibraltar, turn and turn about. Once, he brought me back a wood-and-metal object which imitated bird-calls when twisted. His leisure pursuits were few. He gardened and went to chapel twice on Sundays. He was teetotal. He read his Bible but few other books; I know he enjoyed anything about Scott of the Antarctic, whom he admired.

His wife, my grandmother, spent many years confined to bed with one of those mysterious illnesses which have gone out along with gutta percha, Birkett Foster, and chemist's sealing wax. I used to climb upstairs to see her in her cool room, where long windows looked out on garden and meadow. What sort of woman was she, I wonder? I rather enjoyed being in that room, among the bunches of grapes, flowers, and ornaments; but it was a relief to slip downstairs again and be free.

The Guv'ner's habitat hardly seemed to be in that house. We saw him there only at Christmas. The shop was his proper environment. In the middle of it all he had his office – so much in the middle of it all that the office had no windows. One might look instead into a large safe with a green door. The Guv'ner sat in a swivel chair, with ladies about him on high stools, industriously working at ledgers as if dear Disraeli had never died. But he always had time for me; I knew he loved me in his gruff and inarticulate way, and I would always go to kiss him respectfully good-night on Saturday evenings, when he would press a sixpence into my crafty little palm.

My grandmother died at last. Late in life, the Guv'ner married again. He married one of his cashiers, a nice young lady who looked after the ledgers. It caused no end of a stink in the family. Nobody could talk about it, even decades later, without getting heated. But the old boy did right. His new wife was a marvellous woman in every way, and always very kind to my sister and me into the bargain. She made the Guv'ner happy for the last few years of his life.

All this must sound worlds away to my American readers. It is worlds away to me. In all but date, our little corner of Norfolk in the nineteen-thirties was Victorian in its modes and its thought. Nor had the sun dreamed of setting on the Empire.

When I was thirteen, we went to live at the seaside, at Gorleston-on-Sea. There, father would go down and fish by the old Dutch pier, which was swept away some years later by a heavy sea. He would bring back a bucket full of fish for us and our neighbours. Sometimes we would have crabs. You could buy large crabs, dressed, from the fishmonger in the High Street, for ninepence; they cost almost two pounds now, undressed. And we could buy boxes of soft and hard herring roe – a teatime treat. Mother saw to it that we still ate well. I must owe my health and physique, not to mention my appetite for any exotic dish, to those years of good eating which, compared with the miserable diet of boarding school, were like Heaven to Hell.

My father was a keen fisherman. He liked nothing better than to spend all day in some quiet backwater, preferably on one of the Norfolk broads, watching his line. He took me to Hickling Broad one day. We arrived very early. Nobody was about. Birds were busy over the vast silences of the water. I would have loved it if I had not had to fish.

Only after he died in the mid-fifties did I realize that my father thought of himself as a failure. A failure! That handsome, witty man who worked so hard for us! Impossible! But time brings deeper insights. I can see now how painful it was for him when he sold up his share of the business after the Guv'ner's death and we left Norfolk for good. Nothing was ever the same for him again. He was a humorous man, but his jokes grew more bitter and turned against his family, who must have seemed increasingly a burden to him. He died when my first son, Clive, was less than a year old. Now I have three more children who know nothing of him, Stanley Aldiss.

When I told my father that I was thinking of throwing up my job and becoming a writer, he was horrified. His life experience had taught him to cling to what was. Whereas my life experience had taught me that better things were round the corner. Already, before we left Dereham, I could feel the prison shades closing in on me; well do I know how H. G. Wells felt in his draper's shop, for I was destined for the same fate. I escaped. My father's supreme misfortune was my good luck.

There I pause, looking back at that lad of thirteen. Some things he had already decided. He had decided that he was no more interested in his father's business than was Kafka in similar circumstances. He had decided that he was not interested in the religious rituals droning on round him. But, more deeply, he had decided that he had a contempt for the safe bourgeois way of life in which he found himself.

I was an omnivorous reader even then, although it was mainly trash I read; but I had got hold of a book that firmed up my ideas on the subject. A cell of French culture had penetrated to East Dereham (perfect Bovary country, come to think of it), and I lit on a translation of what could have been Murger's *Vie de Boheme* but was more probably Zola, the mere sight of whose four-letter name always had an hypnotic effect on me. I don't recall what it was, although I can hear a clock ticking as I read it. The novel gave me a longing for bohemian life which, because I have never much gratified it, I have never lost, and a feeling for being socialist as part of life, although I have never been a Socialist with a capital S. Those feelings seemed to be lacking in the circles in which I was brought up.

Along with that went an interest in science. I have mentioned my hero, Sir Malcolm Campbell, the death-defying man who frequently broke the world's speed record. He set up a new world record when I was ten, driving on Daytona Beach, a name I used to recite to myself under my breath. Later, he broke the water speed record. Both his cars and his boats were called 'Bluebell'. I had a little flicker-book, advertising Castrol or another oil, which, when thumbed rapidly, showed the mighty 'Bluebell' surging across Coniston water!

The boys' magazine I took every week was *Modern Boy*, published by Amalgamated Press. I loved *Modern Boy* dearly. Sir Malcolm Campbell used to contribute to it – and Flying Officer W. E. Johns, for his Biggles stories were being published even then. What I was absolutely addicted to was Captain Justice. Justice was an elegant adventurer, much given to wearing white ducks and a naval cap and smoking a cigar. He had various bases round the world, chief of which was Titanic Tower, significantly in mid-Atlantic.

From Titanic Tower, Justice sorted out the troubles of the Anglo-American world in story after story. The stories were written by 'Murray Roberts', the pen name of Robert Murray Graydon. Justice and Co ventured into Africa to find an empire of slaves ruled by strange forces, confronted giant insects, battled with enormous robots, overcame alarming flying machines, survived a world plunged into darkness (the most enthralling of all his adventures!) and also paid regular visits to any runaway planets which happened to be passing through the solar system at the time.

So science fiction entered into and began warping my life

from an early age. My hero-worship changed from one Campbell to another, from Sir Malcolm to John W.

Science also took my fancy. Looking back, I can recall no interest in art or science among the members of our family. But my parents gave me a microscope at the right age; peering down its barrel became one of my favourite occupations for a while. Anything I could get hold of went on those flimsy slides, and what I saw I would draw and colour with watercolour in a special notebook. There was a compelling aesthetic attraction in that microscopic world.

Other landmarks of my journey towards realizing that sf was my main dish I have already catalogued in *Shape Of Further Things* or *Billion Year Spree*. The discovery of *Marvel*, *Amazing*, and *Astounding* on Woolworth's counter. The purchase for a shilling of Alun Llewellyn's remarkable novel *The Strange Invaders*. The continuous reading of H. G. Wells's novels, not only the sf stories but *Tono-Bungay* and *The New Machiavelli*, and so on, which I enjoyed for their socialism. But it was *The Strange Invaders* which persuaded me that I had discovered something worthwhile. Although I enjoyed the magazines – and was particularly mad about Kuttner's 'Time Warp' in *Marvel*, because of its erotic element – I thought they were appallingly written and was a little ashamed of reading them.

Where I got that critical idea from, I cannot tell. By the age of eight, I had begun to appreciate style, the vehicle of fiction, as well as content.

What happened to me at eight was a terrible thing. I have so far painted a cheerful picture. At the age of eight, I was sent away to boarding school, and at boarding school and public school I remained until I was seventeen and old enough to go into the army – whereupon I was promptly whisked abroad to the Far East for four years. So my severance from home and parents began early in life, far too early.

I was sent, like Pip from Joe Gargery's forge, to be educated and to become a little gentleman. The treatment, as with Pip – Dickens was always the perceptive reporter – created a chilled and conventional creature, cut off from his roots. Thousands of English boys endured and still endure the public school system; most of them survive in some way or other. But it seems to me a pernicious system, deadening to a wide sector of life, and it perhaps accounts for much of the legendary coldness attributed by foreigners to the English. Many years of adult life passed before I shook off that cold shadow of exile.

Which is not to say that there is necessarily a great deal wrong with the schools per se. My last school, West Buckland in Devon, was a fine one and I was happy there. Nevertheless, the possibilities for torment in an authoritarian community, within which one is confined for twenty-four hours a day for many weeks at a stretch, are many.

At least school provided some chance for writing and reading. When did I make my first book? I cannot remember. Certainly I was forever making books at prep school, my microscope book among them. By then, I was an authority on prehistoric life and used to give lessons on dinosaurs to other lads at a penny a time (with a cunning mixture of scholarship and commerce which I have never entirely abandoned). Later came my Victorian melodrama period, my epic drama period, my ghost story period, my space story period, my pornography period, my space-pornography period (girls raped by huge vegetables on Jupiter and quite enjoying it), my horror-and-blood period, and so on, until, in the army, I wrote 'Her Dear Dead Body', a sort of erotic detective story. I also kept a voluminous diary.

The diary went on for years and years, growing annually larger and more pretentious. It evolved into a gigantic free-style journal containing many millions of words. I still have it, in something like two dozen volumes. It contains the ramblings of a stranger and is without interest; only a mixture of shame and pride makes me preserve it; after all, getting rid of all those countless days and sentences must have been of some value!

All these sorts of writing, slowly becoming more ambitious, stood me in good stead when it came to attempting anything professionally. Writing by then was an integral part of life.

When I left the army, I had no ambition except to write.

To be propelled back into civilian life in 1948 was extremely disorienting; I had no knowledge of society, except the out-of-date rules I had hazily gathered as a child – though I was fortunate in finding myself in Oxford, where mores were a little fluid. Even while I was still on repatriation leave, I began writing a novel about a soldier's experiences in India, Burma, Sumatra, Singapore, and Hong Kong; it was to be entitled *Hunter Leaves the Herd,* and five chapters were written before I bogged down. The impulse behind it was as much nostalgic as creative. In truth, I longed for the sunlight and the whole ambience of the East. That region, that experience, has remained with me continually. People have less in the East; but they do not seem to suffer from envy as much as we do.

I wanted to be a poet, although I was not familiar with the work of any poet later than Thomas Hardy. I got a job in a bookshop in Oxford, where I came into contact with the physical material of our culture. Bound sets of Macaulay, Gibbon in calf, Richard Burton in folio, Hogarth in elephant folio, were things of romance to me. And of course we were always throwing out books – a useful reminder that, however successful one is, every dog has his day, in Borrow's phrase.

In those dim cloisters, I encountered such splendid eighteenth-century heroes as Candide, Tom Jones, Rasselas the Prince of Abyssinia, Vathek, and the time-haunted Tristram Shandy, while meeting for the first time in complete versions with those redoubtable voyagers Robinson Crusoe and Lemuel Gulliver. Formidable creations, all of them, and all created by authors who project strong *personnae* into the works concerned. Each work, in its way, is a grand entertainment which also constitutes an enquiry into the world.

Fielding, Johnson, and Sterne, in particular, aroused the sedulous ape in me. For some months, my desk was cluttered with Sterne-like entanglements and Fielding-esque disquisitions, written in Johnsonese. Then I moved digs and burnt them all. I began to read that neglected contemporary writer, Eric Linklater, and imitated him instead.

After a while, I took to contributing to the trade paper. The editor commissioned a series called 'The Brightfount Diaries', about life in a fictitious and pleasant bookshop. The rest, as they say, is history, although obscure enough history to bear repeating here. One day, I received a letter from Faber & Faber, from Charles Monteith, saying that I had my fans at Faber's and would I ever think of turning my series into book-form.

I did know the series was successful and, as it happened, I had been thinking of nothing else. So I made the book, my first publishable one; Pearl Falconer – then a fashionable illustrator – drew some delightful pictures for it; and Faber published it, with a pleasing modest success, in November 1955. The edition stayed in print for years and Faber, bless them, never remaindered. They sold me the last thirty copies cheap in the late sixties.

For me, there were few rejected manuscripts, few rejection slips, no starving in garrets. I should feel guilty but don't. There were plenty of years of hardship, when I was too skint to buy myself a morning paper for fear of wrecking the budget, beers were far apart, and I ate at places called British Restaurants.

My regular association with Faber continued through twenty books and seventeen years; a very good partnership. Happily, Charles Monteith was also an sf reader – in the fifties, they were few and far between in England, particularly in any position of power. Charles knew Kingsley Amis and Robert Conquest and Bruce Montgomery (Edmund Crispin), all of whom had been up at Oxford and read *Astounding*. It was a fortifying experience to meet them.

There was no difficulty in following up *Brightfount's* with a collection of sf short stories, *Space Time and Nathaniel*. By this time, I was relinquishing the idea of being a poet – persuaded by reading Eliot, Auden, MacNiece, and John Donne, who showed me what poetry really was. My memorial to that ambition lies in the contents page of *STAN* (we always knew the book by its acronym), where the titles of the three types of story are laid out in octet and sextet form, as in a sonnet. There are fourteen titles.

For Faber to publish this volume in 1957 was an act of faith on their part. I had had only thirteen stories published; a fourteenth had to be hurriedly written to make up the number. Paperback rights never sold until 1966. With my next book, *Nonstop* (retitled *Starship* in the States), I had the same paperback problem. Eventually, rights were sold to Digit for £75 and I was glad to get the money. *Nonstop* has been translated into thirteen foreign tongues so far.

By 1957, I was earning as much money from writing in my spare time as from working from 9 till 5.30 in a bookshop. So I left the bookshop. From that day to this, I have never done an honest day's work, and have lived happily ever after!

Not that the financial position improved greatly at once. I have just come across a note in an old diary for 5 April 1958 which says, 'This is the end of the financial year. I've got £110 less in the bank than I had a year ago. And £20 less in the PO Bank. In fact, we've got £60 left, sum total of our wealth. Ye gods, outlook's black!' Outlook improved during that year, and has never been too perilous since.

It was early in 1957 that the national Sunday paper, the *Observer*, announced the results of its competition for a short story set in the year 2500 AD. My story, 'Not For An Age' tied first and was published in the paper, complete with an illustration by Leonard Rosoman. Since all the British science fiction writers had entered the competition, the ensuing kudos for an unknown was great. The late Arthur Sellings had a story in the top twenty prize-winners. Then it was I learnt that such a thing as fandom existed; I received a letter from Helen Winnick asking me up to the Globe, the pub where London fans met regularly. There I met two young writers, John Brunner and Sam Youd (John Christopher). Sam's famous *Death of Grass* must already have been out by then.

By this time, I had been appointed literary editor on the *Oxford Mail* under W. Harford Thomas. I had been reviewing science fiction and ordinary novels, as well as non-fiction of all kinds, for the paper. My sf column ran from 1954 until 1967, making it the longest regular sf review column ever to appear in a newspaper. It must have been read by thousands of undergraduates (who are called students now). Later, I reviewed sf for the *TLS*, but abandoned it when the standard of work fell so low. I hate to think how many hundreds of books I devoured for the *Mail*. Fortunately, I always had a good appetite. Now I'm doing a stint for Ian Hamilton's *New Review*.

Criticism and creation always went hand-in-hand as far as I was concerned.

My intention was partly to write social novels. John Osborne's play, *Look Back in Anger,* and Kingsley Amis's novel, *Lucky Jim,* embodied for me then much of the experience of my generation – after all, neither author is much more than half-a-dozen years older than I. *Lucky Jim,* over which I howled with laughter, altered something in my approach to life. Laughter is very persuasive.

But there was a bigger persuader: the atomic bomb. When the Bomb was dropped, my division was in India, resting after our bout of involuntary heroism in Burma – and training to be launched against the Japanese in a seaborne assault on Singapore. So I had good reason to rejoice in the flattening of Hiroshima and Nagasaki. My bacon was saved. My admiration for that fine president, Harry Truman, dates from that time.

The new-born nuclear power was something greater than social life, greater than almost all the people (not greater than *all* people: not greater than Truman: for it was he who decided that the bomb remained in the hands of politicians instead of being passed to the generals; that decision forms one of the nodal points of modern history). The Bomb dramatized starkly the overwhelming workings of science and technology, applied science, in our lives.

So I perceived, and have been trying to perceive more fully ever since, that my fiction should be social, should have all the laughter and other elements we associate with prosaic life, yet at the same time be shot through with a sense that our existences have been overpowered (not always for the worse) by certain gigantic forces born of the Renaissance and achieving ferocious adolescence with the Industrial Revolution.

But such matters are best reserved for discussion in fiction, rather than in a chatty memoir.

Since this piece is addressed in part to an American audience, I will seize on the chance to examine my dealings with the States. It is a curious thing for a writer to think of his natural audience as being in another country, although not too strange for me.

One reason was what I have called the shadow of exile which loomed over me. Another was the whole American dream under which I was brought up – or under which I brought myself up, to be more accurate. I was a movie fan from an early age, encouraged by my cousin John. All that I admired in the cinema was American. Then again, the sort of music that moved me most deeply was American, the blues and jazz. The same with all the music we called 'hot' in my adolescence.

The best ideas, too, seemed to be American. The States stood then as a bastion of freedom and continued revolution. It was a sad thing to see that image crumble after the war; at the same time, the American view of Britain as a gallant little fighting island was collapsing. Particularly before the second world war, when more and more of Europe seemed to turn into an armed enemy camp, the lights of America burned bright, viewed from English shores.

Then of course there was sf. Not that it ever could be said to paint a cheerful picture of the States; very far from it; but it radiated an image of a land of dynamism and change. This I apprehended as very different from Britain, with its oppressions, unemployment, class structures, and trading difficulties (all of which existed in the States also, as I failed to realize when a lad). I did get the message that the most exciting sf came from New York.

The war. France fell. The boy of fourteen watched with mingled fear and excitement as his father brought his two guns out of the cupboard, handing the lighter one over and saying, 'You'll have to use this when the invasion comes, so we'd better get some practise in.' The invasion never came. Britain miraculously survived, right on the edge of black Europe. Our great ally was the USA, across the Atlantic. Americans were very much treated as heroes. Liberators of Europe and all that. Times change; it ill becomes an sf writer to complain of the fact. Change is the material from which his cloak is cut.

All of which made it natural that I should write my science fiction with America in mind. That first novel *Non-*

stop, was part of American fiction. I had read and been fascinated by Robert Heinlein's *Common Sense,* about the interstellar ship on which a catastrophe has occurred, although I was struck at the same time with the poverty of characterization and feeling in it. My novel was designed at least in part as a response, an antidote.

Another thing. At the time I began to write for publication, there were really only two going sf magazines over here, *Authentic* and *Nebula.* I disliked the *Authentic* format, which had long boring stories in it by people like William Temple and Sidney Bounds (it improved later under E. C. Tubb's editorship). *Nebula,* edited by Peter Hamilton in Glasgow, was more exciting. I found an issue (No. 3) in Freshwater, Isle of Wight, read it, and decided that I could do almost as well as the authors performing there. Hamilton took a lot of trouble trying to make the stories I submitted publishable, but without much success – for one thing, I've always disliked rewriting at editors' behest.

Then Ted Carnell's magazines got going on a regular basis. Ted can never be enough commended for exercising that principle of punctuality to which he adhered, for his sane good humour, or for his scrupulous honesty in professional and financial matters. But it was always apparent that most of his authors were little better than illiterate, and were short on imagination too. Jimmy Ballard has said of them that they were 'the most dingy and pathetic bunch of third-rate ex-journalists' he had ever met; so they were. In fact, they were feebly copying an ageing American tradition. Many of their stories were rejects from American magazines.

It was a poor thing to talk with an assumed American accent in a British magazine. I have no doubt that it was because of this kind of down-at-heel tradition that the axe fell and revolution, signalled by Moorcock and his feathered hordes, had to come.

Even before Moorcock's day, there were only two authors I could read with interest in Ted's magazines. One was me. An author should always read with care his writings when they appear in print, when sufficient distancing has set in for him to be able to perceive his errors and victories. The other was J. G. Ballard. His record for not writing American retreads was always unblemished.

Before us, Arthur C. Clarke had always used an English idiom instead of the bogus Yankee employed by some of our chums.

At first, events moved more happily for me in the States than in my own country. I was lucky to have Truman 'Mac' Talley as editor at Signet; he really seemed to care, and I appreciated his advice. When he received the manuscript of *Hothouse* (which he insisted on retitling *The Long Afternoon of Earth* so that it did not fall among the horticultural section), he altered it throughout very extensively in pencil. Every page had something changed. He sent it to me to look at. I was horrified. I wrote back and said I would prefer that the novel should not be published rather than that it should be published in such mutilated form. He wrote back, 'Okay', and printed my text as written.

Under Mac, the best of my early titles appeared in the States, neatly packaged with Powers covers, and I was proud of them. I was also getting a response from Anthony Boucher and Fred Pohl, men whose work I respected. The atmosphere was sharper and more intellectual in New York. And I was grateful to Don Wollheim at Ace for publishing my more shaky early attempts.

It was a stimulating time in which to enter the lists. Not a great deal seemed to be happening in England then, apart from John Wyndham and John Christopher. I admired and still do admire the latter's *Death of Grass* (called *No Blade of Grass* in the States), and his very funny and clever novel, *In the Year of the Comet*. There was also Arthur, whose writings I greatly enjoyed; but his distinctively English style was generally exported to New York.

In the States, much more was going on; all the other contributors to this volume were already making a considerable mark on the world. Pohl's *The Space Merchants*, in collaboration with Cyril Kornbluth, was already on the way to being accepted as a classic. Bester had exploded his two great fireworks, *The Demolished Man* and *Tiger! Tiger!* (*The Stars My Destination*), leaving considerable retinal damage in my case. Silverberg was already filling all the available magazines; I had the pleasure of meeting him in 1957. Knight was still writing fiction, often with a humorous emphasis much to my taste, whilst his book of reviews, *In Search Of Wonder*, had already appeared. (I must have read that volume more often than any sf novel, with the possible exception of *Earth Abides* and *Out of the Silent Planet*.) Harrison's *Stainless Steel Rat* and *Deathworld* had already appeared, paying enough for him to bring his family to Europe at the start of their long peregrinations.

Kingsley Amis's *New Maps of Hell* appeared in 1960. In many ways, it must be regarded as a special event. It did put sf on many maps. Amis was the first man to lecture on sf in a university, taking it as a serious subject for discussion, and his book remains exemplary in its wit and literacy, even if its scholarship is a little hasty. *Hell's Cartographers* is a title that reflects back some of Amis's heat and light.

It was as part of the hospitality I enjoyed from US sf readers that I received a shield from the 17th World SF Convention nominating me 'Most Promising New Author'; there were a Hugo and a Nebula to come later.

I still gain encouragement from that 'Most Promising New Author' plaque. It was a sign that someone cared, and I took it as such. I was incensed when a Mr Devore of Chicago later suggested the plaque be withdrawn.

(It's true that, later still, the Australians voted me 'World's Best Contemporary SF Writer', but I suspect that was a friendly conspiracy by Lee Harding, John Bangsund, and Bruce Gillespie. Still, the title looks good on dust jackets.)

An author's career is an haphazard matter, subject to chance like most things. I suffered some misfortune in the States, changes at Signet and trouble with agents; meanwhile, success started coming my way in my own country.

Writing from England in 1974, I could list many troubles under which the country labours, and many vexations from which the individual suffers. But the sixties were in some ways a halcyon period. It is difficult to encapsulate what happened but, in my view, the Romans were busy becoming the Italians. The British had lost or relinquished most of their empire and, what's more, the Goth was within the gates of the capital. The Goths were civilized people, as were the waves of Italians, Indians, Pakistanis, Chinese, and Americans who, for their different reasons, began to invade England. They still help to make London one of the pleasantest and most cosmopolitan capitals in the world.

The sixties was the time of 'Swinging England', the Beatles, Mary Quant, Flower Power, permissiveness, and all that. More deeply, personal relationships opened out, people became much more frank, would make friends more easily, and would more readily tell those they disliked to go and find another pad. This was a general phenomenon, by no means confined to the very young – although that particular revolution had its storm-warning in 1961, when a schoolgirl called Helen Shapiro bounded into the national consciousness singing 'Don't Treat Me Like a Child' and 'Walking Back to Happiness'. It was a great time. I don't recall the country feeling so pleasant.

For me personally the weather also set fair. I too had my freedoms. In 1965, I remarried. The adorable Margaret Manson became my wife. That long shadow of exile of which I have spoken had at last dissolved. It proved to have been an exile from my true self.

The effect of this beneficent change upon my writing was slow but undeniable. One can see it by comparing the stories in one of my early volumes, such as *Canopy of Time* (which appeared in the States in different format as *Galaxies Like Grains of Sand*), with those in my latest collection, *The Moment of Eclipse*. A Cambridge reviewer said of the earlier volume that the stories were perfect, classically perfect, almost too perfect; whereas the later stories are never content with a static form, and shape and content form a living whole, varying as needed. The dynamism is redirected.

It was in the mid-sixties that Mike Moorcock took over *New Worlds*. There one was allowed to cut one's capers – to the advantage of all, and especially to the advantage of oneself. I must say something about *New Worlds*, although that subject is entered into more fully in *Billion Year Spree*.

We can identify two streams in science fiction, two streams which have now (though uneasily) become one: what I will call the 'once-for-once-only' stream and the pulp stream.

The 'once-for-once-only' stream is a direct literary response to a new factor or a change in society, generally brought about by a technological development, as are most societal changes. The first good example is Mary Shelley's *Frankenstein* (so much better a book than all the horror movies allow), provoked by new sciences, new discoveries (the opening up of the South Seas for instance), and new philosophies, such as the evolutionary speculations of Erasmus Darwin. The line of inheritance then goes on through – shall we say – Verne, de l'Isle Adam, Butler, Bellamy, Wells, Kafka, Huxley, Skinner, Orwell, *et al*. The books of these men are once-for-once-only responses to or examinations of some new aspect of the world.

The other stream is the pulp stream. When Gernsback started his magazines in the late twenties, he invented sf as a genre, a category. No chance of the 'once-for-once-only' approach here! By their very nature, the pulps appeared regularly, with a regular amount of space to fill. So modern sf was established, wherein a lot of underpaid authors rather frantically cribbed or sparked ideas off each other – at its rare best, the process did become some sort of a meaningful dialogue (for more on that subject, I must ask you to consult the intros and commentaries in Harry's and my *Astounding/Analog Reader*, 2 vols.).

The pulp stream also witnessed the triumph of the editor over the writer. It was something we missed in England, whether because writers are more individualistic or editors are poorer, I don't know.

But the great distinction to be made between the two streams in their heyday is that whereas the 'once-for-once-only' stream was, by its nature, a critical literature, even in the case of its most noted practitioner, H. G. Wells, the pulp stream quickly turned to power-fantasy and escapism. Here, the great practitioner is Edgar Rice Burroughs, one of the best-selling, if not the most bestest-sellingest, sf writers of all time. Burroughs' influence has been pervasive and often detrimental; among Tarzan's descendants is certainly Heinlein's Michael Valentine Smith of *Stranger in a Strange Land*.

It is up to everyone to pick the bones out of their own reading preferences; I've already declared my preferences in my history. Sf is the best-equipped of all literatures to indulge in power-fantasy; it encompasses the universe, and it can give us the infinite policing powers of the human mind, as well as the gross material conquests that lie beyond the atom.

But for a writer to indulge himself and his readers in these ways is ultimately to ruin his credibility as a writer. As a real writer. The disgrace that the sf community still (perpetually?) thinks it is in is precisely the shame it shares with pornography, of transforming a man into an organ of conquest in a knocking-shop of wish-fulfillment.

Mike Moorcock, in kicking the old gang out, allowed in the more traditional kind of sf, responsive to the current situation. There were excesses, but excesses are part of every revolution. The four-letter words, the sex, the indulgence in style for its own sake – all these were in defiance of the old pulp tradition; so was the attention paid to the other arts. This is what opponents of the new wave, like Sam Moskowitz, Isaac Asimov, or, more literately, Robert Conquest, never seem to have grasped.

It is disappointing that someone of Conquest's critical standing refuses to comprehend that this new wave had much in common with many previous revolutions, major and minor; it was reacting against the decadence it superseded. Kingsley Amis shares Conquest's general view, of literature as of politics, but as a popular novelist Amis is more aware of the writerly necessity for breaking new ground, as his continuing exploration of genres shows.

Moorcock's revolution was always part-powered by American writers like Thomas Disch, John Sladek, Norman Spinrad, Samuel Delany, Pamela Zoline, Kit Reed (all of them, incidentally, people of great charm), and other exiles who visited London from time to time, as well as English writers like Mike, Ballard, David Masson, Charles Platt, Lang Jones, and me. It found sympathy with a whole lot of people who were out there reading sf occasionally but unhappy about its limitations. And when I sought a grant for *New Worlds* from the Arts Council, we could rely on im-

Magic and Bare Boards

mediate support from a wide range of people in the arts and journalism who enjoyed sf, Angus Wilson among them. From then on, sf has prospered widely in England, and not just in a narrow commercial sense, cut off from other arts. To the arts sf can contribute whenever it, or any author who wishes to write it, ceases indulging in arabesques of power-fantasy. Of course, power-fantasy always sells. That's not what I'm arguing.

It may be that early promises were not entirely fulfilled. Such is the way of early promises. Good writers are always too few. But Spinrad remains a considerable talent who will forge further yet. Disch will recover from his present doldrums. While Kit Reed, in such books as *The Better Part* and *Tiger Rag*, has proved herself a considerable psychological novelist. That elusive man, S. L. 'Chip' Delany, already has a large fan following.

While this excitement was going on, I was involved with other matters. Margaret and I bought an old Land-Rover in 1964 and headed for Jugoslavia, where we travelled all of the six republics that make up the state. A wonderful country, a great experience, tremendous to be able to snatch six months out of life. We've never managed to fit in a similar expedition since. Out of the Jugoslav trip came my one travel book, *Cities and Stones.*

Margaret and I *recognized* each other from our first meeting, which meant that we could stand a lot of mutual nonsense, and do so even with an amount of pleasure.

It was important that she recognized me clearly as I was. From then on, I became able to realize myself; my writing changed in accord with the mysterious gear-changes which carry individual evolutions forward. With my first wife, no such recognition took place. Indeed, as that marriage was approaching the last stages of destruction, I said to a certain person whose business it was to know us both that one of my anguishes was that, while I felt I had a clear picture of Her, she had no picture at all of Me. This was confirmed. It is impossible to live day after day with a shattered mirror. Rapport is the sun of existence.

The early sense of formlessness with which I had been afflicted was a search for identity. When I found it, it was startling and protean. The years of exile brought their recompense. Through a new understanding of myself, I was better able to understand others. I have a quick empathic sense; now I try to use its findings to warm the essentially cold medium of modern sf.

One amazing incident on the Jugoslav trip. We had a letter from Harry Harrison in May, c/o the British Embassy in Belgrade, saying that he and Joan were going to drive from Denmark, where they were living, to Hungary in July – a distance of about a thousand miles; they would look us up in Jugoslavia if we named a time and place. It sounded a bit remote, but we wrote back saying we'd be in Makarska on the afternoon of 24 July, in the local camp (we saw from the map that there was a camp, although we had never been there). The mail went astray then. We got no answer. But we rolled into Makarska camp a couple of months later – and the Harrisons turned up ten minutes after we did.

Harry and I had already begun collaborating. With the aid of Tom Boardman, we put out *SF Horizons*, a little review of sf. We issued only two numbers, but it seems to have been influential, not least on us. We went ahead with other collaborations. The most successful collaboration has been Harry's idea for an annual *Best SF*, although my role there is merely as a talent scout. Our recent *Astounding/Analog Reader* in two volumes is doing well. But our partnership has been most fruitful for the insights into writing we have been able to give each other. The fact that we never cheat or let each other down has helped a good deal, too.

It is generally assumed that my main contribution to the Moorcock era lies in *Report on Probability A* and *Barefoot in the Head*. Both certainly appeared in *New Worlds* (*Barefoot* in chunks as 'The Acid Head War' stories). In fact *Report* was written some years earlier, in 1962. After a while, a writer grows too firm in his own ways to be actively influenced by anything new but, in 1960, I was much persuaded by the French *nouveau roman*, the anti-novel, as practised

Magic and Bare Boards

by Michel Butor and Alain Robbe-Grillet (Marguerite Duras was less to my taste).

I admired their scrapping of many literary clichés. I was attracted by the way that Robbe-Grillet and Duras translated readily into cinematic terms. In particular, I was stunned by the Robbe-Grillet-Resnais film, 'L'Année Dernière à Marienbad'. with its temporal confusions, mysterious agonies, and alien perspectives. It still embodies for me many of the things I set most store by in sf (while many other valuables are to be found in Luis Bunuel's recent film, 'Le Charme Discret de la Bourgeoisie').

Robbe-Grillet's novels are not exactly works one wants to read through many times. But Michel Butor's *Passing Time* is less austere, and to be recommended as a permanent book.

From these exemplars I took courage. I would cleanse my prose of its antiquities. So I developed the central situation in *Report*, a situation charged with a drama which is never resolved. Moreover, I withhold the emotion involved, so that a reader must put in emotion for himself.

Later, I met Anna Kavan, author of *Ice*, and found that she too had been haunted by 'L'Année Dernière'. That brave woman took her life before she could learn of her new reputation, to my lasting regret. She was marvellous, and it is entirely fitting that a cult is now growing about her name.

After Moorcock had published *Report*, I was able to sell it as a book; Faber published it in hardcover and Sphere in paperback, where it still reprints merrily. Unfortunately, I have not yet been able to secure a French translation. It is a novel that owes much to the cool Paris of the intellect.

In the States, *Report* seems to have secured none of the supporters which a book of its nature requires in order to gain ground. For it does need close attention, particularly if one has been nourished on a diet of pulp. My staunch friend Larry Ashmead published it in hardcover from Doubleday. None of my regular paperback publishers such as Signet would support it. Eventually it appeared from Lancer, but clearly it has not met with the same response as in England. A pity. It is the novel in which I came nearest to fulfilling my intentions, and its essence remains with me in a way I could claim for few of my other novels.

Barefoot is more ambitious. I believe it has its triumphs. There again, it has met with a mixed reception in the States. Larry again backed it. The paperback publishers again shied like startled virgins. Ace eventually produced rather a pleasing edition. From the start, the novel had its supporters. My particular gratitude went to Jannick Storm, who translated it into Danish – a great accomplishment.

Doubleday finally pulped their hardcover edition. It sold fewer copies than had the Danish translation (in a country of only four million people!). But eccentrics like Harlan Ellison, Norman Spinrad, Theodore Sturgeon, and James Blish have aired some of the novel's virtues to a reluctant public, and there is a chance that it will survive and flourish in the States as it does in England.

The growing band of academics should espouse the cause of novels which venture to be unpopular by breaking new ground. As far as I know, only Charles Platt has used *Barefoot* in an sf course so far.

The form that *Barefoot* takes is entirely dictated by its content. If you write about a Europe overtaken by drugs, how do you best convey the experience to the reader? I had no doubt about the answer: you plunge him in to that world as deep as you can. And you do that by the chief means at your disposal – the use of language. By the deployment of suitable phraseology, you make him feel what it is like to belong in an entire culture gone hippie and yippie. The logic cannot be faulted, however you judge the end result.

The book's not just style. It is full of things, ideas, images. It took me almost three years to write and, when I'd finished it, I felt I had written myself out of sf. I wrote ordinary novels instead – *Hand-Reared Boy* and *Soldier Erect,* both of which went straight to the top of the best-seller lists in England, although they did less excitingly in the States. They embodied too British an experience, maybe. *Soldier Erect* is probably the best of all my novels, shot through with pain and humour.

As a result of the Moorcockian revolution, sf has achieved a widely based reputation and readership. There were years when it looked as if Ballard and I were the last of the breed and no more sf writers were coming along. Now the situation has changed, with many younger authors such as Christopher Priest, Mark Adlard, and Ian Watson coming up. Bob Shaw has already arrived.

Unfortunately, sf writers, like everyone else, tend to grow conservative as they age, which is why new talents, techniques, and topics are continually necessary. A writer should set his own house on fire if he finds too much dogma lurking there. Try something new. In Bester's phrase, go for broke.

Some of the greatest sf writers have been subversive and gone for broke. Olaf Stapledon is the supreme example. What courage and imagination in *Star-maker*! Plagiarised often, never rivalled! – although Stanislav Lem's *Solaris* possesses something of Stapledon's quality.

Most of the science fiction being written is disappointing, and not merely on literary grounds; so many of its basic assumptions are fossils of thought. The philosophy and politics behind the average sf novel are naive; the writer takes for granted that technology is unqualifiedly good, that the Western way of life is unqualifiedly good, that both can sustain themselves for ever, out into galaxy beyond galaxy. This is mere power-fantasy. As I have often argued, we are at the end of the Reinaissance period. New and darker ages are coming. We have used up most of our resources and most of our time. Now nemesis must overtake hubris, for this is the last act of our particular play.

The knowledge should be a challenge. We should not be dispirited. 'May you live in interesting times' was an ancient Chinese curse; whatever we die of, it will not be boredom. The human spirit has to be continually tested. By whom? Why, by man himself. There is no one else.

One thing is certain, as Orwell said: when the world-state dawns, it will be neither Christian, white, nor democratic. But there is a long way to go before that.

Meanwhile, the Western way of life has the termites under it. The extravagance of Europe, of Japan, of the USA, is being curbed. Our foundations were built not upon stone, not even upon sand, but upon oil, and cheap oil has come to an end. These our memoirs are being written during the

Great Power Crisis of the Seventies, when the Twentieth Century skidded to a halt. Readers must forgive our concentration on minutiae – to which I now return.

Philip Dick is one living sf author whose writings I admire and enjoy consistently. Dick is a natural subversive. He has a quality often found in great writers: humility. He seems to keep himself open and vulnerable, just as he writes about vulnerable little people. Dick made a brave speech at the 1972 Vancouver Convention, where he spoke of an ill-used girl he knew and then said about the future, 'I can only imagine it as populated by modest, unnoticed persons like her'. This loving quality in Dick balances nicely with all his seedily glittering wonders. Silverberg has that quality too, markedly in *Dying Inside*. Dick does not have to make his events plausible; the internal plausibility is always there.

One of the traditions of the novel which has been most staunchly defended over the decades is that fiction should be more plausible than life. Not too many coincidences, no over-exaggerated caricatures, as few flat characters as possible, no preposterousness. Anthony Trollope is one of the great practitioners here; whereas Charles Dickens fails on all these counts, although the scope and power of Dickens's mind is such that he has far more to offer the reader than Trollope. While it is true that the descendants of Dickens are many and often unexpected – Kafka for example – nevertheless, the other tradition of 'nothing implausible' still rules.

Science fiction cuts across this dividing line. Sf that stirs my imagination often boasts a major implausibility (maybe with attendant minor implausibilities hanging from it like subordinate clauses), which the writer then gradually makes plausible. That is, he integrates it with the world picture we already accept, so that our view of the world is thus changed. One good example of this process is in Jack Williamson's *Darker Than You Think*, where we are slowly forced to take a darker view of our own ancestry than normal. More sophisticated examples lie in Kafka's two great novels, wherein almost nothing happens that could not happen in real life, until we realize that it is precisely the *banality* of life that defeats us.

One element in the contributions to this book, and in its

very inception, is phenomenal. It will be self-evident to sf fans and a cause of amazement to those who know little about science fiction. I mean the loyalty we all show to our chosen medium. Bob Silverberg confesses he felt that loyalty even in the days when he was exploiting it to the tune of several million words a year. Other writers who have gone beyond it – financially, like Arthur Clarke, popularly, like Kurt Vonnegut, or artistically, like J. G. Ballard – still recognize the tremendous power of that abstract idea of sf, an attempt, however crude, to build some sort of philosophical and metaphysical framework round the immense changes of our times brought about by technological development – a development which has largely obliterated the ramshackle old frameworks of medieval thought and organized religion.

Apart from writers of the comic-apocalyptic, such as Terry Southern, Thomas Pynchon, Joseph Heller, Philip Roth, and so on – all of whom apparently owe a debt to sf – the mainstream novel singularly fails in exactly those areas where sf is strong; it fails to interest itself in that abundant wilderness existing outside the narrow zone of activity covered by an average newspaper.

It is infuriating the dull way in which sf writers cling to the same topics over and over. The number of writers who actually *invent* are few. All the same, I feel the loyalty. Did I not, I should never have written that complex volume, *Billion Year Spree*. The brief lives recorded here have been devoted to an obscure and unpopular genre (as it was until a few years back, when we had made our reputations). Julius Kagarlitski calls sf 'the intellectual novel for lowbrows'. If it is so, then it is a new genre, and we are among the first to succeed in it.

Unfortunately, genre materials wear out. I long ago swore off FTL travel and ESP in my writing (unless for comedy effects) because (a) I felt both subjects were refuges for tired minds, (b) they had been overdone to death, (c) while I could not say that I absolutely disbelieved in either concept, it was apparent that a writer who rambles on about concepts he only pretends to understand or believe in is going to become a purveyor of drivel, and (d) that it is often an advantage for a writer to accept limitation of subject-matter, particularly in a field where he can get away with almost anything after two sentences of double-talk.

This voluntary restriction of subject matter has prevented me from turning out a regular ten novels, or five novels, or two novels, or even one novel, a year, unlike many of my competitors. It has made me think harder and care more about what I do write.

Not only do genre materials wear out, but the form itself wears out, and the form of sf is still essentially that of the Gothic or post-Gothic (Leslie Fiedler has much to say on this topic), with a mystery posed, hints of danger, a thread of suspense throughout, and a final revelation of some ghastliness. It is hard to resist the idea that to continue to use this form, patented at least as long ago as the turn of last century, is to put oneself in danger of obsolescence; although, in view of the threatened obsolescence of the Western way of life, this could be merely in accord with the times – but the most interesting writers are never content to be merely in harmony with their world.

I can see the problem. I'm still looking for a solution.

There are a number of stop-gap solutions. Two of the contributors to *Hell's Cartographers* are noted practitioners of such solutions. Harrison has his own patent brand of comic-apocalyptic which uses as material not so much reality as sf itself; I'm thinking of *Bill, the Galactic Hero, The Technicolor Time-Machine, A Transatlantic Tunnel, Hurrah!* (which his US publishers plonkingly retitled *Tunnel Through the Deeps*), and the *Stainless Steel Rat* books. In *Bill* one can detect among the strata of Harrison's comedy the fossil bones of Heinlein's *Starship Troopers* and, deeper yet, the crumbling foundations of Asimov's planet Trantor.

Bester's novel, *The Stars my Destination,* is an earlier example of cannibalism, wherein all the elements of gaudy science-fantasy are seized up and kneaded into one tasty cake. Bester really ended that dynasty by doing the job definitively. Of course, there are minute intellects around who have not noticed the fact, and continue to do it over yet again.

These, as I say, are stop-gap solutions to the problems of a dying art (not that I don't think that all arts are not perpetually dying and almost-perpetually being renewed). I have another solution in my recent novel, *Frankenstein Unbound.*

Barry Malzberg's *Beyond Apollo* is a novel which uses the traditional elements of a space journey but, by setting it in retrospect and within the mind of an astronaut, equates the journey with a man's exploration of his own life and motives, and shows something of the inter-relation of the two. Incidentally, it is often a very funny novel.

Malzberg's format may appear complex at first, but he is not wooing complexity for its own sake; his complexity is the measure of Evan's, the astronaut's, mind. We should respect those writers who go out on a limb; they bring home the triumphs and the failures that the rest will be using casually, or casually avoiding, in a few years' time. Best-selling authors don't need our respect to anything like the same degree; they're working with the discoveries of the day before yesterday, often without knowing it. And they are generally richer than the pioneers.

Talking about solutions in the abstract is one thing. It's quite another thing when the individual writer shuts his study door, sits in front of his typewriter, and stares infinity in the face. Every writer has to work out his own solution in specific terms. Most writers are interested in little beyond a financial solution, although they may seek fame or notoriety as well. Whilst admiring the sort of writer who struggles to keep beer in his fridge and his mistress in dresses, whilst indeed admiring the whole idea of brave defeat and going-down-fighting, I am addicted to the idea of success. I naturally mean success in my own terms – any other kind of success is a defeat.

The problems of the serious science fiction writer cannot differ greatly from those of the serious writer. If the novel itself sinks, then sf itself will soon follow down to the ocean bed. I cannot think the novel will founder yet; there is still so much to be said for it, both for the understanding of life that it brings, and for the sheer convenience of its format. One of the qualities it does not now enjoy which it used to do is that very quality after which it was named: novelty. But the sf novel possesses novelty still.

Novelty may be the elixir which keeps an sf reader reading. It is less attractive to the general reader. In consequence, a good science fiction writer may be more neglected than an average writer or (certainly) an average playwright. An extreme instance of this is that great experimental writer Olaf Stapledon.

Such blind attitudes may change. This volume is itself a hopeful token of change. Meanwhile, we have our own successes, of which we are the best judges. I have written a number of books which I believe contain something like a creative vision, no matter in what other ways they may be flawed. Although I see my true strengths to lie in the short story field, I have novels for which I cannot but feel some warmth; most of them are involved with the portrayal of landscape, such as *A Soldier Erect, Report on Probability A, Barefoot in the Head,* and *Greybeard,* all of which depict figures in a landscape. *Non-Stop* and *Frankenstein Unbound* show figures swallowed by their landscapes. So, I suppose, does *Hothouse,* a novel from which I always feel distanced, perhaps recalling the miserable circumstances under which it was written. *Cryptozoic (An Age)* has landscape as surrealism, *Male Response* landscape as comedy. *Eighty-Minute Hour* has an exploded landscape.

Being a self-conscious man, I am well aware of how – in England if nowhere else – one can be both famous and remarkably obscure. It is curious to have arrived at a point where one's standing in this way so precisely matches character.

Damon Knight, who has read what I write here, complains that I begin my piece interestingly with concrete details of childhood, only to fade into the twilight of theory. It may be so. But the theories now mean more to me than childhood.

Lest I have been too abstract, let me add a portrait of the author as a middle-aged scribe. I am many people. Most of my opinions and emotions come in cycles, as does the weather – I am strongly influenced by the temperature, like an old allosaurus. As a youngster, I mistrusted this apparent shifting sand of character: how disgraceful that one's opinions should change with the company. Now I have learned to live with and profit from the phenomenon; it is of tremendous value to an author to be able to play the chameleon, to have an empathic sense. My empathic sense carries me away, and what can be disastrous in real life becomes a triumph on the page, where one is one's characters.

I am cynical and sentimental, foolish and wise, wanton and puritanical, courageous and cowardly, religious and atheistic; not all at once but in series. I hate exhibitionism, perhaps because there is a streak of it in me.

Some things are permanent, though. Permanent is the belief that the human species does not improve or deteriorate rapidly from one generation to another. But the emphasis changes. The America of Ford and Nixon suffers largely from values derived from advertising; there is too much eagerness to sell the product, irrespective of the worth of the product. One sees this among the self-advertisers of sf. And one sees their success. If you keep telling the world you're good, it will read your books and believe they're good. Very saddening. The false values Fred Pohl warned against in *The Space Merchants* are taking over.

The England of today suffers from national exhaustion. I mentioned my three uncles. All joined the Army at the beginning of the First World War, all were captured and made prisoners by the Germans, an ordeal from which they were slow to recover. My father was gassed and involved in the debacle of Gallipoli in that same war. All my nearest and dearest male relations were scarred by that ferocious struggle; and many of their generation emerged into a world bereft of values.

The shame of Munich occurred when I was a schoolboy. The Second World War broke out when I was twelve. The map of Europe turned black. I used to have nightmares in which I was pursued and shot by the Gestapo. Murder and destruction were the commonplaces of our youth. Our minds were peopled with warlords : Stalin, Churchill, Eisenhower, Chiang Kai-Chek, Hitler . . . .

Britain emerged from that second great war broken and apathetic. To my mind, it will need another generation before the trauma is played out.

Responses to the havoc and grandeur of this mental desolation are many; I feel a sort of wonder at the years gone by – which actually seem to include the First World War for, although I was not born until long afterwards, I listened avidly to the stories my uncles and parents told me. Since then, we have come through the attritions of the Cold War and Vietnam. The Renaissance period has been ended by our own innate violence.

Inevitably, acts of kindness, deeds of bravery, works of art, are dwarfed by the landscape of destruction in which they take place.

Inevitably, we are of our times; writers can do well to move beyond those times, as well as merely depicting them.

I will end on a note of gratitude for the fortune that has been mine, much of which has come to me through writing. Sf fandom, with its essential kindness and relish for the sort of nonsense I relish, has been the only society I ever felt I belonged to; for once I left Norfolk, I never belonged anywhere again – not even at my own hearth for many years. I have had the pleasure of meeting many of sf's leading writers; there was that moment in Rio de Janeiro when Harry was in his finest form, lining up two gentlemen to greet me and saying, 'Brian, I want you to meet A. E. van Vogt and Robert A. Heinlein'.

I have visited many exotic and ludicrous spots, and have good friends abroad, particularly in Scandinavia, which to me is the best slice of the world – except for the fact that its climate is just slightly chillier, darker, and cooler than England's. At home, my luck is as good, with an early Victorian house which is not unlike my grandfather's old home in Dereham, a jolly family to fill the house, and a wife I adore.

Lest I make the picture too rosy for general credence, let me add that I regret having no faith – for belief in Catastrophe is no faith – more especially since I have lost hope in the idea of Reason as a guiding light. Even a loving family does not entirely compensate for a sense of isolation; nor do beautiful women and good friends erase the knowledge that life and success are mere temporary accidents. The days come and go; the enemy is never forgotten.

Yet I finish this memoir (if memoir it is) on a mild January afternoon with a fire burning and a tranquil country view from my window. Margaret prepares dinner while the children play with a friend. Tonight there is a party. Tomorrow offers new excitements. In the circumstances, a display of stigmata would be inappropriate.

how we
work

Robert Silverberg

It was all much simpler long ago, in the old days when I was a high-volume producer of fiction. I worked a rigid schedule, five days a week, throughout the entire year, with six or seven weeks blocked off for holidays. I kept a sheet on which I listed, day by day, everything I was committed to writing over the next three or four months, and I simply did my daily stint, knowing I'd always be able to complete my allottment. The schedule looked something like this:

    March 20 Ace novel pp 140–165
    March 21 Ace novel pp 165–190
    March 22 AM finish Ace novel; PM short story 3000 wds
    March 23 Campbell novelet pp 1–25
    March 24 Campbell novelet pp 25–50

And so on, incredibly, month in month out. Like a machine. Getting the ideas was no problem; they arrived mysteriously out of the air, like radio broadcasts, while I was reading or strolling or listening to music. I jotted them down on handy scraps of paper – often nothing but a title (titles usually came before plots for me, and still do) and a brief summary of

213

theme ('Earthman falls in love with bizarre alien woman'). The morning I was due to begin work on a story, I would elaborate the summary into a two-paragraph outline, pick some characters, give them their names and physical descriptions, and start work. Into the typewriter would go a sheet of white paper, a piece of carbon paper, and a yellow second sheet; and, hour after hour, the first and only draft of the story would emerge. I worked from nine in the morning to half past eleven, took a little more than an hour for lunch, and put in another stint from quarter to one or so until about half past two. Somehow this regime produced twenty to thirty pages a day of publishable copy, and everything I turned out this way sold. *Everything*.

But, as readers of my early stories know, the prose was simple, functional stuff, the plot showed signs of improvisation, the narrative flow was often congested with padding: when no inspiration came I nevertheless kept my agile fingers moving and the action, however inconsequential or irrelevant, spinning. As I matured this method of work no longer sufficed for me, and by the time of my first 'new' fiction – in the mid-sixties – I was very much more careful, doing detailed outlines before beginning, pausing to rewrite scenes that didn't seem acceptable as they came from the typewriter, going back to put in inserts, in short doing a great deal of planning and revising. Still, most of what I was publishing through 1967 or so was basically first-draft stuff – written more slowly, conceived with greater care, but even so not subjected to any systematic process of overall rewriting. My years as a high-volume producer had given me skills of expression and improvisation that allowed me to say what I wanted to say clearly and effectively in a single try.

What I wanted to say, though, became ever more complex and difficult to express, and during the late sixties my working methods evolved toward what they are today, so very different from my habits of fifteen years ago. I still work a faithful five-day-a-week routine, although my hours now run only from nine to noon, and the holiday weeks are more frequent. I no longer try to set a fixed schedule of pages per day, however, being content to work at whatever pace is necessary for each day's task; and so, whereas in 1957 I could tell you on 3 October what I would be writing on the 12th of December (and almost certainly be right), I now have no idea how long it will take me to finish any project. I used to do short stories of up to 7,500 words in a single day; now they require, sometimes, six to eight weeks, and writing novels, once a job of two or three weeks, has become an endless procedure.

I still begin with a title and a brief statement of theme. Then, on the backs of old envelopes, come structural notations having to do with overall form and texture of the work, lists of characters, bits of background data, suggested sequences of chapters. I usually have the beginning and the end of any story fairly clear before I start; the middle is subject to development once the story acquires life of its own, and so I constantly write memoranda to myself as I go along. (The final paragraphs of *Born With the Dead* presented themselves to me, unbidden, while I was watching 'Last Tango in Paris', and quite distracted me from the movie; the moment the film was over I grabbed pen and paper and wrote everything down, feverishly, before it vanished. Some day I must go back and see the second half of 'Last Tango' again.)

I never try to get away with one-draft writing any more. Using old letters, advertising circulars, bits of manuscript, or any other sheets of paper with one blank side, I write (single-spaced) a paragraph or two, go back and do it again, do it three or four times if necessary, then try another passage, and so on until I have a thousand words or so of work that I consider acceptable. At this point I usually type a fair copy, double-spaced, and put it aside; then I continue with more rough work, and so I proceed through the story, now doing new material, now revising, now retyping, the final manuscript constantly growing as I plough onward into new territory. Very frequently I discover that I have been premature about committing the early pages of a story to final-copy form: it has become almost customary for me to halt, thirty or forty pages along, realize I've made a false start, consult frantically with my wife (who has the unique privilege of seeing works in progress, and only in their earliest phases, when I'm least sure of myself) and go back to page one. This creates a mound of blank-on-one-side waste paper out of what for a while had been my 'final' draft, but I recycle it into the drafts to come.

Here are some samples of the rough-draft process:

> I pondered for a couple of days. Break my word to Carvajal and save Qu
>
> But could I let Quinn mess himself up?
>
> Half an hour after I left Carvajal I could see no reason for not telling Quinn
>
> Half an hour after I left Carvajal I was ready to warn Quinn to skip the Kuwait dedication. I didn't call him.
>
> I didn't put through an immediate call to Quinn, but it was close. Once Carvajal was out of sight I found myself wondering why I had decided to remain silent. Carvajal's inflexible
>
> I didn't put through an immediate call to Quinn, but I came close. As soon as Carvajal was out of sight I found myself wondering why I would hesitate at all. Carvajal's insights into things to come

And so on. All of these are possible openings for a scene; in the end I chose a variant of the last one. Choices I once made automatically and unconsciously I now must work out on paper, and there seems no way around it. At first I was restless and bothered by the inescapable need to do all this fussy sentence-by-sentence tinkering; now I accept the reality that my work will no longer flow as it once did. My output now is less than a tenth of what it was in my most prolific days. I suppose by some standards I'm still a terribly productive writer, but it doesn't seem that way to me, not with a net output of 800 words or so per day. There are times when I miss the old ease of production; but I do prefer today's results.

Alfred Bester

'Writeing is a nag – ' is a line from one of Ring Lardner's superb stories, 'A Caddy's Diary'. It sums up my attitude toward my work; it isn't a knack, it's a nag, a damned compulsion, and this is how I handle it.

I've often said, whilst living abroad, that it was difficult for me to learn another language because I was too concentrated on learning my own. This has more meaning than a mere cop-out. In my opinion it's essential for a writer to think, speak and write the identical language. This takes a tremendous amount of self-discipline and training.

Next, preparation and dedication. It's tough explaining preparation. It means that every item of life, no matter how minute, must be observed and noted. You never know when it may become useful, perhaps never, but it must be there waiting. I don't know how many times I've combined notes made years apart into one story. This means that the author must split his personality. Half of him is participating in the scene; the other half is watching himself and the other members of the cast keenly. It's rotten. It's hell. It's a price an author must pay.

Dedication: I don't write two hours a day, or four or eight; I write twenty-four hours a day. I can't help myself. I keep thinking story, even in my sleep, not as an observer but as a participant. I'm inside the story. I'm all the characters. Of course it must be understood that many of these stories never come to fruition, let alone writing. I pass them off as fantasies and let them go. A few of them still haunt me, however, and I often wonder whether my unconscious is making its own notes.

My writing, naturally, is the sum total of my education and experience. I studied music at college and am extremely sensitive to tempo and timing. It was pointed out to me once that I usually write in a presto three-quarter beat. No argument, although I try very hard to relieve it occasionally with a four-four andante. I was deeply affected by the energy of Dickens, Reade and Dostoievsky, and have sometimes been criticized for my razzle-dazzle style. I can't help that. I'm compelled to try to match their dash because I regard writing as an entertainment for myself and the reader, raree show which will amaze and amuse.

I'm sometimes condemned for being an elitist in my lifestyle and my writing. I don't think that's true but I don't defend myself. All I can say is that I am what I write and write what I am and it's up to the reader to keep up with me. I never try to put the reader down, but I'll be damned before I write down. I have too much respect for people to do that.

I return to the questions of discipline and split personality. After many years I learned to edit myself. This means that I'm both writer and editor. I recall one of my publishers giving me the manuscript of a science fiction writer and asking my opinion. 'It's dull,' I reported. 'Well,' he said, 'he's a rather dull writer.' 'No,' I said, 'he makes a silly mistake. He accepts the first idea that comes to his mind.' This is something I cannot permit myself to do. The editor in me nods and says, 'Yes, but that's obvious. Surely you can come up with something better, my boy.'

And I try. God knows, I try! With what success I don't

know, but I try. I was once rebuked for being a perfectionist. So I am. What destroys me is the conviction that I've fallen so far short of perfection. This is what nags me into writeing and writeing and writeing.

Harry Harrison

Writing about writing can be a very tricky business. It seems very pretentious to talk about how one goes about the physical act of writing – yet who can deny the hideous attraction of the topic. The *Paris Review* series of interviews were supposed to get the reader inside the heads of the great authors, but about all I can recall of them is Hemingway saying that every good writer had an inborn automatic shit detector, and Simenon writing 5,000 words a day in a scruffy hotel and X-ing out each day boldly on the calendar until the end of the book was reached within two weeks.

With this love-hate aspect of writing in mind the writerly act has been tucked into this corner of the book. Read it if it interests you, pass it up and I shall not mind.

Writing is a fragile act. When one is pulling language, thoughts, ideas out of thin air, or the turgid subconscious, any disturbance disturbs. Harlan Ellison makes it a point to write in the middle of booming, drunken parties but, no drinker himself, I feel that what he writes there reads as though it were written in some place like a booming, drunken party. I'm sure he does his best work in the quiet of his study because I know of no serious writer who does not need his solitude, his sitting and thinking time, in addition to his writing time. Even the familiar, no matter how peaceful, can intrude. Brian, I know, goes to a cottage on the Thames when he needs that sort of quiet. Alan Nourse has an A-frame deep in the Washington woods, totally deserted. I take the camper to the beach in Mexico where I can neither talk nor be talked to. Not that any of us lack peaceful studies at home, we all have fine ones. But there are times when a bit of Walden Pond is needed by all of us.

Not that non-writing others always understand. In Mexico Joan literally beat a 'friend' away from my study door with a broom because he knew old Harry didn't mind talking to him at the time. Joan's mother, a paragon of virtues in all other ways, does not realize the basic needs of a writer or she would not have opened the door when I was writing, as she did once years ago when we were staying in her home, and say, 'Harry, since you aren't doing anything, would you go to the store for me.' A writer's family understands; my daughter knows when I have that glassy look in the eye and am staring into space that I am not to be disturbed because I am 'working'.

That is part of the working time. What is needed next is the sitting-at-typewriter time which is when the penny finally drops. During my freelance art days I found I worked best from noon to about four the following morning but, thankfully, I have changed my schedule since then. I know some who still work these kind of hours. I find that a regular daylight schedule is more productive.

In the morning, anywhere between eight and ten, I go to the studio (called that instead of study or office by reflex from the art days) and put in a day's work. When I am writing I emerge at cocktail time in need of strong drink. When I am editing I emerge at the same time in greater need since most editing is such drudgery. When I am working at a piece of fiction I stay with it for as many days as it takes. Early on, in honour of the christian work ethic, I used to work the six day week and take Sunday off. I found this broke the motion of a book so I began to work straight through on the first draft. Since I average about 2,000 words a day this means at least a month of continuous writing. That's fine. It also means weeks off at a time when others are in their offices. There are really only three advantages to the free-lance life. (1) You can live wherever you wish. (2) You can work the hours you want. (3) You can wear comfortable work clothes and old shirts while on the job and save a fortune in suits and white shirts.

I work from an outline always, more or less detailed, but always an outline. Many pages for a book, just a firm idea in mind for a short story. I know writers who start a story with no idea how it will end; I would rather die first. I am a firm back-plotter and must know the ending before I begin, then expend writing energy disguising the fact that I always know what is coming next.

My study contains a long desk, formerly from a drafting room, cut down so the whole thing is at typewriter height. On this are in and out baskets for correspondence, a holder for paper and stationery, the telephone – with a switch to turn it off so it won't ring – and a calculator so I can figure how much money I am owed at any given time.

Some few years ago Joan rubbed in an awareness of a basic financial question. I had always bought cheap second-hand typewriters, and the one I had decaying at the time had cost £20 second-hand, had been made in East Germany, which meant that American repair men would not work on it (it was a commy machine), and I had written seven books on it which amortized out at $7.1428 a book (the calculator, remember?) not even counting the short stories. I was looking around for another cheap wreck when she told me that everything the family ate and drank, everything physical in our lives, came from the typewriter – so why was I being so chintzy? Buy the best. It was a good argument and I did. An IBM selectric, the writer's friend. I have never regretted this action for a moment since.

Books and books ago I found it hard to start work each day, a variation of the writer's block we have heard so much about. I discovered that if I did my correspondence first I could get the fingers flicking about and the typewriter humming. Then I would trick myself and slide in paper and try to write. It usually worked. Things are better now. Most of the time I can approach work, begin and end.

To begin I read the pages done the previous day. I give them a quick proofing but no elaborate rewriting – though I do make marginal notes like BAD! OUT! REAL CRAP! to cue myself on the second rewrite. Having reread the one day's work, but no more, I slip white paper and carbon-set into the machine, take a deep breath – then turn the machine off and think a bit. Then I write.

The carbon-set is a must. Early in life I found I needed copies of letters uncopied, carbons of manuscripts lost in the mail and such. Now a carbon goes in with anything, other than labels or envelopes, that I put in the machine.

I labour this way until the first draft is done. Less than a week for the usual short story, the mentioned month at least for the novel. If the work to hand is a book I take an extra large drink after I type those fine words THE END and lay the whole thing aside for a bit. A week usually. Joan and I take a weekend in Mexico, or some such place, and sun, water, food and drink cleanse the mind. Then I begin the rewrite, something that gets progressively harder each time through. I do try to get through the book at least five times. I write very tightly and rarely do more than change words right on the page, punctuation, grammar, the usual thing. When this is finally done I emit what is called an intense sigh of relief. Some writers retype their mss, thereby finding a chance for more rewrite, but since I am the world's worst typist I bundle the entire thing off to my typist, the pearl-beyond-price, Mrs Fitzhamon. (First making a xerox of the rewritten ms. which differs a good deal from the carbon.) She lives near Brighton and makes no errors and finds all of mine, and if you have ever had a bad or indifferent typist you will understand just how good a superlative one can be.

That is it. By the time the typing is done I am well into the next piece of work and planning the one, two or three pieces ahead of that. At the same time earlier stories or books will be at the publisher or being published. When people ask me 'how is the book coming' I can respond only by blinking a glassy eye and muttering 'which one?' This is no act because at any given time I may have at least four or five books somewhere in the area between idea and on sale.

It may be art, but it is business too. That is why I have an agent who earns, ten times over, the ten percent for his labours.

Damon Knight

I work at a large wooden desk made for me by a carpenter years ago at a cost of $40; it has a well for the typewriter and open shelves on either side for paper, letterheads and envelopes. As far as I can see there is only one thing wrong with it, and that is that the desk is so big that it tempts me to pile all sorts of things on it, and I am forever trying to clear it off. The desk faces a wall lined with bookshelves. I found out years ago that I could not work facing a door or a window. Someone might come in through the door, and there is usually a tree outside a window; then I watch the tree and forget to write.

I use blue second sheets. It is absurd that the colour should make any difference, but it does – I need something to distinguish the work from final copy, otherwise I get self-conscious and freeze up. When I began writing I used yellow second sheets, the cheapest kind, but now I dislike them.

I once had a Frieden Flexowriter on trial – a marvellous machine, with a tape cutter and reader built onto the chassis of an IBM Model A electric typewriter. It cuts an eight-channel tape, and you can feed the tape back in, make any corrections you like while the machine cuts a second tape, then feed in the corrected tape and watch it chunter away by itself turning out final copy. If I were very rich I would own one of these machines, but they are expensive and delicate. Ideally, every professional writer would have one of these now, and would furnish a tape to be used in typesetting along with each manuscript. Later we all ought to have computer terminals which would do the same thing more efficiently, and would also provide instant information, correct our misspellings and typographical errors, etc. With sophisticated programming they might do a lot of the routine work of writing as well; in some kinds of commercial fiction there is no reason why they shouldn't do most of it.

By the time I feel ready to start a short story I usually have a pretty clear idea of its form, and have written down a list of scenes. A novel is different, and I always write reams of background material first. Then I throw out most of it and write more. This is a terribly inefficient way of making a novel, and it partly accounts for the fact that I have written so few.

I am particular about the names of characters, and at one time kept a list of good ones, crossing them off as I used them. Names in stories should have the variety and absurdity of real names. They can be used to suggest what part of the country a character comes from, what his parents were like, etc; they can also be used, as Hammett used them, to give subliminal cues about people in a story.

I write one draft and correct it heavily for style, etc. If part of it gets too bad, I cross it out and write in a new version; I often throw pages away and start over, but I try to keep the work up to a satisfactory level as I go, rather than running out a complete first draft and then correcting the whole thing. This is not efficient, either.

I think I can tell by the look of a page whether it is well proportioned or not. If I know where I'm going in a scene it will come out in approximately the right form and length, but if I am just noodling around hoping for inspiration to strike, it will go on drifting forever.

I always throw away beginnings. If the beginning is wrong, the rest of the story will be wrong, but if it's right the rest of the story will spin itself out of the first sentence or two.

I model characters after people I have known, but they always take on their own personalities, and I never know what they're going to say until they open their mouths.

I once tried to write a series of stories with titles derived from the running heads of Donald Day's *Index to the Science Fiction Magazines.* 'Stranger Station' was one of these.

Frederik Pohl

How do I write? Any way I can. There is a disciplined way, an inspired way and a way of desperation. The inspired way is most pleasurable; it is joyous to conceive a story, sit down at the typewriter and bring it to birth in a single sitting. Unfortunately inspiration hardly ever lasts past the first ten pages, so that only works for short stories, and not many of them. The way of desperation is surest, the times when I have so boxed myself in that I have no choice but to write. I try to avoid the post-deadline, bills-due, editors-screaming sort of desperation that makes it hard work because it is uncomfortable, and also because often enough it produces bad work. But sometimes it produces good work, too – I cannot say why sometimes it is the one and sometimes the other – and anyway, without at least a little desperation I am not sure I would finish many stories.

So year in and year out I mostly rely on the disciplined way. For me the procedure is simple. Once a day I sit down at my typewriter, roll a sheet of paper in and do not get up until I have produced four pages of copy. If I am going well, maybe I'll produce more; but however badly things are going, I will produce those four or die for it. It's as simple as that. Sometimes it takes forty-five minutes to write the four pages, sometimes twelve hours. But when I am on my quota system editors smile at me, I meet deadlines, I produce satisfying amounts of material and all the world is mine.

Is what I write in this soulless and stultifying way any good? Sometimes yes, sometimes no – like what I write in any other way.

What do I do if it's bad? I put it away and work on something else, till the ageing process has had a chance to work. Then I take it out and look at it, and most times I can see what is wrong and what I need to do to fix it. (I never submit first drafts. As I have mentioned elsewhere, I make it impossible to submit first drafts by typing them on the backs of old circulars and fund appeals.)

Provided I have not boxed myself into a deadline, that almost always works; I put aside what is going badly, and work instead on something that goes well – until it too begins to go badly, and then it gets put aside in turn. It's a slow way to write. Most of my novels are three or more years in the works for that reason. Some have been ten. Short stories have been five years from first page to publication. In fact, I have short stories started much longer than five years ago that haven't been published, or even finished, and some of them never will be. A good thing about being a successful writer is that everything you write gets published. A bad thing is that it gets published even if it shouldn't be. So I try to censor myself and not send out a story until I am pretty sure it's as good as I can make it – sometimes I've later come to think I was very wrong – which means that I have quite a few stories in one stage or another which I don't offer for publication. I suppose that, counting everything, there must be well over a million words: five books, three of them actually completed, twenty or thirty shorter pieces, and God's own quantity of (at least temporarily) abandoned fragments. Several times I have decided against publication not only after finishing a work but even after signing a contract and receiving an advance on it; three of the books were in fact contracted, and I bought the contracts back, because I didn't like the books well enough to want to publish them.

If imposing the four-page-a-day rule on myself works all

that well, why don't I do it all the time? Human frailty, that's
why. Partly it is rebellious unruliness in my head, but partly
it is a matter of losing quality after a while; I go stale and
need fresh inputs.

What are my inputs?

Science is one of them; as I have said, I am a fan of
science, it is the greatest of spectator sports for me. Because
many scientists were, or are, science fiction readers I have
the opportunity quite often to spend time with men who are
doing fascinating kinds of research; and as they like to talk
about what they are doing, and I like to listen, there is a lot
of good conversation to add to the magazines and journals
and books and papers and symposia and speeches. That is
probably my favourite perquisite, but surely next to it is the
oportunity to do a good deal of travelling. I usually get out
of my own country two or three times a year at least, and
inside it I have managed to visit forty-eight of the fifty
United States. (If anyone cares to offer me a lecture engagement in either Alaska or North Dakota I'm available any
time.) And then – well, I read a lot, and I permit my curiosity
to lead me into out of the way places. I've taken formal
courses, in the last six months, in things like guitar-playing,
ballroom dancing and transcendental meditation. I'm a
trustee of a Unitarian church, and of a private school for
retarded children. From time to time I am involved in
politics; and within the last year or two I've made my debut
as folk-singer, night-club comedian and actor – all very
amateur, to be sure. But interesting, informative – and
inputs. I do not pretend that I do these things because I want
to write about them, but some of them do show up in what I
write, and I don't see how I could write well without them.

Where do I work? On the third floor of our home, in a
four-room suite – three are mine, the fourth (since she began
doing anthologies and painting covers on her own) my wife's.
It is a wickedly profligate consumption of space, and I love
it. Everything is here: three desks, four typewriters, two
kinds of recording equipment, file cabinets full of manuscripts, correspondence, documents and reference materials.
We are plagued with books – thirteen of our fourteen rooms
have bookshelves in them, and so do two of the halls. But the

books on the third floor are my working library: scientific books, six shelves of them in the northwest room; political books in the northeast; histories, language guides, encyclopedias and so on in a passage between two of the rooms; my own published work spread out wherever there is room for it, mostly in the southwest room and the hall. God knows what we'll do if we ever move.

But really I don't need it all, not for more than one or two sidelights in an average work, which I could of course as readily pick up in a public library if I had to. It is convenient, but not essential. Some of the best writing I've ever done has been with a portable typewriter perched in my lap, in a hotel room or a bus station, on a plane, wherever. A few years ago while my wife was taking a nap in our California hotel room I sat on the sunny balcony outside our tenth-floor window, looking out over the old 20th Century-Fox lot, and in about an hour and a half I had written one of the short stories I'm most pleased to have done, 'I Remember a Winter'. It's a fragile sort of story, and if I hadn't written it right then when it formed itself in my mind I don't suppose I would ever have written it at all.

When do I work? Optimally, at night – starting at midnight, and continuing until I have done my quota for that day, whereafter I read a little, eat something, listen to a little music and go to sleep, generally about sunrise. (My old friend, Cyril Kornbluth used to say, 'If God had meant man to be awake by day He wouldn't have given us the electric light.') This makes problems when I interface with the real world. Publishers and university people in particular have a foul habit of trying to telephone me in the morning, when I am generally asleep. But I won't change; from midnight to six there are no phone calls, the household is asleep, no one comes to the door and that is how I like it. I am all too easily distracted. Years ago I used to try to get my family to tell callers I was out in the morning. Now they just say I am asleep.

Being a writer is difficult; you not only need the talent and technique to write, you also need the discipline to make yourself do it, and the critical judgment to know when you are done. If you are a bricklayer, say, people tell you what to do – 'twelve courses of glazed yellow, ten yards long, staggered and faced with stone at the gate – ' and when the wall is up you are through. If you are a writer you have to set yourself a task, make yourself do it, and evaluate the result when you are done, with little or no real help from anyone. To be sure people will *try* to tell you what you should do, and give you all the criticism you want, maybe more than you want, once it is irretrievably in print; but the only opinion that really matters is your own.

The way I write is the way every other writer writes: the best I can, in whatever way I can; and that is the Whole of the Law.

Brian Aldiss

The most important thing first. I never submit outlines or synopses of novels to publishers. For better or worse, generally worse, my novels are entirely mine. Only when they are finished do agents and publishers get a look. That way, art or whatever-you-call-it and commerce do not get too mixed up. Nine out of ten writers, I'm told, must have an advance before they begin writing; but that's not my way.

I've never written for radio or tv or the films. I have often written for free – but no longer, with four children and several publishers to support.

I'm one of those fools who likes to think he is writing for posterity as well as the present. I know, I know. But my older children, Clive and Wendy, read my books voluntarily; it would be nice to think that their children could enjoy them too.

Science fiction used to be regarded as ephemeral; ephemeral is a relative term, but experience indicates otherwise. All the sf that I ever wrote is now in print and continually being reprinted. Several of my collections of short stories, from *Space, Time, and Nathaniel* onwards, remain in print in various editions, and at least three of them have sold towards 200,000 copies each – a figure that would be phenomenal outside the sf field but must have been exceeded many times over within the field. Which suggests that it is worth expending time (i.e. love and care) over even the shortest pieces.

Much of my time – Harry says the same thing – is spent doing nothing. I suppose I work about nine months of the year and, during that nine months, I do a six-day week every week. I'm in my study by 9.30 or 10, remaining there till about 4.30, with an hour or two break for lunch, when I may, or more likely may not, take a stroll. For half of those days, my time is spent answering correspondence from all over the world – I must be mad to do it. Half of the rest of the time, I do nothing, either sitting and gazing relaxedly out of the window at the twentieth century unfolding, or walking about twitchily with ideas half-formed, occasionally picking out a book from the shelves and reading an odd page. Only in the rest of that time do I actually manage a little fiction.

My study is at the top of the house, a spacious and comfortable area with cacti, sofas, an easy chair, three desks, and thousands of books. Phone, radio, tv, cassette-player, electronic calculator, photo-copier, intercom; but no booze or cigars. I never smoke or drink when I'm writing, except on occasions at the end of the day when I'm getting a bit ragged.

When really absorbed, I like to work in the evening, but there has been less of that in recent years. Small children impose regular hours on authors; there is nothing so bourgeois as children. A verse of Clarence Day's comes to mind at this juncture:

> Who drags the fiery artist down?
> Who keeps the pioneer in town?
> Who hates to let the seaman roam?
> It is the wife, it is the home.

An understanding wife is one of a writer's great assets. Not only is Margaret my first and shrewdest reader, she makes it easy for me to slip off for the odd week to a cottage in the depths of the country, where I work in absolute peace, sometimes writing for twelve hours a day (but I never go without being clear about what I wish to write).

The other thing a writer needs is a good agent. My agent, Hilary Rubinstein, owns the cottage I use as refuge; the loudest noise you ever hear there is the dropping of apples in the autumn into the long grass. Several recent novels have been finished in Willow Cottage.

Generally, I am serene when writing. Between times, I am occasionally depressed to reflect on how much of my art I have never learned and probably never can learn; I can't bear to think of Leo Tolstoi. (Even thinking of his wife is bad enough; she wrote out *War And Peace* for him five times in longhand.)

People always want to know how long novels take to write. Novels impose different schedules, just as they need different approaches. The fastest novel I ever wrote was *Dark Light Years*, because I did it in a fit of anger. It was all complete in a month – but I did nothing else in that month except write or do nothing. *Barefoot In The Head* occupied me for over two years. The average time is about a year. *Billion Year Spree* took the best part of three years to write. Now that I'm moderately successful, I want to spend more time over novels – instead, I seem to spend more time over correspondence.

I have a nice secretary, Pam Woodward, who comes in two mornings a week and will do extra when needed. I also have a typist, Jill Watt, who lives near Bristol and is good on sf as well as typing. And Margaret does a thousand jobs, including looking after all the financial side and managing SF Horizons Ltd. I have never typed out the final draft of any of my own novels or stories; that surely is a job for a professional.

Writers' blocks are unknown to me (he said nervously), perhaps because I have never flogged out copy for cash and still actively enjoy the building of sentences and paragraphs. Of course I get stuck occasionally, but one develops remedies for sticking as for hangovers. There are one or two critical books which can always get my associative and creative juices flowing again – John Livingstone Lowes' *The Road to Xanadu*, Caroline Spurgeon's *Shakespeare's Imagery*, and – unfailingly – Mario Praz' *The Romantic Agony* (a title I have been known to repeat in incantatory monotone while drunk). I rely increasingly on free association for the series of short stories at present under way.

Apart from this series of short stories (about the Zodiacal Planets), I also have on the stocks another series of short stories about an imaginary utopia called Malacia. Four of this series have appeared in Damon's *Orbit* and eight more are planned, but they are among the most exacting I have ever written. The idea is that eventually they will form a book called *The Malacia Tapestry*. There are two novels taking shape, one at present entitled *Moreau's Other Island*, which is intact in first draft, and has been for many months; I am dissatisfied with it, and leave it on one side to mature. The third Horatio Stubbs novel, successor to *A Soldier Erect*, is largely visualised in my head, and should be the next thing I write after editing this book. It will probably be called *A Rude Awakening*.

When I work on a novel, I compose on to a slow typewriter – it is some years since I forced myself to graduate from fountain pen and loose-leaf book, thank heaven! As the pages come out of the machine, they are placed in a pile face downwards, so that I cannot see what I have just written. This is to prevent disillusion. A creative glow is the great necessity for that first draft; by resisting reading back, I can sustain that glow, thinking how wonderful was my vision. Only when the draft is complete and finished dare I go back and read what is written. How much of the vision escaped between head and paper! Disappointment is always great; but hope still abounds, and creative hope mixed with critical discontent carries me through the re-write and/or second draft. Then there comes a sort of lull, where second thoughts creep out of the basement of the subconscious like swine-things in William Hope Hodgson's *The House On The Borderland*. They can be incorporated in the final draft correction, which is almost purely critical in feel. Then the raddled and ratty old typescript goes off to Jill Watt.

It looks better when properly presented. Hopes rise again, and you send the typescript copies off to your agent in good heart. The publisher's proofs bring you to the nadir of hope: the material is stale, you no longer laugh at your own jokes, weep at your own tragedies, blench at your own truths. But, with luck, the whole thing looks much more imposing when you get your six bound complimentary copies. Thus encouraged, you turn like a stag at bay to face the baying of the reviewers. . . .

selected
bibliographies

Novels and Short Stories

Revolt on Alpha C, US 1955
Needle in a Timestack,
US 1966, UK 1970
To Open the Sky, US 1967,
UK 1970
The Time Hoppers, US 1967,
UK 1968
Thorns, US 1967, UK 1969
The Masks of Time, US 1968,
as Vornan–19, UK 1970
Nightwings, US 1969, UK 1972
The Man in The Maze,
US & UK 1969
To Live Again, US 1969,
UK 1974
Up the Line, US 1969,
UK 1975
Tower of Glass, US 1970
The World Inside, US 1971
Son of Man, US 1971
A Time of Changes, US 1971,
UK 1974
Moonferns and Starsongs,
US 1971
The Book of Skulls, US 1972
Dying Inside, US 1972,
UK 1974
Unfamiliar Territory,
US 1973, UK 1975
Born with the Dead, US 1974
The Stochastic Man, US 1975

Non-Fiction

Lost Cities and Vanished
Civilisations, US 1962
The Old Ones: Indians of the
American Southwest,
US 1965
Scientists and Scoundrels:
A Book of Hoaxes, US 1965
The Auk, the Dodo, and the
Oryx, US 1967, UK 1969
Mound Builders of Ancient
America, US 1968
Mammoths, Mastodons and
Man, US 1970, UK 1972
The Realm of Prester John,
US 1972

Editor

New Dimensions, Vols 1–6,
1971–6
Alpha, Vols 1–6, 1970–5
The Mirror of Infinity,
US 1970, UK 1972
Science Fiction Hall of Fame,
US 1970, UK 1971

Awards

Hugo: Most Promising New
Author, 1956
Hugo: Nightwings, 1968
Nebula: Passengers, 1969
Nebula: Good News from the
Vatican, 1971
Nebula: A Time of Changes,
1971

I'd be delighted to fill your request for a bibliography but the hell of it is that I can't. I've sometimes wondered whether it's Freudian; I always dismiss my past and concentrate on the present and future. As a result I don't remember three-quarters of the things I've written, and certainly not the dates of anything. Would these paragraphs serve?

> Began professional writing in 1938. Wrote science fiction, mystery and adventure stories, then comics (*Green Lantern – Captain Marvel* – etc.), then radio (*Charlie Chan – The Shadow – Nick Carter* – etc.), then TV (*Fireside Theatre – The Winchell Show – NBC Showcase – Fred Astaire* – etc.). Switched to magazine feature writing for *Holiday* and *Rogue* magazines regularly; others occasionally. Four novels, three short story collections, one popular science book.* Only award: the very first *Hugo*. Am not at all glamorous; merely a working stiff.

Novels and Short Stories

The Demolished Man,
  US 1953
The Rat Race, US 1955
The Stars My Destination,
  US 1956, as Tiger! Tiger!
  in UK
Starburst, US 1958
The Dark Side of the Earth,
  US 1964

Non-Fiction

The Life and Death of a
  Satellite, US 1966

Novels and Short Stories

Deathworld, US 1960
The Stainless Steel Rat,
    US 1961
War with the Robots, US 1962
Deathworld 2, US 1964
Bill, the Galactic Hero,
    US 1965
Plague from Space, US 1965
Two Tales and 8 Tomorrows,
    UK 1965
Make Room! Make Room!
    (filmed as Soylent Green),
    US 1966
The Technicolor Time
    Machine, US 1967
Deathworld 3, US 1968
Captive Universe, US 1969
The Daleth Effect, US 1970
One Step from Earth,
    US 1970
Planet of the Damned,
    US 1970
Prime Number, US 1970
The Stainless Steel Rat's
    Revenge, US 1970
Stonehenge (with L. E.
    Stover), US 1971
Montezuma's Revenge,
    US 1972
The Stainless Steel Rat Saves
    the World, US 1972
A Transatlantic Tunnel,
    Hurrah!, US 1972
Star Smashers of the Galaxy
    Rangers, US 1973
Queen Victoria's Revenge,
    US 1974
The Lifeboat (with Gordon R.
    Dickson), US 1975

Juveniles

The Man from P.I.G., US 1968
Worlds of Wonder (editor),
    US 1969
Spaceship Medic, US 1970
The California Iceberg,
    US 1974

Editor

Apeman, Spaceman (with
    L. E. Stover), US 1966
John W. Campbell: Collected
    Editorials from Analog,
    US 1966
Nebula Award Stories 2 (with
    Brian W. Aldiss), US 1967
Four for the Future, UK 1969
The Year 2000, US 1970
The Light Fantastic, US 1971
The Astounding-Analog
    Reader (with Brian W.
    Aldiss), US 1972–3
Astounding: John W. Camp-
    bell Memorial Anthology,
    US 1973
Best SF, US 1967–74 (with
    Brian W. Aldiss)
SF: Author's Choice, Vols
    1–4, US 1968, 70, 71, 74
Nova, Vols 1–4, US 1970, 72,
    73 & 74

Awards

Nebula: Make Room! Make
    Room!, 1974

Novels and Short Stories

Hell's Pavement, US 1955
A for Anything, US 1959
Far Out, US 1961
In Deep, US 1963
Beyond the Barrier, US 1964
Off Centre, US 1965
The Other Foot, US 1965
The Rithian Terror, US 1965
Turning On, US 1966
Three Novels, US 1967
World Without Children and
    The Earth Quarter, US 1970

Biography and Criticism

In Search of Wonder,
    US 1956; rev. ed. US 1967
Charles Fort, Prophet of the
    Unexplained, US 1970

Translations

13 French Science Fiction
    Stories, US 1965
Ashes, Ashes by René
    Barjavel, US 1967

Editor

Orbit Vols 1–15 (US 1966–74)
    and many other anthologies

Awards

Hugo: Best Book Reviewer,
    1956

Novels and Short Stories

Alternating Currents, US 1956
The Case Against Tomorrow,
US 1957
Tomorrow Times Seven,
US 1959
Drunkard's Walk, US 1960
The Man Who Ate The World,
US 1960
Turn Left At Thursday,
US 1961
A Plague of Pythons, US 1965
Digits and Dastards, US 1966
The Age of the Pussyfoot,
US 1968
Day Million, US 1970
The Gold At The Starbow's
End, US 1972
The Abominable Earthman,
US 1973

with C. M. Kornbluth

The Space Merchants,
US 1953
Search The Sky, US 1954
Gladiator-At-Law, US 1955
Wolfbane, US 1959
The Wonder Effect, US 1962

with Jack Williamson

Undersea Quest, US 1954
Undersea City, US 1958
The Reefs of Space, US 1964
Starchild, US 1965
Rogue Star, US 1969

Awards

Invisible Little Man Award,
1963
Edward E. Smith Memorial
Award, 1964
Hugo: Best Editor, 1966–8
Hugo: Best Short Story (with
C. M. Kornbluth) The
Meeting, 1973
President, Science Fiction
Writers of America, 1974

Novels and Short Stories

The Brightfount Diaries,
UK 1955
Space Time and Nathaniel,
UK 1957
Non-Stop, UK 1958, as
Starship, US 1958
Canopy of Time, UK 1959
Male Response, US 1959,
UK 1961
Hothouse, UK 1962, as Long
Afternoon of Earth,
US 1962
Airs of Earth, UK 1963
Dark Light Years, UK 1964
Greybeard, UK 1964
Best, SF Stories of Brian
W. Aldiss, UK 1965, as
Who can Replace a
Man?' US 1965, Rev. ed.
1971
An Age, UK 1967, as Crypto-
zoic!, US 1968
Report on Probability A,
UK 1968, US 1969
Barefoot in the Head,
UK 1969, US 1970
The Hand-Reared Boy,
UK 1970, US 1970
A Soldier Erect, UK 1971,
US 1971
The Moment of Eclipse,
UK 1971, US 1972
Frankenstein Unbound,
UK 1973, US 1974
The Eighty-Minute Hour,
UK 1974, US 1974

Non-Fiction

Cities and Stones: A Travel-
ler's Jugoslavia, UK 1966

The Shape of Further Things,
UK & US 1970
Billion Year Spree: The
History of Science Fiction,
UK & US 1973

Editor

Penguin Science Fiction,
UK 1961
More Penguin Science
Fiction, UK 1962
Yet More Penguin Science
Fiction, UK 1964
Penguin Science Fiction
Omnibus, UK 1973
Best Fantasy Stories, UK 1962
Farewell Fantastic Venus,
UK 1968
Best SF 1967–74 (with Harry
Harrison), US & UK
1968–73
The Astounding-Analog
Reader, Vols 1 & 2 (with
Harry Harrison) US 1972–3,
UK 1973
Space Opera, UK 1974

Awards

Hugo Special Citation: Most
Promising New Author,
1958
Hugo: Hothouse, 1962
Nebula: The Saliva Tree,
1965
BSFA Vote: Britain's Most
Popular SF Writer, 1969
Ditmar: World's Best Con-
temporary Science Fiction
Author, 1970
BSFA: Moment of Eclipse,
1972